IMAGES
of America

AROUND WALNUT COVE AND DANBURY

On the Cover: Pictured from left to right, Sheriff Wesley Dunlap, Deputy Nolaska Alley, Deputy Bryant Nelson, Deputy Clifton Joyce (Sheriff Mike Joyce's father), and Deputy Henry Dunlap have just captured a liquor still in Stokes County. (Courtesy of Margie Dunlap.)

IMAGES
of America

AROUND WALNUT COVE AND DANBURY

Kyle A. Berrier

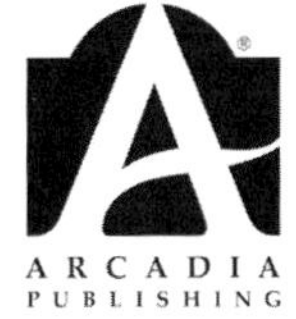

ISBN 978-1-4671-2102-6

Published by Arcadia Publishing
Charleston, South Carolina

Printed in the United States of America

Library of Congress Control Number: 2013945586

For all general information, please contact Arcadia Publishing:
Telephone 843-853-2070
Fax 843-853-0044
E-mail sales@arcadiapublishing.com
For customer service and orders:
Toll-Free 1-888-313-2665

Visit us on the Internet at www.arcadiapublishing.com

This book is dedicated to those who came before us and took these photographs, making the preservation of Walnut Cove and Danbury's history possible.

Contents

ACKNOWLEDGMENTS

When deciding to undertake the task of publishing a pictorial history, I didn't quite realize the daunting task brought forth. From there, I turned to my neighbors and friends for help, and the response was overwhelming. I would like to start by thanking Patti Dunlap, whose help was tremendous in the identification and gathering of photographs, and Jerry and Yvonne Rutledge for their effort and knowledge of obtaining many early photographs of Walnut Cove; without their efforts, this book would not be complete. I also would like to thank Don Richardson, and Rick and Kim Ferrell for their encouragement, advice, and identification of individuals within the photographs. Other contributors I would like to thank are Martha Fowler (daughter of Dr. Jack and Nancy Helsabeck Fowler), the Stokes County Historical Society, Hannah Rothrock, Linda Neal Alcott, Phil and Pamela Joyce, Margie Dunlap, Jerry and Sarah Stephens, Charles Rodenbough, Debbie Cummings (Davis Chapel Historical Association Inc.), Dianne F. Bullin, Tommy Young, James Harbuck, Lois Dodson Smith, Hazel F. Bowles, and Barbara F. Tuttle. While old photographs are a passion of mine, meeting these fine individuals was worth all of the effort. Sitting down to listen to their stories and memories taught me more than any book I have read. Without the people who helped during this process, this publication would not have been possible. Thank you all so much.

INTRODUCTION

One hundred twenty-five years have passed since the town of Walnut Cove was incorporated in 1889, but it was well established much before then. The first known settler in the area known as Walnut Cove today was Ben Young. He settled near present-day Oldtown Road around 1750. Over the next 100 years, an establishment known as the Town Fork Settlement emerged. One settling family in particular was the Lash family. They had a large plantation and eventually opened many businesses including, but not limited to, a general store, livery stables, and, reportedly, a bar. This area eventually became known as Lash. As it is evident, the name "Lash" did not stick. Instead, the area became incorporated as Walnut Cove. The name is reportedly from the abundance of walnut trees growing in the area. As time passed, Walnut Cove grew and became a very large and thriving town. Along with the efforts of Dr. William A. Lash, a descendant of an original settler, the railroad came in just in time to transform the town into what many remember as Walnut Cove. Throughout the early 20th century, new buildings were erected, and many still remain today. Some that remain are buildings of Mercantile, Ford Motor Company, Tuttle Motor Company, Fulton's Store, Neal Hardware, and Alley's Maytag. In June 2013, Walnut Cove lost a building known to many as the Dodson Hotel. This structure was built by Wesley Dodson in 1912 and boasted many modern-day conveniences, such as running water, sewer lines, and electricity. Travelers often found rest there on their way to Winston-Salem or the mineral springs located above Danbury. These springs were frequented by visitors who knew of the water's healing purposes.

Danbury, first named Crawford, was chosen as the county seat in 1849. A new courthouse was to be erected in 1851. The mid-1800s were a time of growth for Danbury. Nathaniel Moody built a tavern in 1854, Wilson Fulton built his brick house in 1859, and Samuel Taylor built a home in 1849. These three structures became important in the community. Moody also built an iron works in 1843, located just south of Danbury. During the Civil War, this ironworks supplied the Confederacy with iron for a period of time. In 1864, Gen. George Stoneman, a Yankee, stormed through Danbury, burning much of his path. He and his troops quartered in Moody's tavern. While there, the general learned of the ironworks that supplied the Confederacy and ceased its operation. The surviving home Fulton had built became the Stokes County Historical Society's museum more than 150 years later.

The communities of Walnut Cove and Danbury are among the best-kept secrets of the South. These communities are nestled around the Sauratown Mountains in Stokes County and are often referred to as "God's Country." The beautiful landscape is just the beginning of the true beauty of Walnut Cove and Danbury. Without the people of these towns, they would be nothing but an empty shell. The voices that echo from the area are held by deep roots, roots that eventually run together. With neighbors that are always willing to lend a hand, no one ever stands alone. Our ancestors would be proud of the community we have inherited and embraced.

Throughout the years, many people and businesses have come and gone, and the streets may not be as vivacious as they once were. But sometimes, you can still feel the presence and hear the sounds of the people from yesteryear. This book is a glimpse into the years that have since gone by.

One

The Early Years

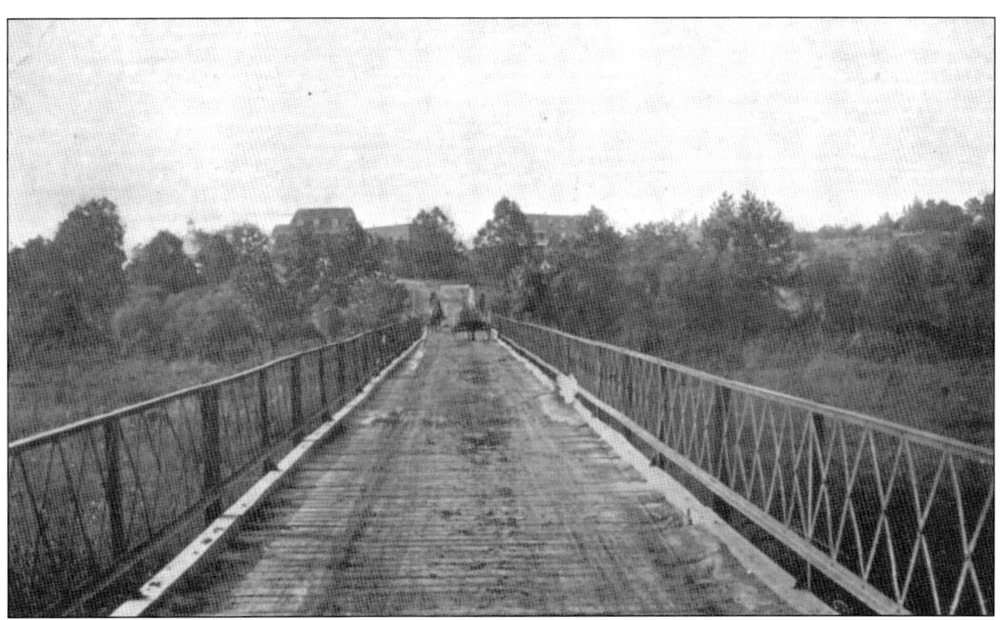

Town Fork Bridge, seen here in 1915, is still the entryway to historic downtown Walnut Cove. In the background, the Vaughn Hotel, Mercantile Building, and Dodson Hotel can be seen. (Author's collection.)

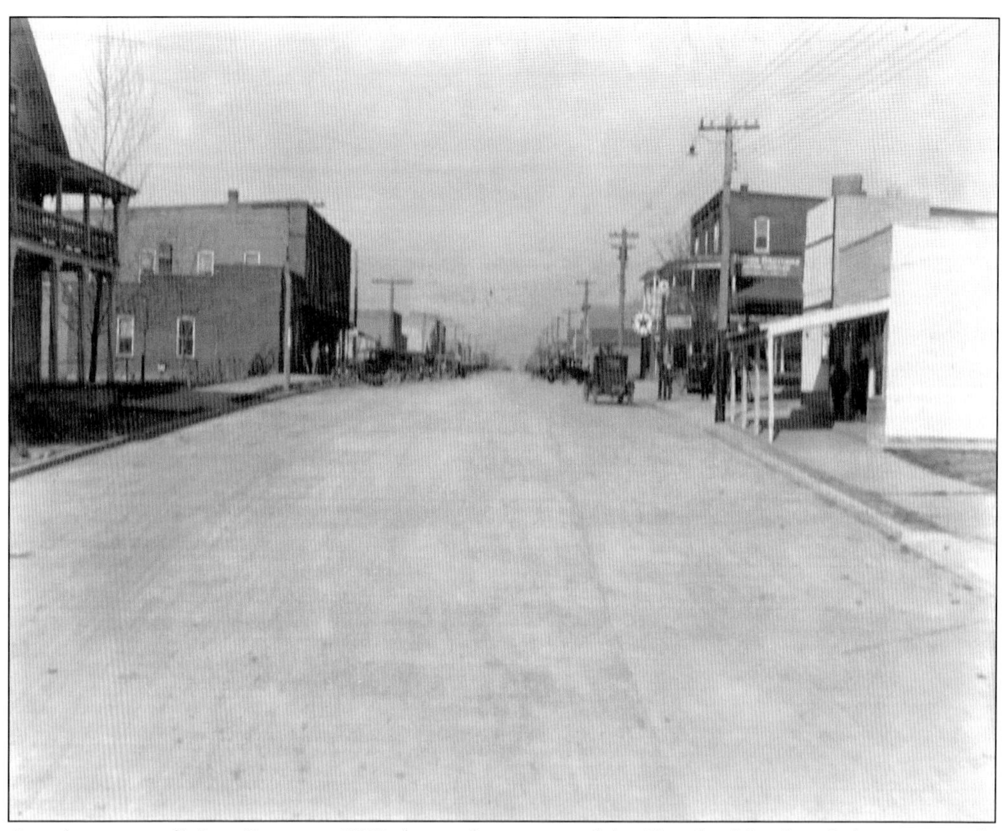

Another view of Main Street in 1922 shows the corner of the Vaughn Hotel and the mercantile building on the left. The Dodson Hotel can be seen on the right. (Courtesy of Barbara Fulton Tuttle.)

BURROUGHS-FOWLER FUNERAL HOME
WALNUT COVE, NORTH CAROLINA

Nº 1376

March 21 1959

RECEIVED FROM Virgil Mitchell

Seventy one + 65/100 DOLLARS

FOR His Share. Funeral of Mr W H Mitchell

$71 65/

BURROUGHS-FOWLER FUNERAL HOME

I.K. Burroughs Secy Treas.

This 1959 receipt was for funeral services at Burroughs-Fowler Funeral Home owned by Ivey Burroughs and Luther Fowler. It was located on Main Street in Walnut Cove. Fowler later sold his interest in 1962, and Burroughs remained in business. In 1972, a new funeral home was built on Highway 65, and it is still in use today. (Author's collection.)

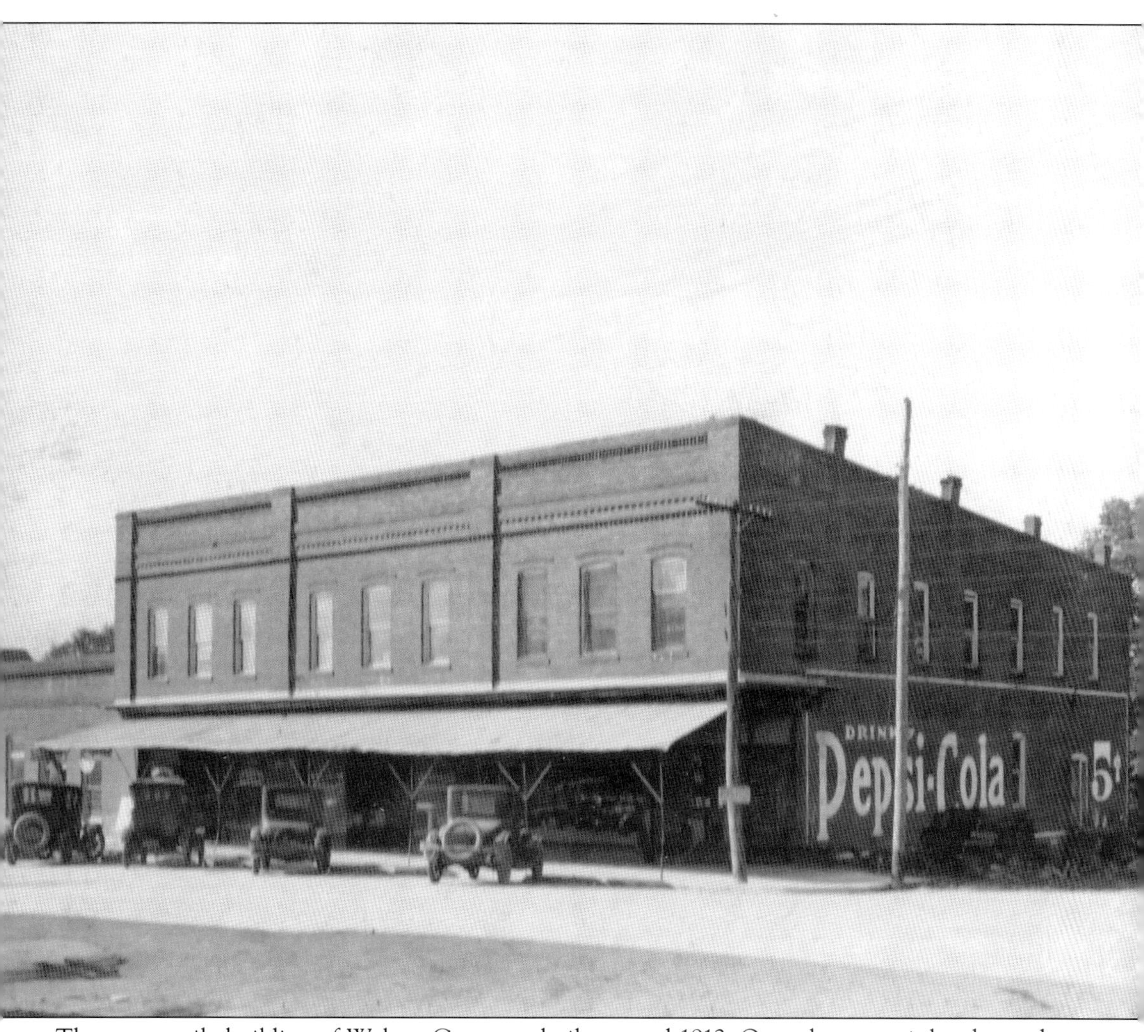

The mercantile building of Walnut Cove was built around 1912. Over the years, it has housed many businesses, such as the post office, hardware stores, undertaking businesses, drugstores, and presently the Law Office of Jerry Rutledge. (Courtesy of Barbara Fulton Tuttle.)

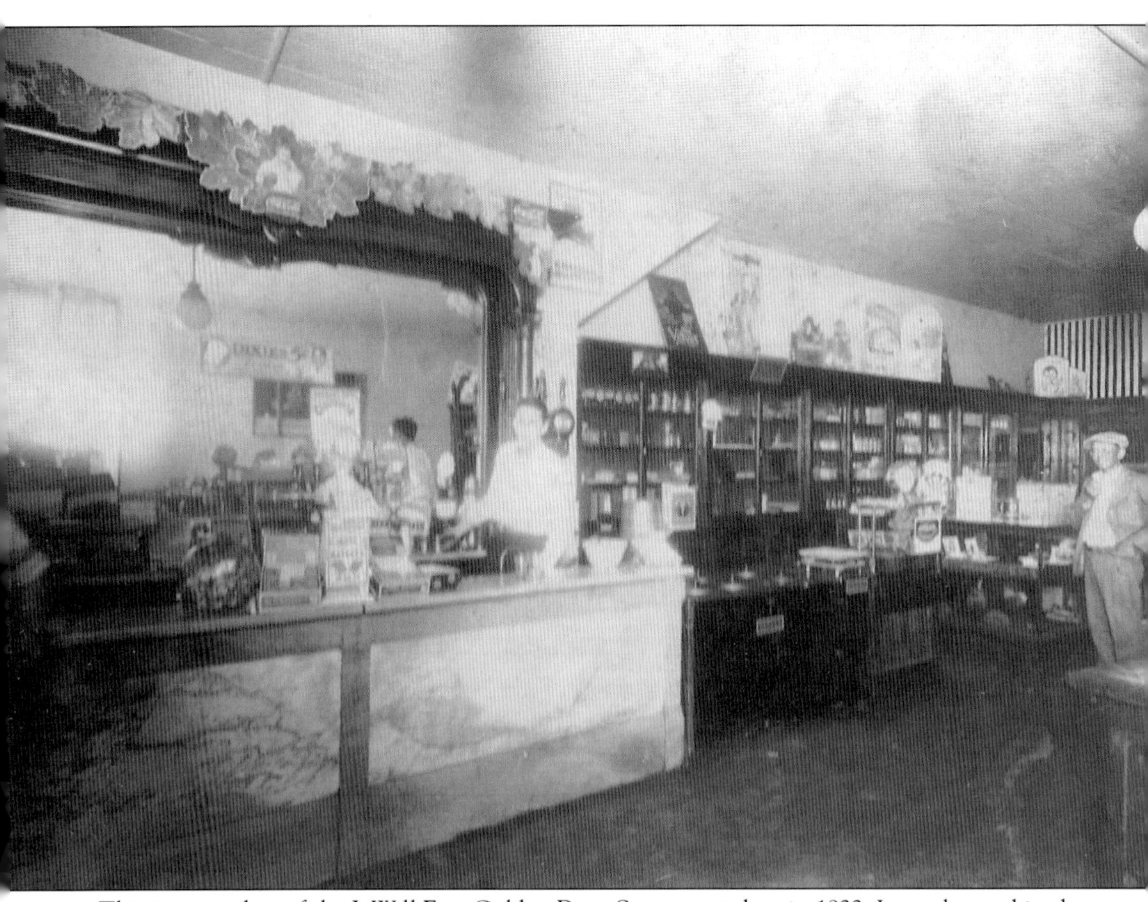

This interior shot of the J. Will East Golden Drug Store was taken in 1922. It was located in the mercantile building, which is presently occupied by the Law Office of Jerry Rutledge. (Courtesy of Barbara Fulton Tuttle.)

DODSON HOTEL
Mrs. Dolly Fair Dodson, Manager

No.

Walnut Cove, N.C., March 25, 1929

Pay to the order of Bank of Stokes Co. $76.28

Seventy-six & 28/100 Dollars

For Ins. Prem. 16.88 59.40 76.28

To BANK OF STOKES COUNTY
66-463
5
WALNUT COVE, N.C.

Dodson Co. Estate
By Dolly Fair Dodson, Admx.

This check came from the register of the Dodson Hotel. Built in 1912 by Wesley Dodson, the hotel featured its own water, sewer lines, and electric system. The hotel was a popular stop for traveling salesmen and people heading for the resorts near Danbury. (Courtesy of Lois Dodson Smith.)

DODSON HOTEL
Mrs. W. G. Dodson, Proprietress

WALNUT COVE, N. C., 192

Room # 1
1 Iron bed, mattress & springs
1 wash stand
1 Dresser
1 Table
1 Chair
1 Lamp
1 Bowl & Pitcher
1 slop jar
2 Shades
1 soap dish
2 Dresser scarfs
2 Towels
2 Sheets
2 Pillows & cases
1 Spread
1 Blanket
1 Drugget
1 Rug.

Found on this hotel stationery is an inventory of the contents of room No. 1 at the Dodson Hotel. This room featured more amenities than others, but every room had at least a bed, dresser, washstand, and slop jar. (Courtesy of Lois Dodson Smith.)

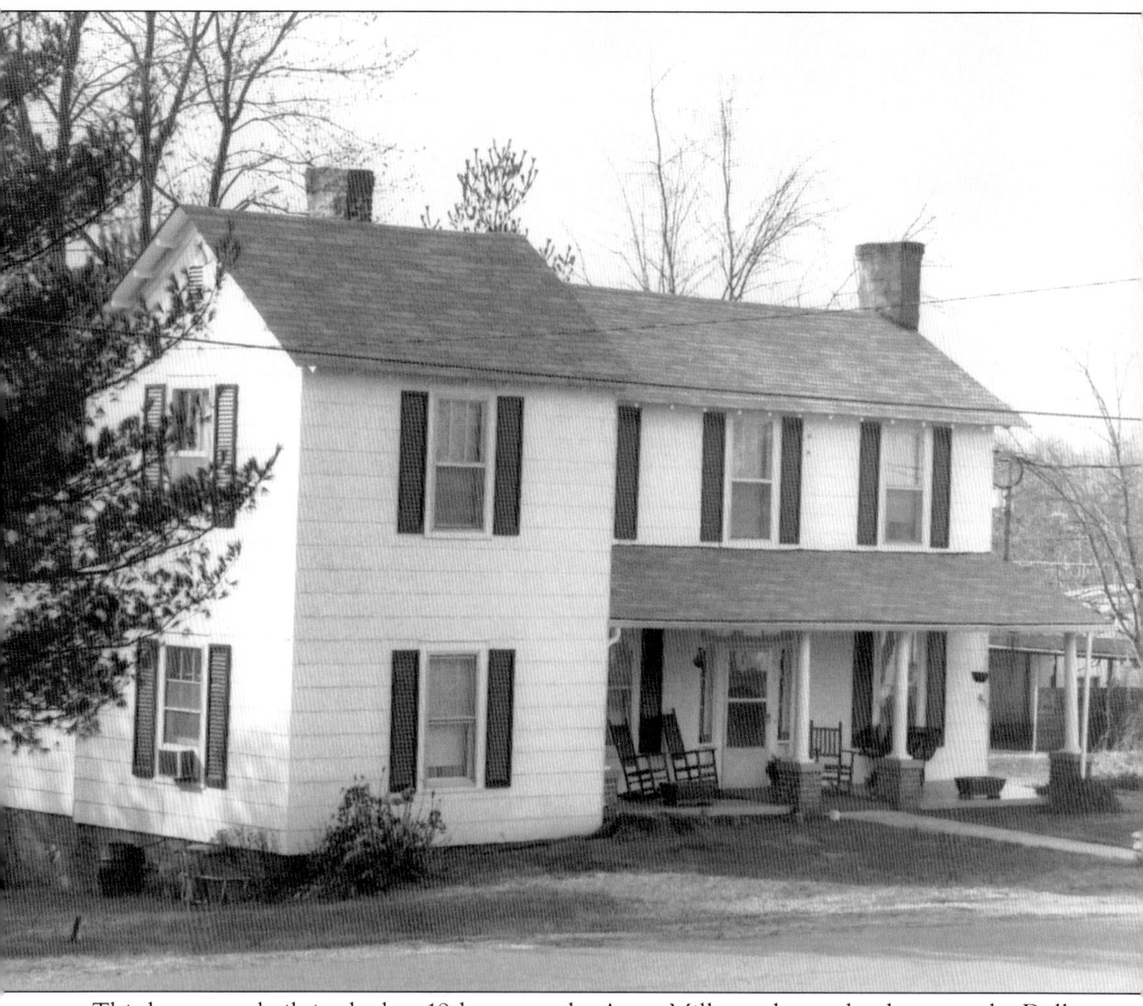

This house was built in the late 19th century by Amos Miller and served as home to the Dolly Fair Dodson family after the death of her husband, Wesley, in 1924. The late Lois Dodson Smith, a prominent member of Walnut Cove and daughter of Dolly Fair Dodson, lived in this home for many years after her mother. (Courtesy of Lois Dodson Smith.)

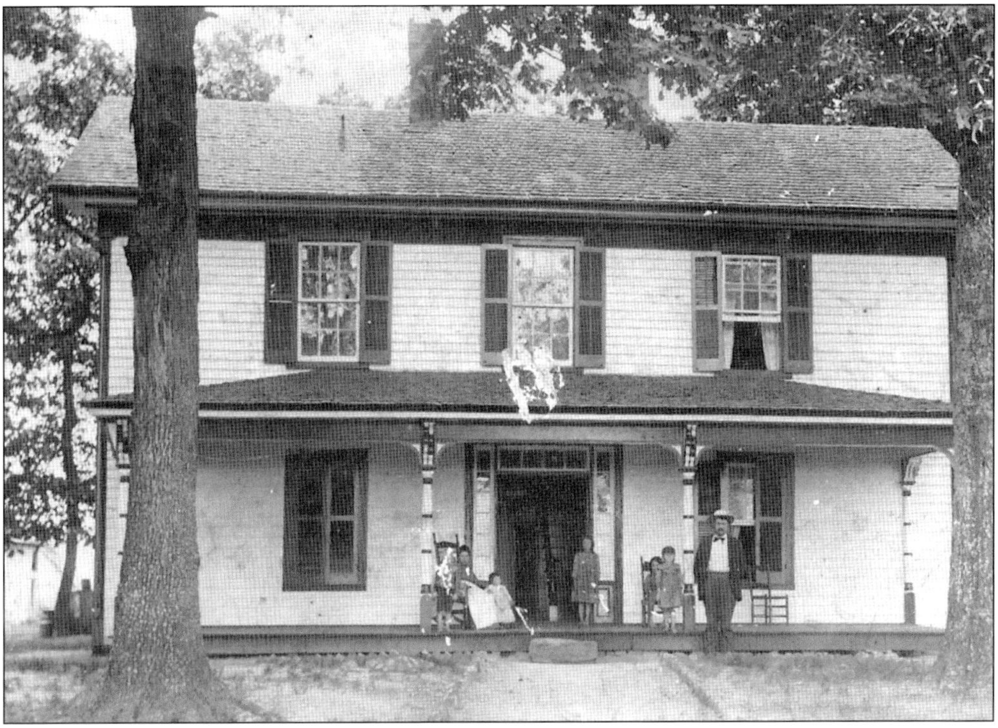

The Woodruff family was important in the development and success of Walnut Cove. In this 1905 photograph is the Woodruff home that stood on Summit Street. This image was captured before the addition of bedrooms and the renovation of the porch. (Courtesy of Barbara Fulton Tuttle.)

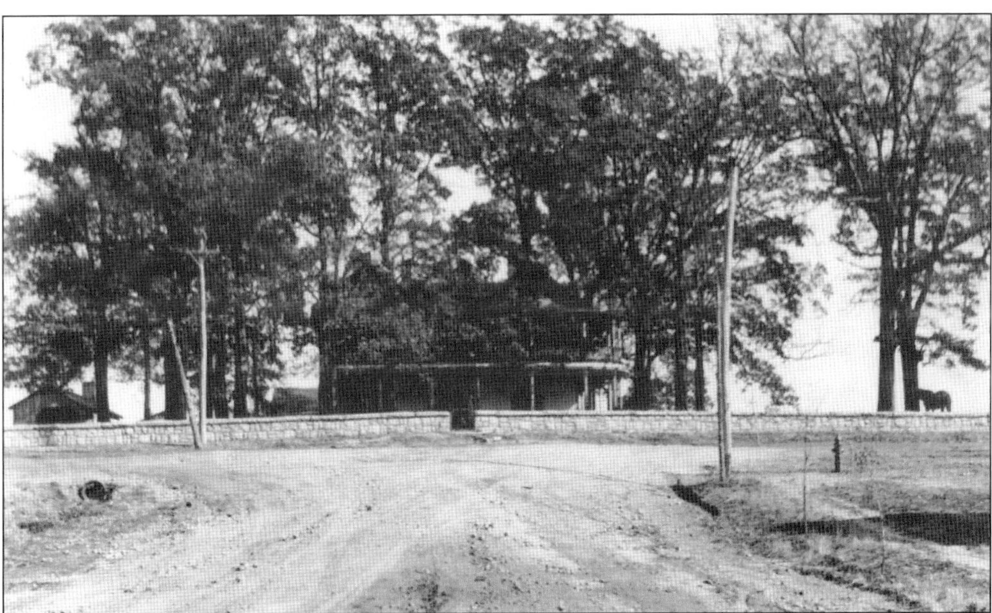

This photograph of the Woodruff home was taken around 1925 after renovations. Notice the large granite wall surrounding the home, which still remains today. The horse seen in the side yard was named Duke. (Courtesy of Barbara Fulton Tuttle.)

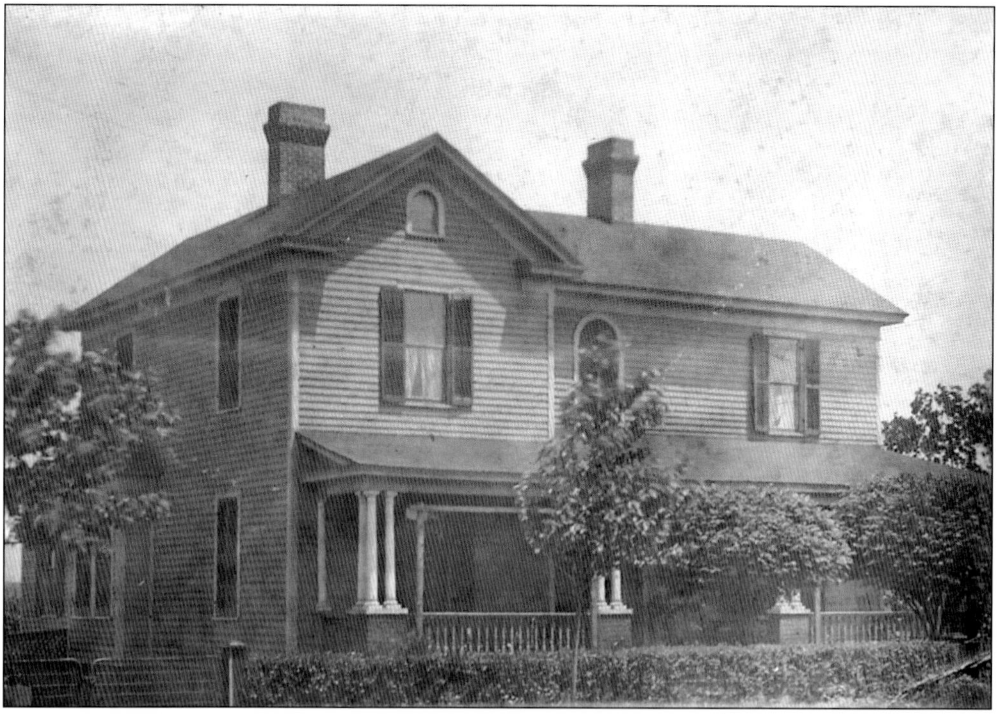

William F. Bowles built this house in 1910 after his marriage to Lilly Fair. It is seen here a few years after its completion. It has been the property of Christ Episcopal Church for many years, and has been used for functions and meetings. (Courtesy of Lois Dodson Smith.)

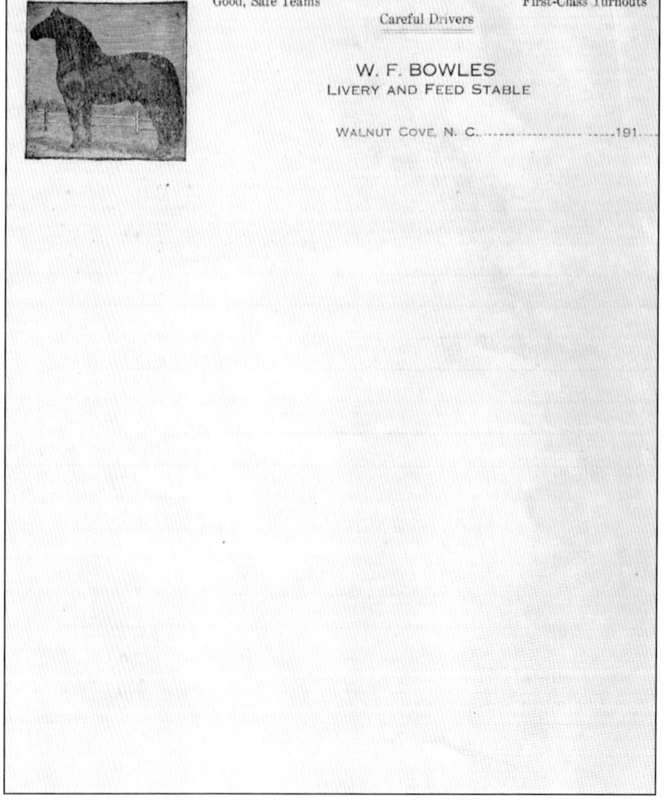
Good, Safe Teams
Careful Drivers
First-Class Turnouts

W. F. BOWLES
LIVERY AND FEED STABLE

WALNUT COVE, N. C.......................191....

Bowles, a key character in the early success of Walnut Cove, was a known businessman. This stationery was from a livery stable that he operated in the early part of the 20th century. (Courtesy of Hazel F. Bowles.)

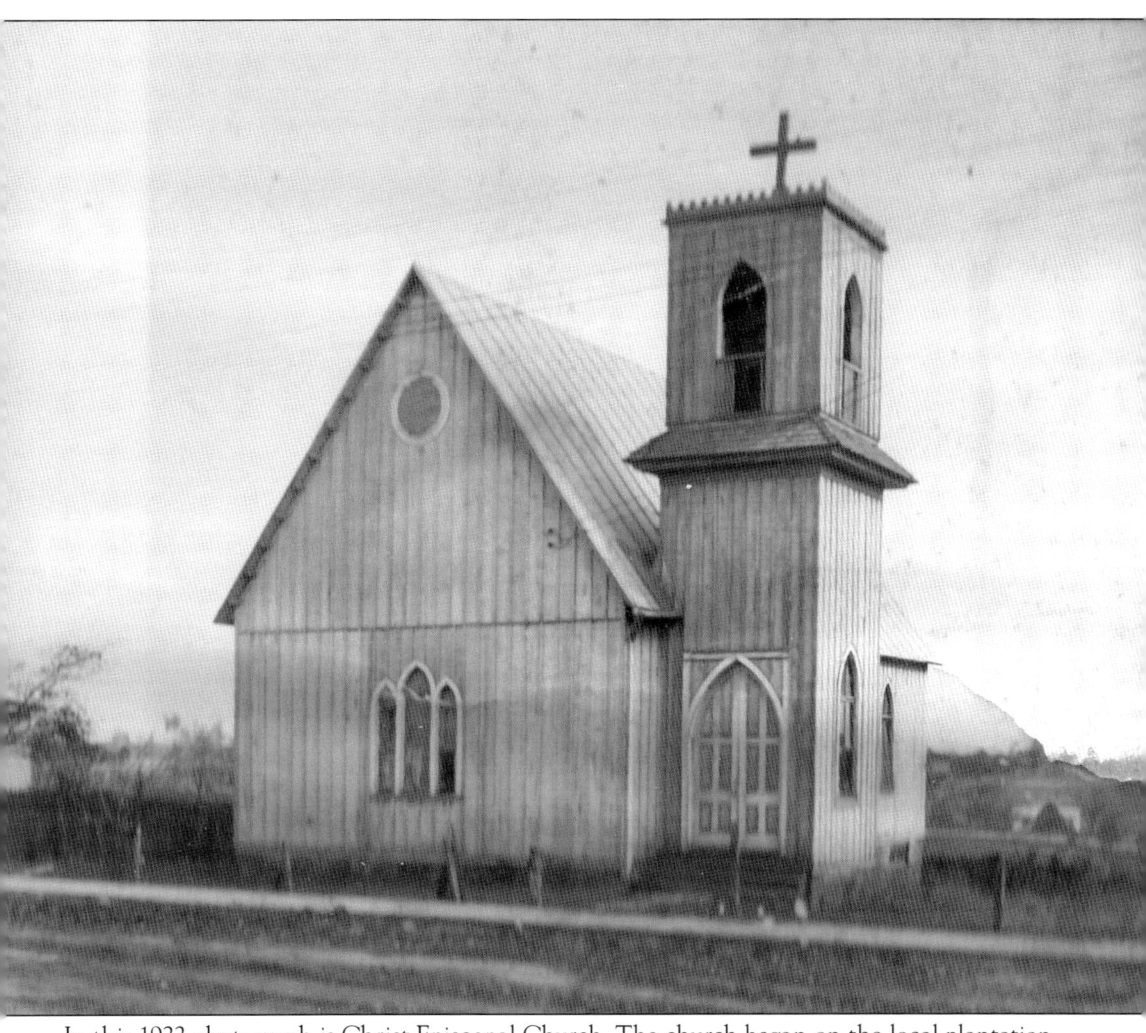

In this 1922 photograph is Christ Episcopal Church. The church began on the local plantation of the Hairston family, and many of the stained-glass windows bare the family's name. Built in 1886, the church was originally located where the Walnut Cove cemetery is today; it was moved in 1909. (Courtesy of Barbara Fulton Tuttle.)

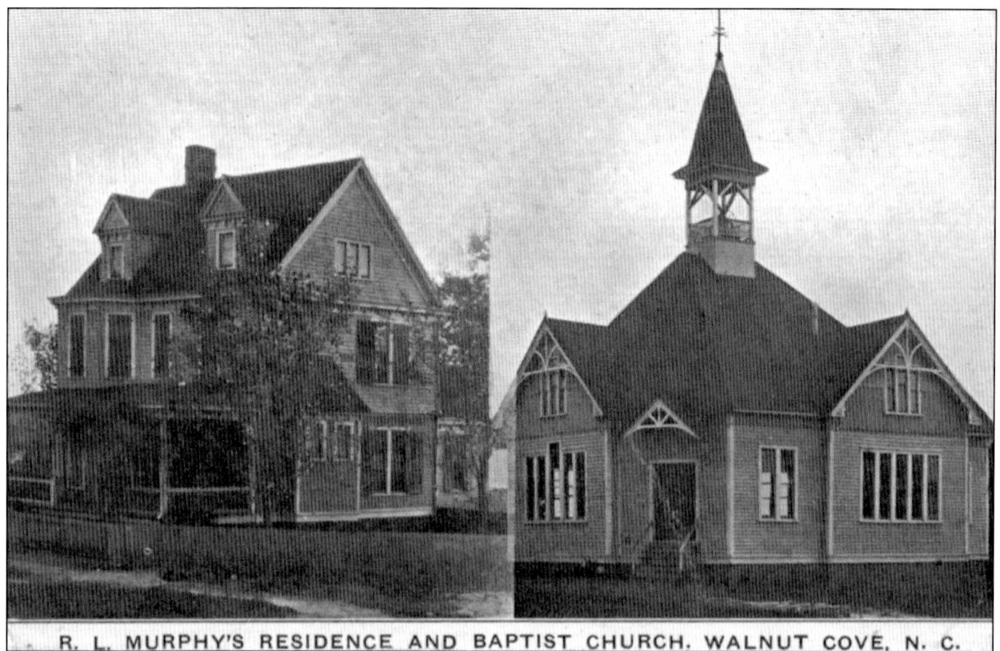

On the left, "Murphy's Castle," built by R.L. Murphy, is shown around 1915. This beautiful late-1800s home still stands on Summit Street. On the right is the earliest building of First Baptist Church. Although housed in a new structure, it is still a very active congregation. (Courtesy of Wayne and Louise Biby.)

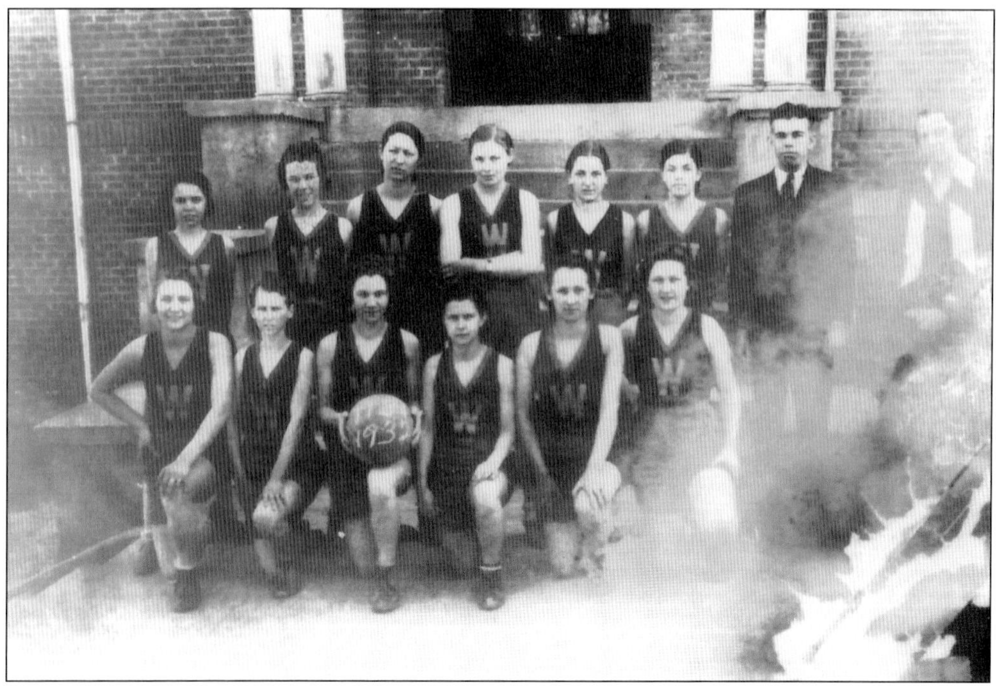

The Walnut Cove School basketball team is pictured on the front steps of Walnut Cove School in 1932. (Courtesy of Durwood and Patti Dunlap.)

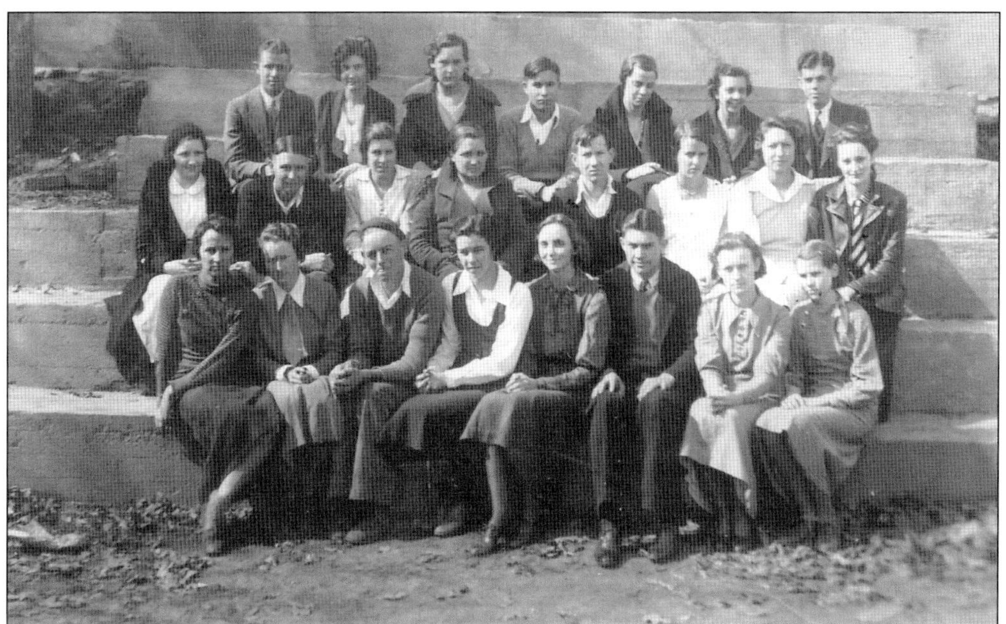

Walnut Cove School's class of 1932–1933 poses for this photograph on the steps leading down from Summit Street to Walnut Cove School in 1932. (Courtesy of Durwood and Patti Dunlap.)

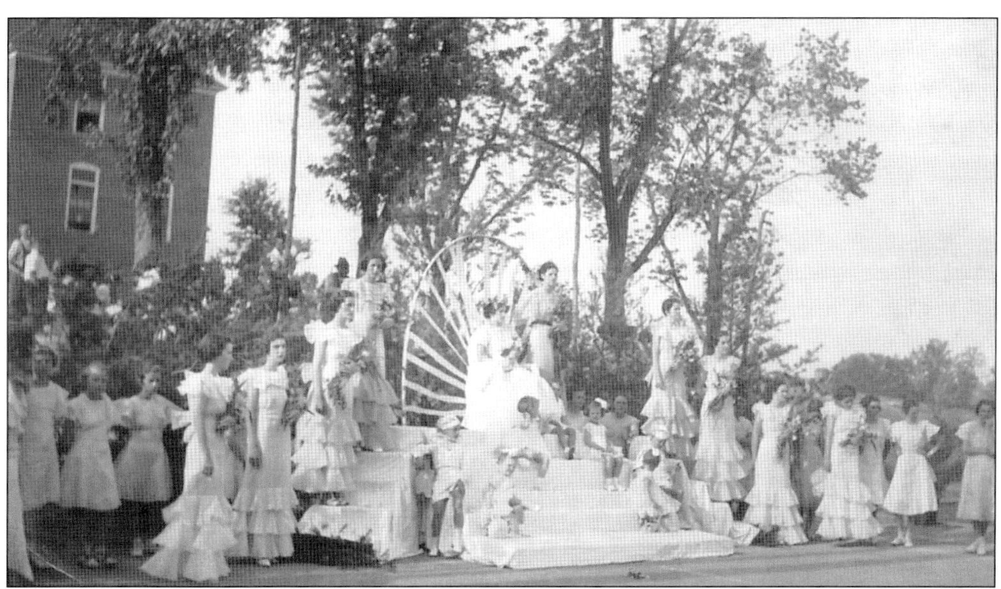

An annual tradition was that of the May Dance. Shown here is a May Queen celebration at Walnut Cove High School in the 1930s. (Courtesy of Dr. Jack and Nancy Helsabeck Fowler.)

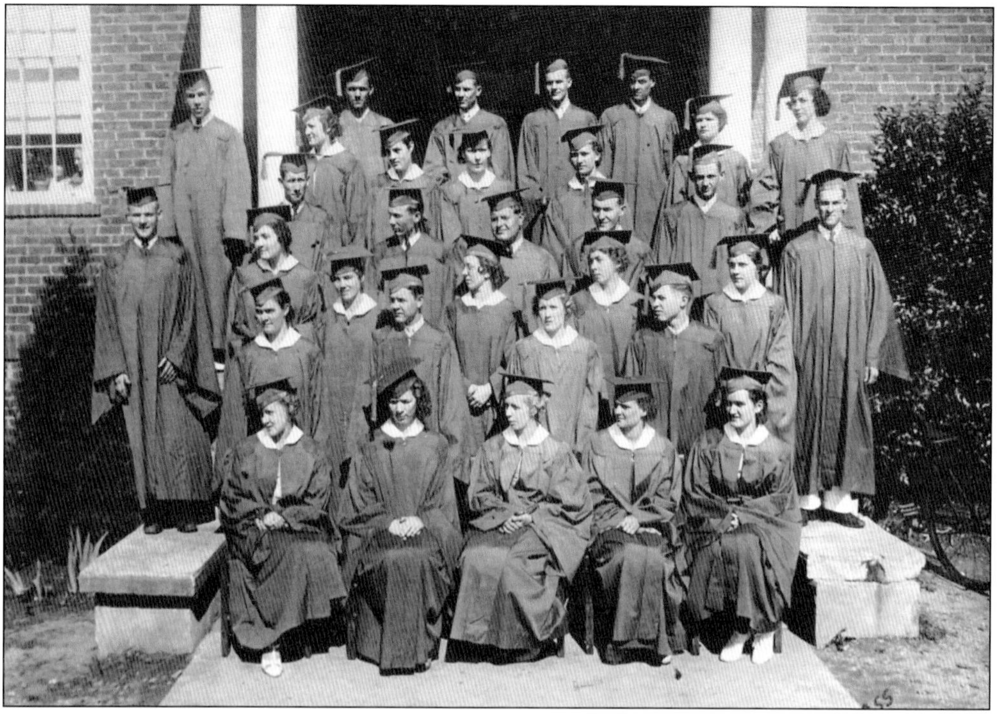

The 1935 class of Walnut Cove High School gathers on the steps to pose in their caps and gowns while anxiously awaiting graduation. (Courtesy of Lois Dodson Smith.)

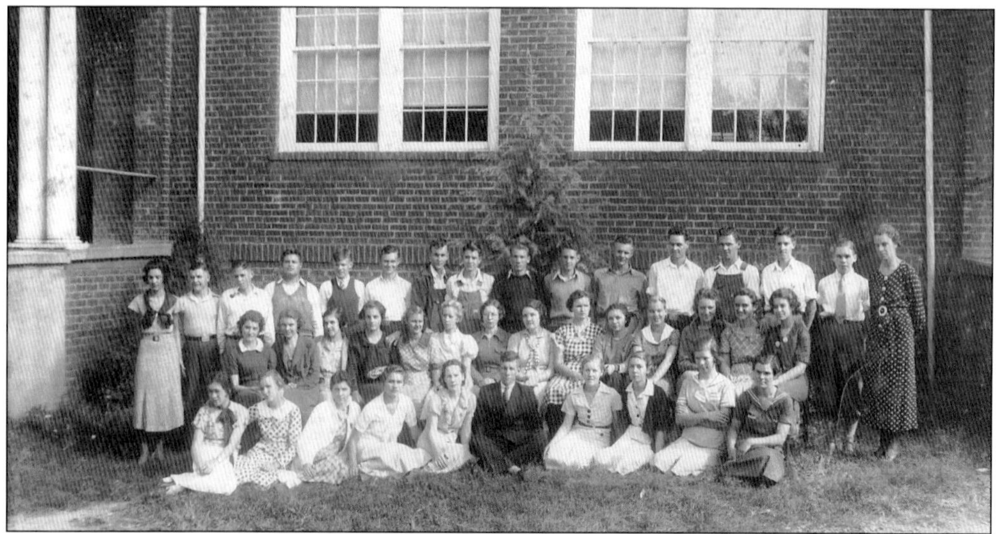

Pictured is the Walnut Cove class of 1935. They are, from left to right, (first row) Nellie Duggins, Dorothy Lackey, Ida Morgan, Lennis Flinchum, Mary Russell, Herman Fulp, Hazel Bowles, Lois Smith, Nellie Venable, and Margaret Burton; (second row) Sara Flinchum, Mary Powell, Marie Fitzgerald, Annie Neal, Mary Lasley, Louisa Mounce, Geneva Flynt, Florence Gerry, Thelma Priddy, Nell King, Evelyn Tuttle, Virginia Hensdale, Virginia Burton, and Lois Martin; (third row) teacher Mary Neal, R. Vaughn, Barlow Bowles, Hiram Adkins, Harry Hutchison, Maria Brown, Harry Smith, J. Wall, Posey Rhodes, Sam Kirby, Paul Craig, Theron Wood, Joseph Lasley, Gordon Wood, and Briggs Neal. (Courtesy of Lois Dodson Smith.)

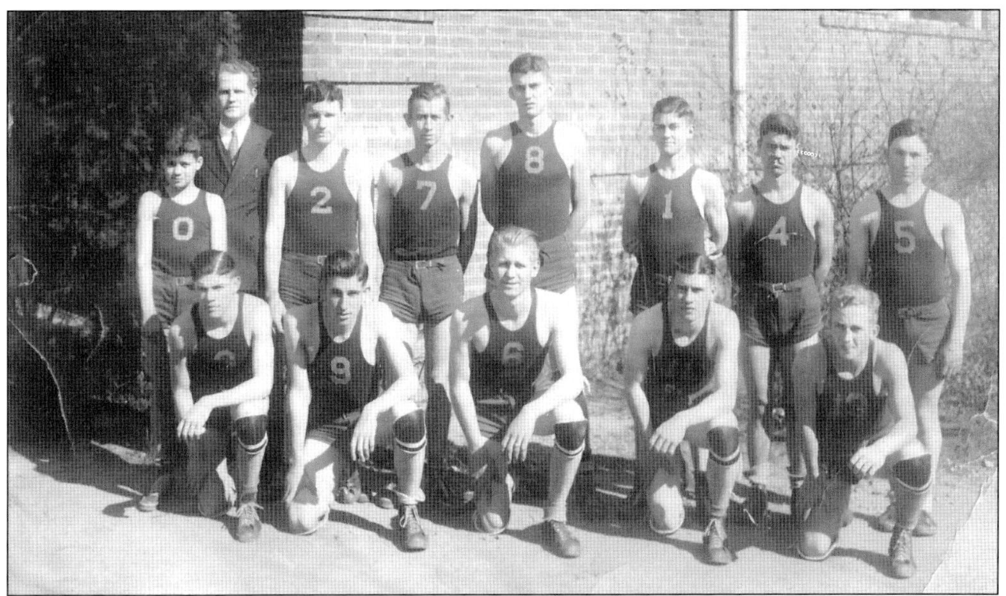

The Walnut Cove School Basketball Team of 1938–1939 lineup is pictured here. No. 0 is Jack Gentry, No. 2 is Ray Sisk, No. 7 is Wesley Dunlap, No. 8 is Beverly Christian, No. 1 is Byron Hill, No. 4 is Buck Wall, No. 5 is Arthur Brown, No. 3 is Walter Sands, No. 9 is Dunkle Dunlap, No. 6 is Esca Carroll, No. 11 is William Smith, and No. 12 is Tom Crews. (Courtesy Durwood and Patti Dunlap.)

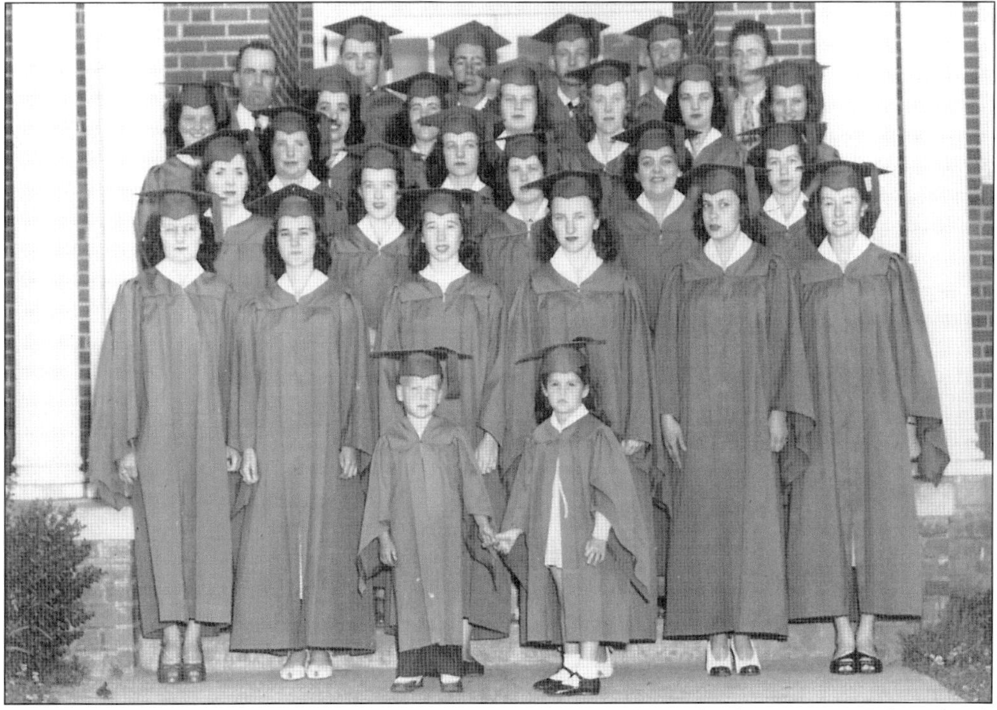

A Walnut Cove High School class poses for this photograph on the front steps of the school. Mascots were always typical during this era. Note the two small children in the front holding hands. (Courtesy of Margie Dunlap.)

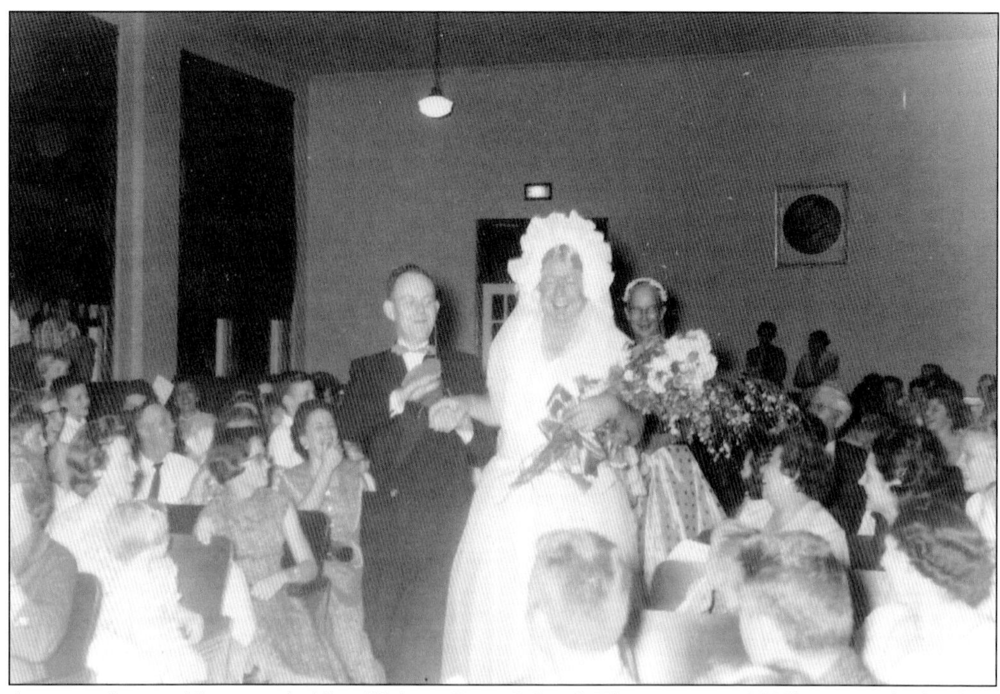

A womanless wedding was held at Walnut Cove School. The groom is Al Ellington, the bride is Pete Donaldson, and the attendant is Bill Bailey. (Courtesy Richard and Kimbyl Alley Ferrell.)

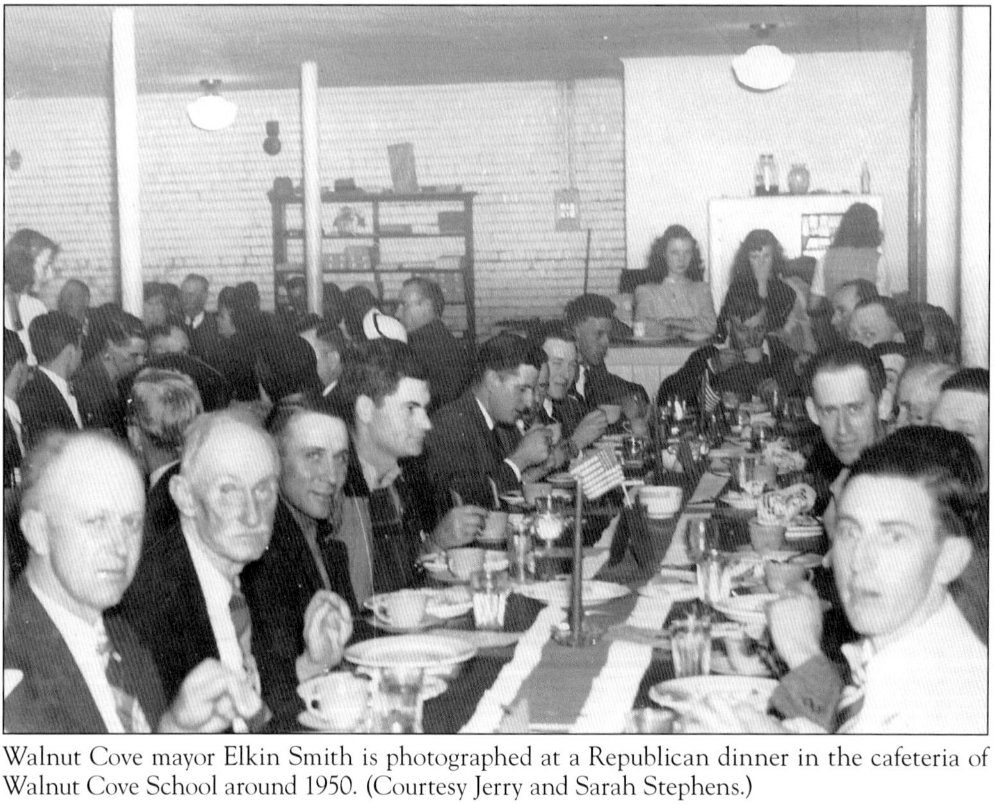

Walnut Cove mayor Elkin Smith is photographed at a Republican dinner in the cafeteria of Walnut Cove School around 1950. (Courtesy Jerry and Sarah Stephens.)

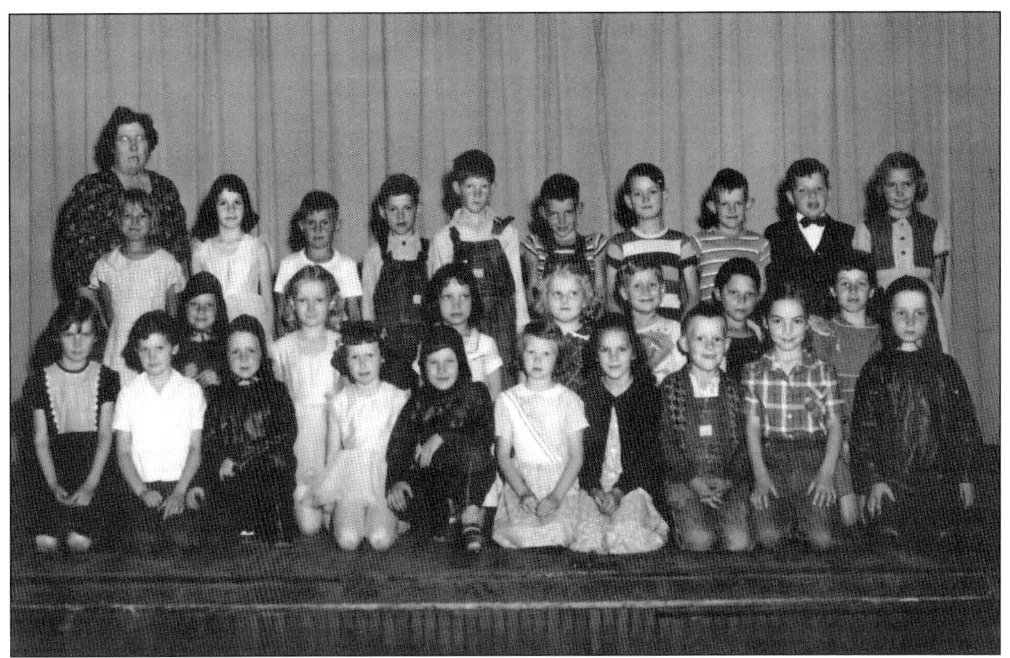

Janie Tuttle's class of 1951 poses after completion of a play at Walnut Cove School. (Courtesy Jerry and Sarah Stephens.)

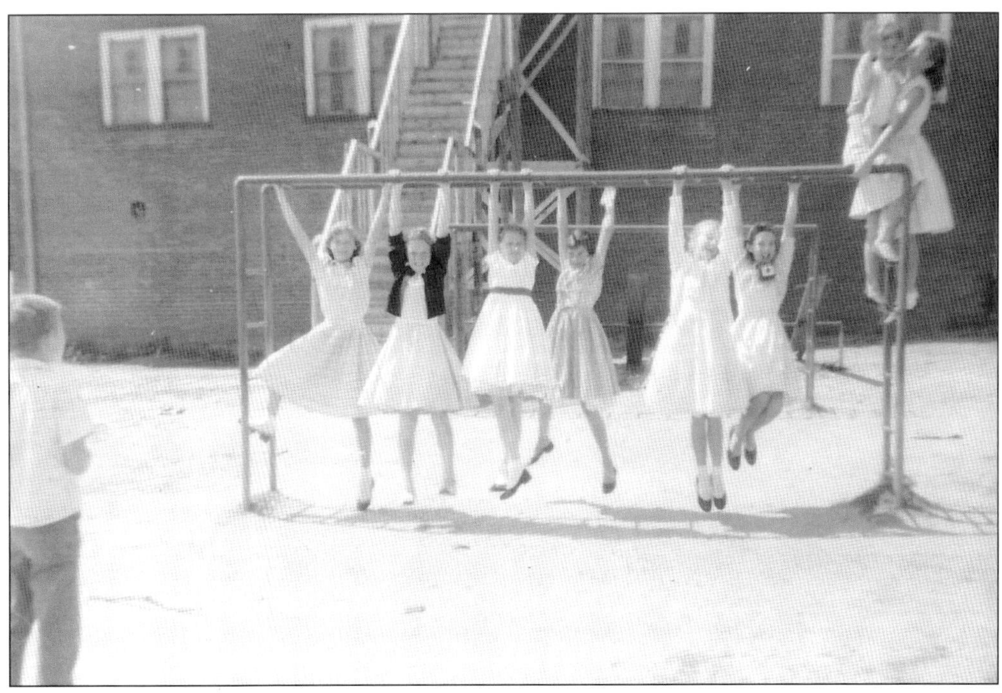

Young girls play on the monkey bars outside of Walnut Cove School in the 1950s. (Courtesy Jerry and Sarah Stephens.)

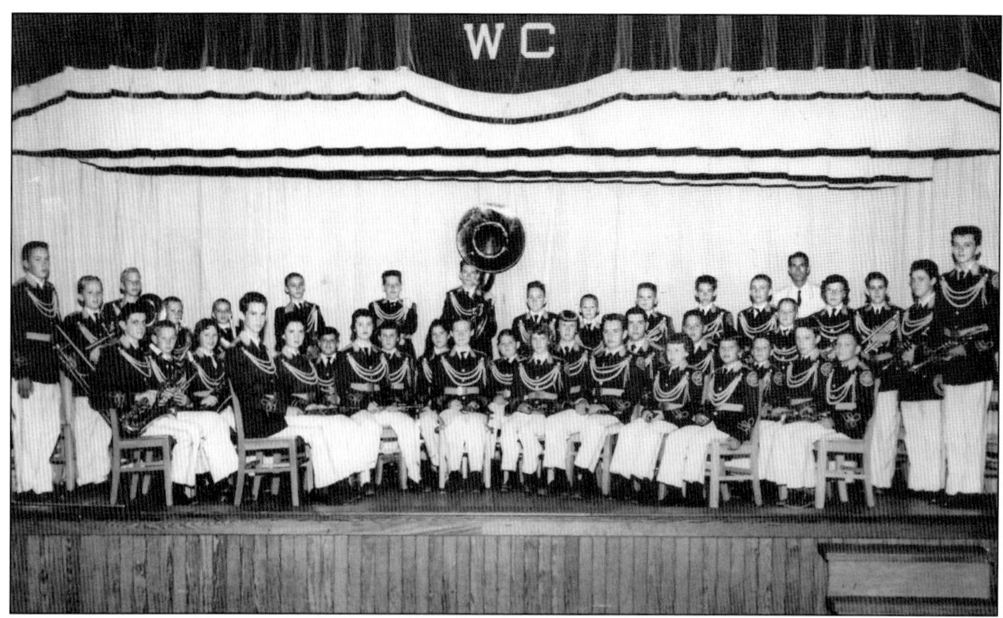

School bands have been known to encourage a sense of school spirit. Walnut Cove School's band proudly poses around 1958. (Courtesy of Margie Dunlap.)

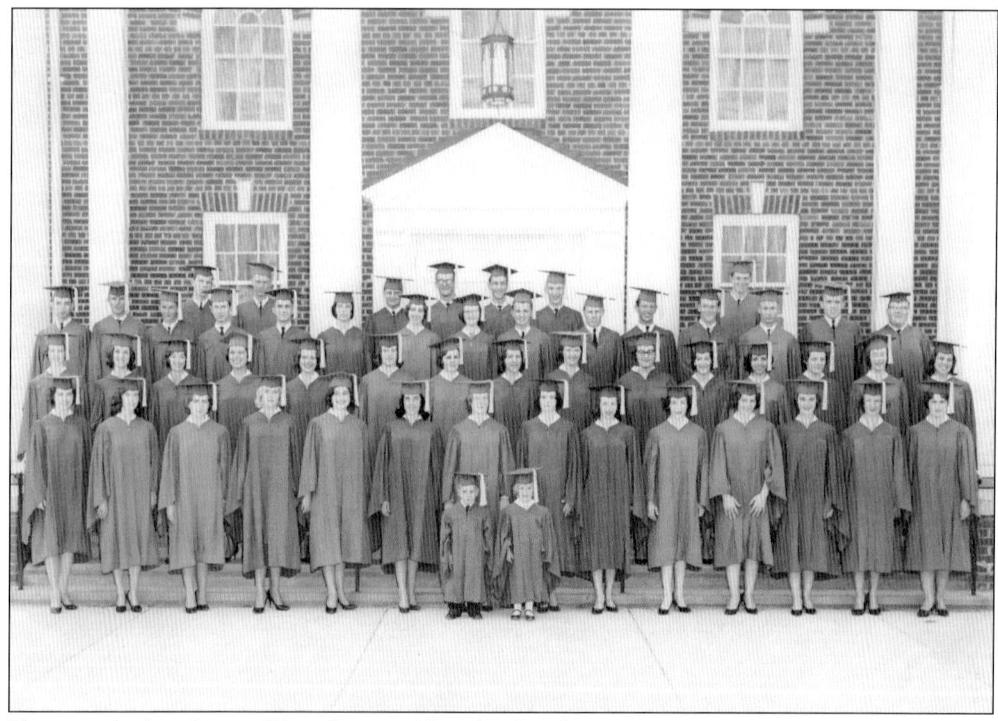

Photographed in front of First Baptist Church of Walnut Cove is the last class that graduated from Walnut Cove High School in 1964. The school consolidated when the larger South Stokes High School was built. (Courtesy of Jerry and Yvonne Lewis Mitchell.)

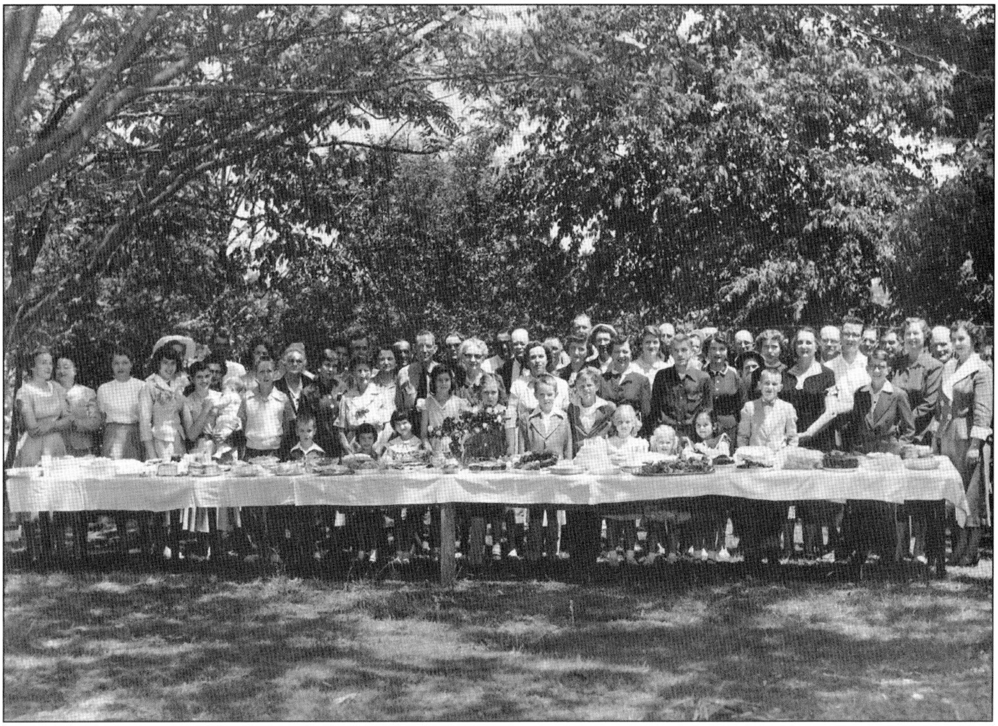

Family gatherings have been a time of coming together for many years in Stokes County. Seen here is a birthday party for Burchie Ray Dunlap, who lived on Summit Street. Also pictured are community members such as Jack and Barbara Gentry. (Courtesy of Durwood and Patti Dunlap.)

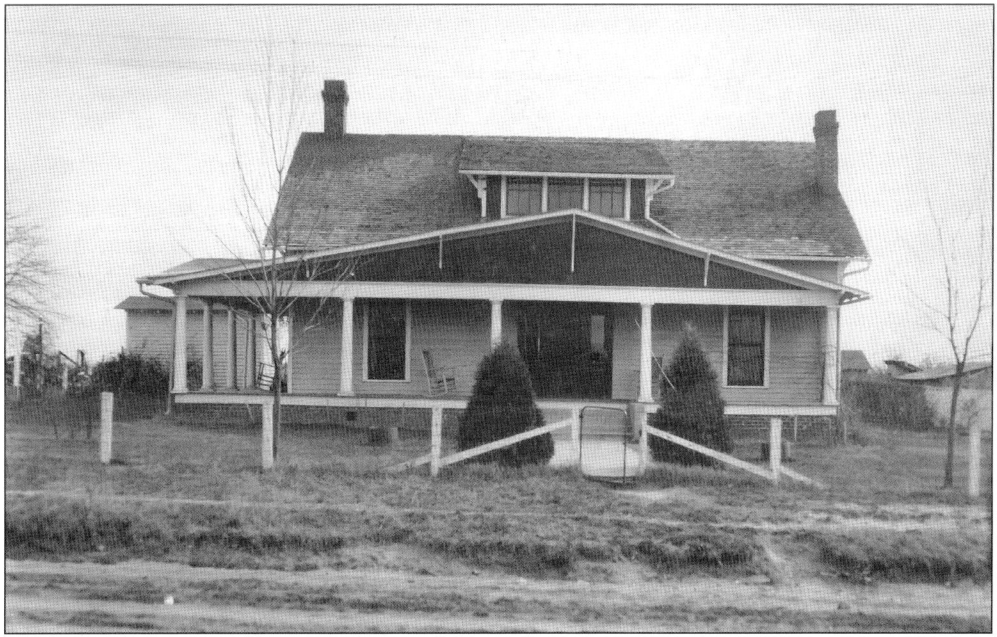

This house was built by the Neal family in the early 1900s. It served as the home of George Neal Sr. and remained in the Neal Hardware Co. family with ownership by Erna Neal until a few years ago. It is located on Summit Street. (Courtesy of Linda Neal Alcott.)

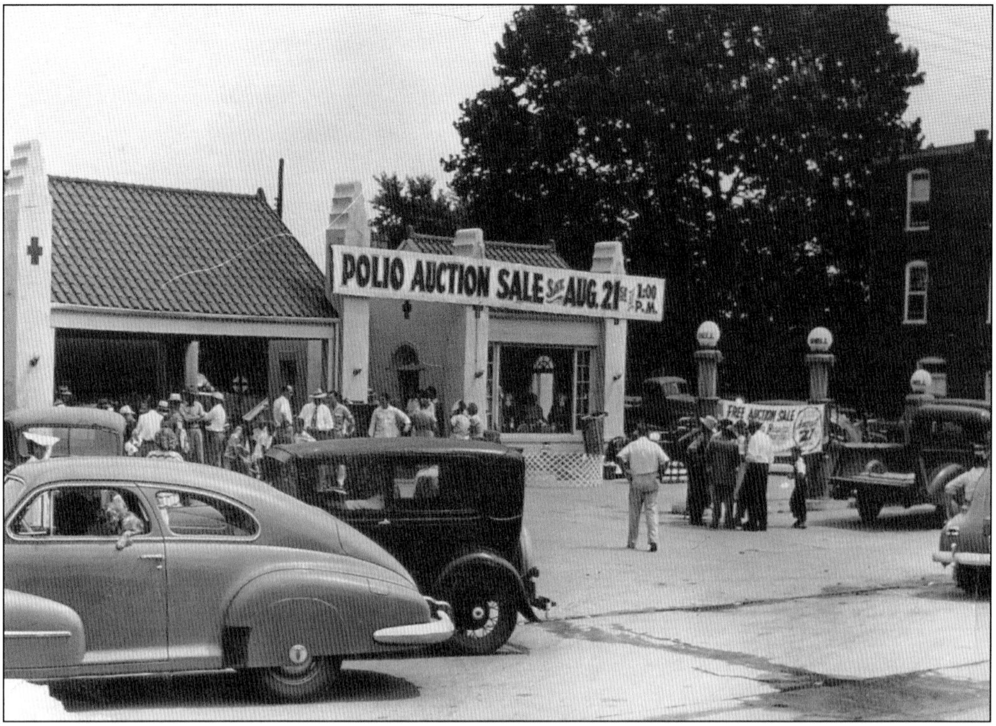

This scene is of a benefit auction for those affected by the polio epidemic in the 1940s. (Courtesy of Mary Finland Landreth.)

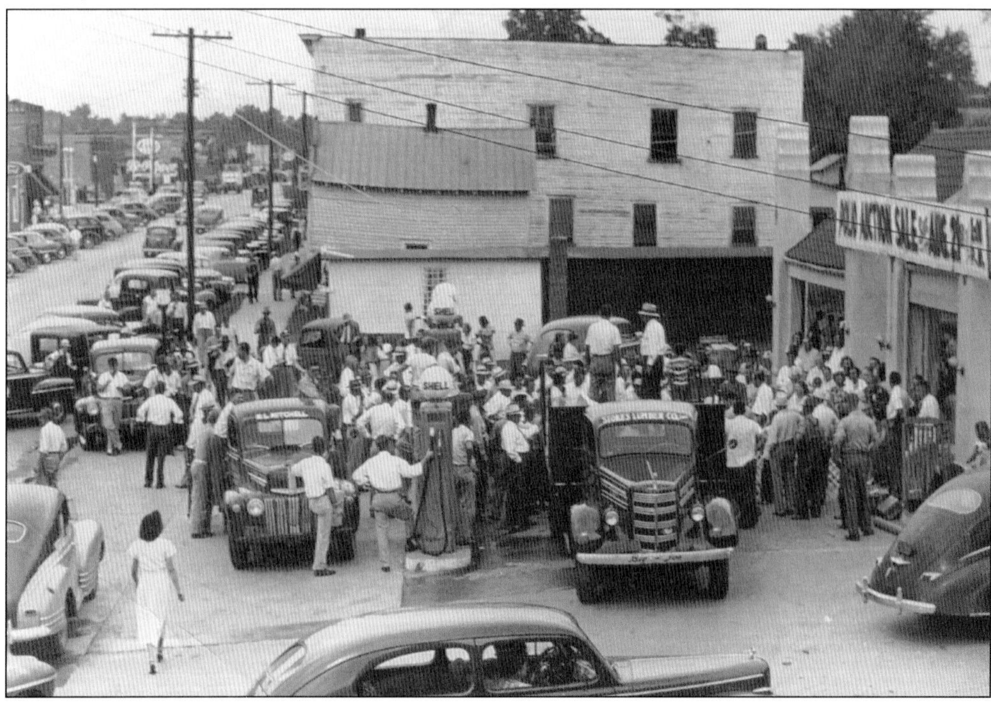

Another view of the polio benefit auction was captured here from the balcony of the Dodson Hotel. M.L. Mitchell's meat truck is visible in the crowd. (Courtesy of Mary Finland Landreth.)

Vernon's Grill was a favorite hangout for the community members of Walnut Cove, and many organizations, such as the Rotary Club, held meetings there. Owner Kathleen Vernon stopped cooking at the grill long enough to pose for this photograph in the 1960s. (Courtesy of Lois Dodson Smith.)

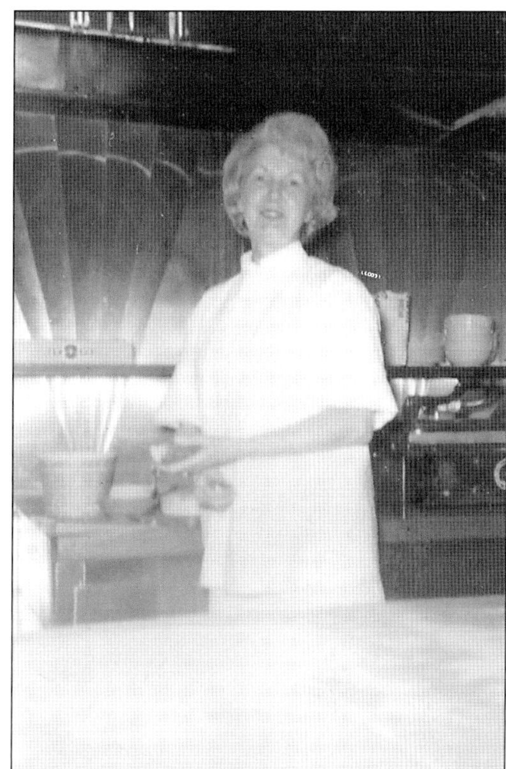

This early shot captures the Walnut Cove Ford Motor Company. Notice the visible gas pumps on the curb of the road. In recent years, this building served Tent and Canvas Works, but it remains in much of its original state. (Courtesy of Barbara Fulton Tuttle.)

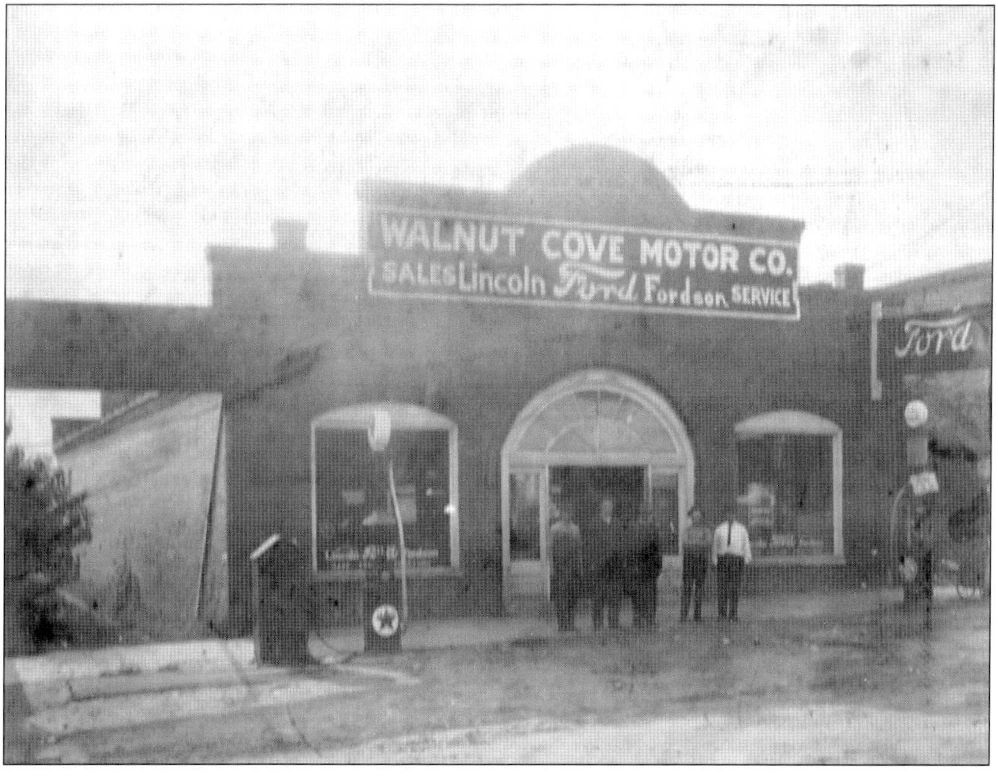

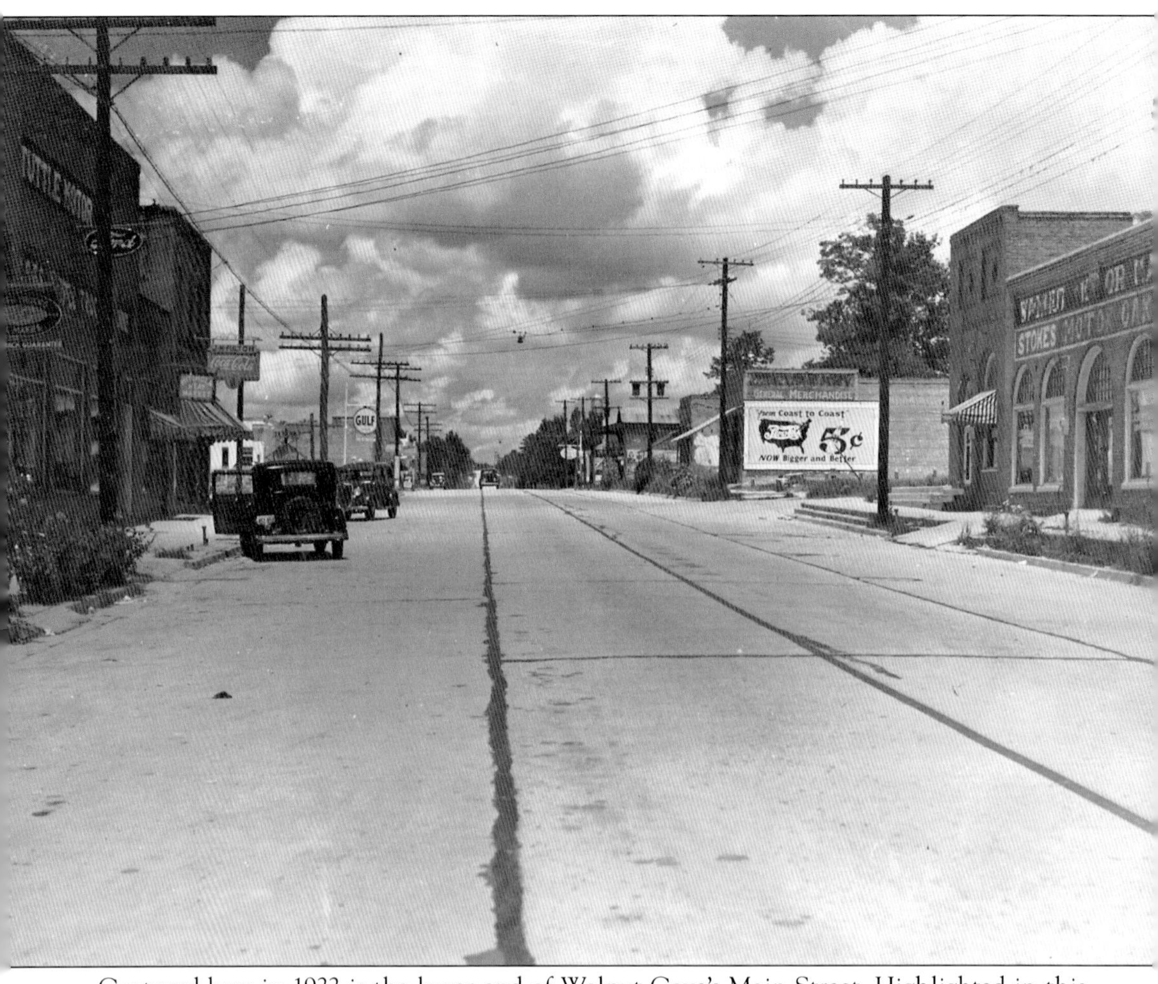

Captured here in 1922 is the lower end of Walnut Cove's Main Street. Highlighted in this photograph are businesses such as Tuttle Motor Company, Stokes Motor Car Company, Mitchola Meat Market, and Crews Barbershop. (Courtesy of Barbara Fulton Tuttle.)

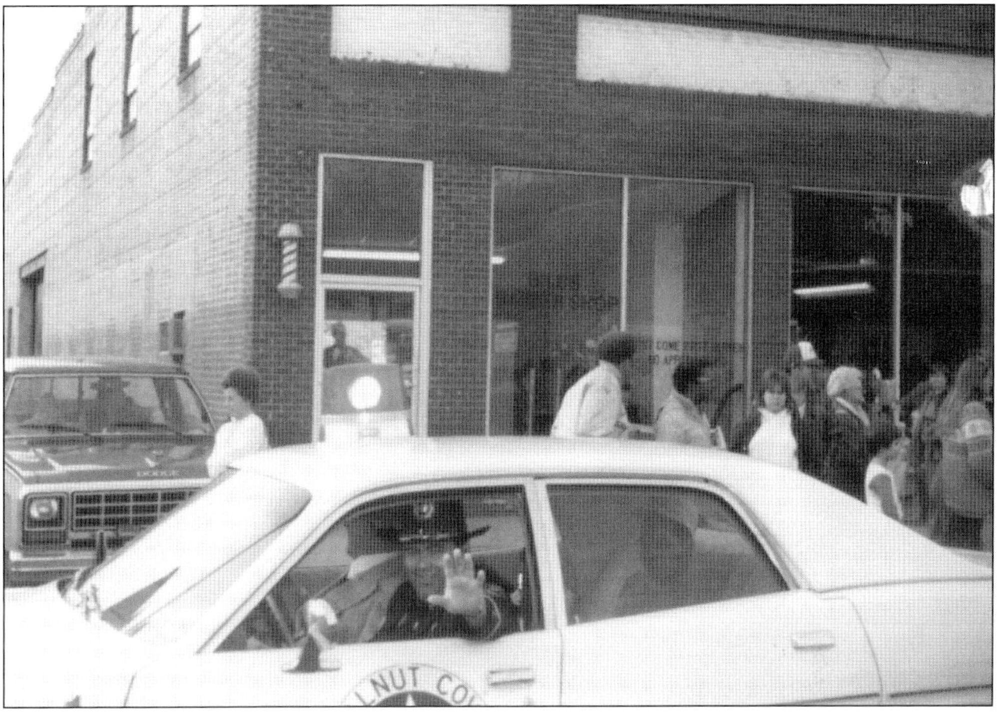

Mike Joyce, former sheriff of Stokes County, is seen here waving from his patrol car during the 1985 Christmas parade. Bill's Barbershop is in the background. (Courtesy of Tracey Brown Edwards.)

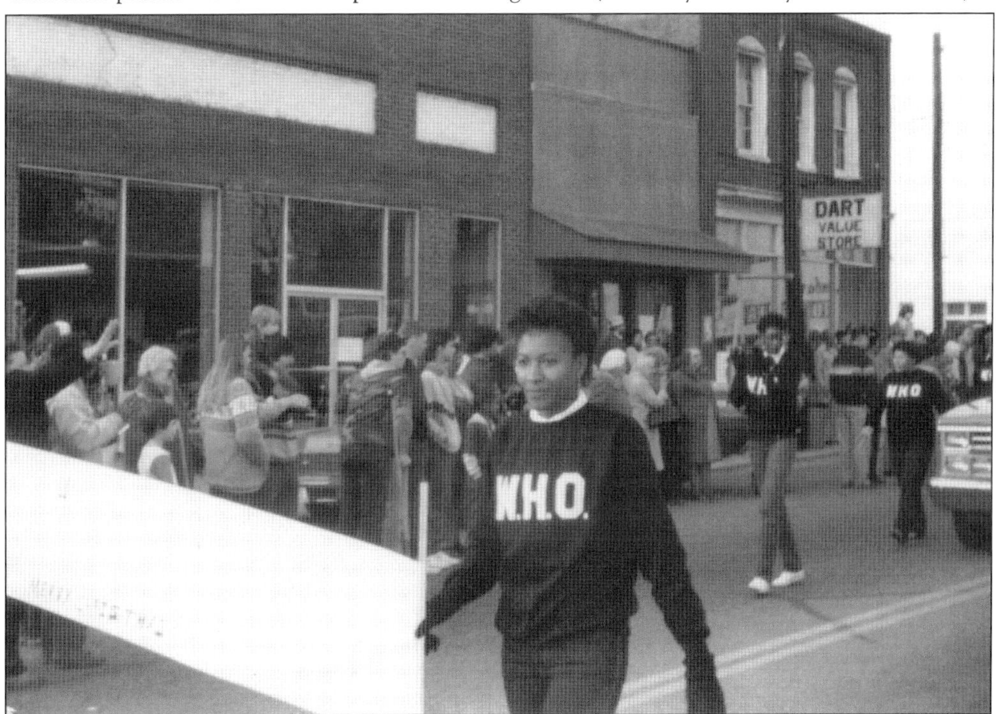

Ada Linster marches in the 1985 Christmas parade. In the background, Sue Tuttle's Beauty Shop and Dart's Variety Store can be seen. (Courtesy of Tracey Brown Edwards.)

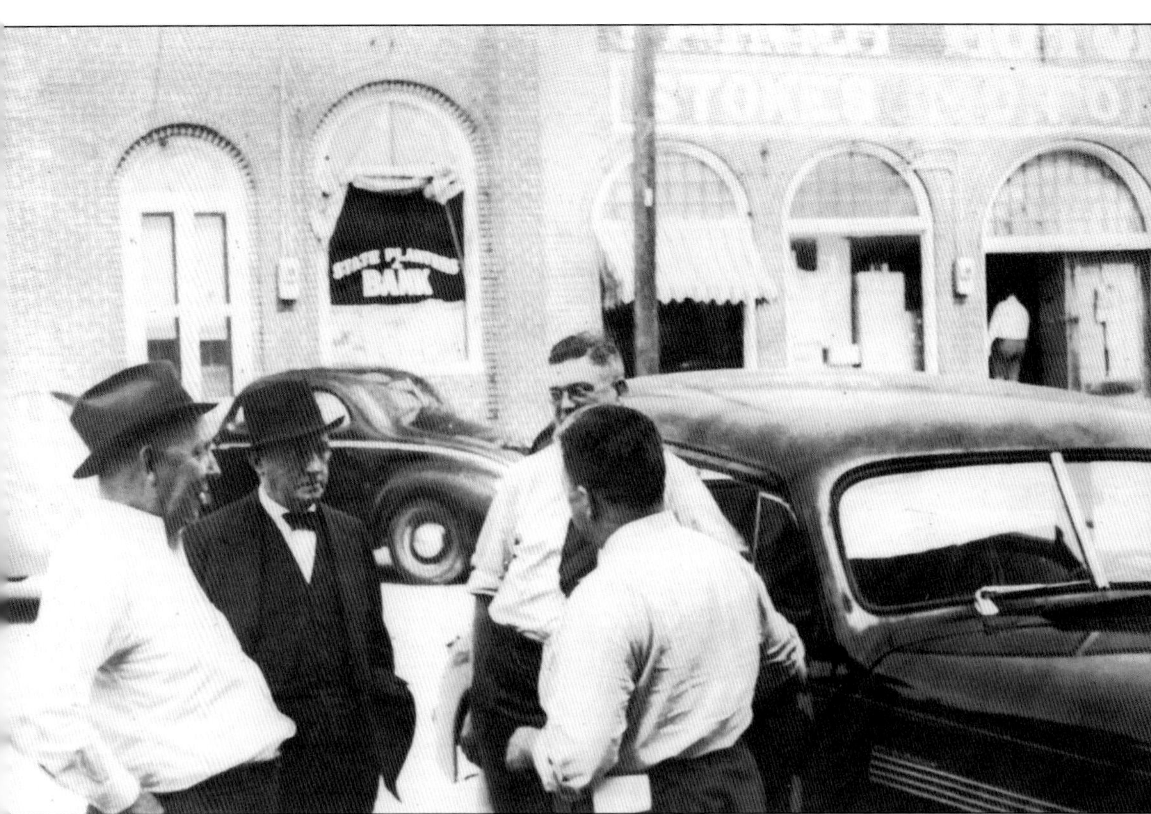

Main Street in Walnut Cove was not only a place to shop but also a place to converse. A favorite topic amongst the local men was politics, which is probably what Jacob Fulton (standing next to the car, facing the camera) and these men were discussing. In the background is State Planter's Bank. (Courtesy of Barbara Fulton Tuttle.)

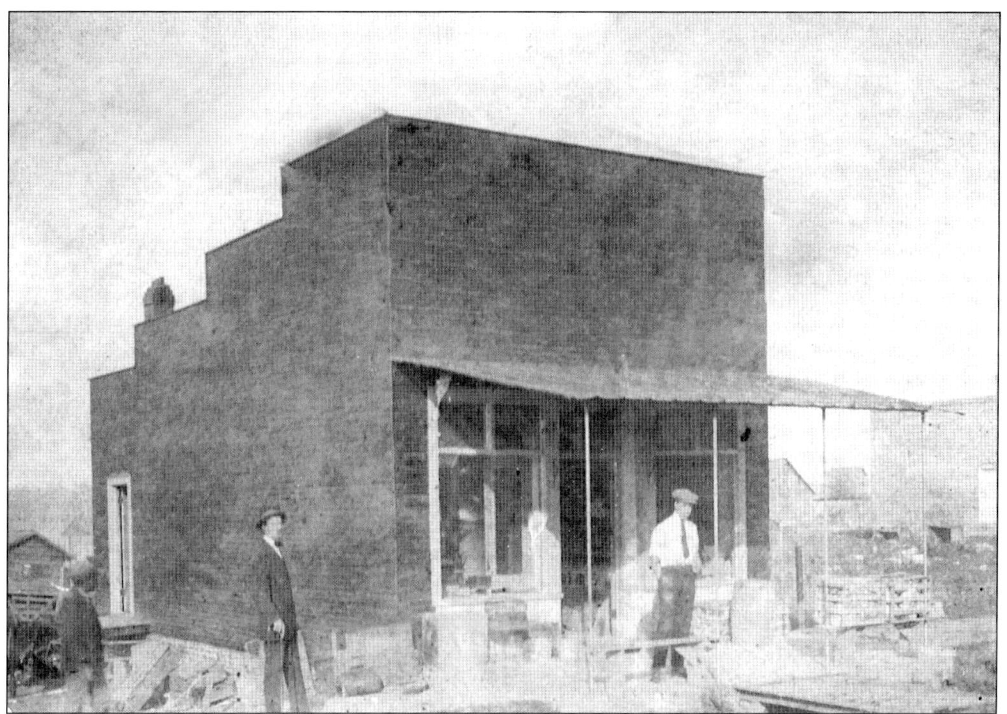

Photographed in the early 1900s, Paul Fulton and R.F. Reynolds (editor of the newspaper) stand proudly in front of the original Fulton's Grocery. (Courtesy of Barbara Fulton Tuttle.)

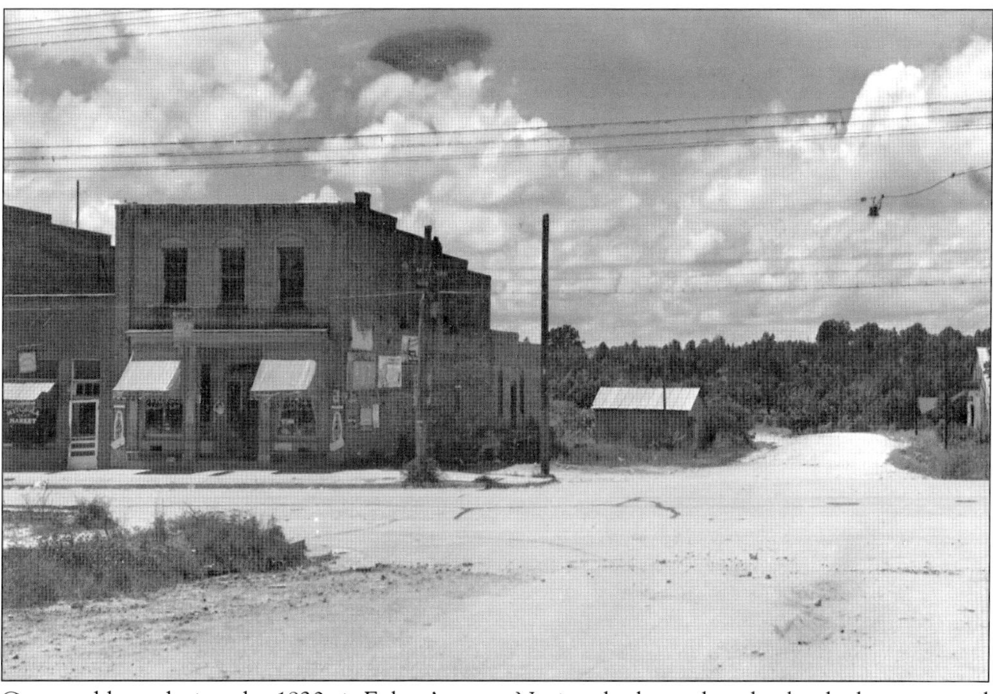

Captured here during the 1930s is Fulton's store. Notice the huge thunderclouds that surround the building. Mitchola Meat Market can be seen in this photograph as well. (Courtesy of Barbara Fulton Tuttle.)

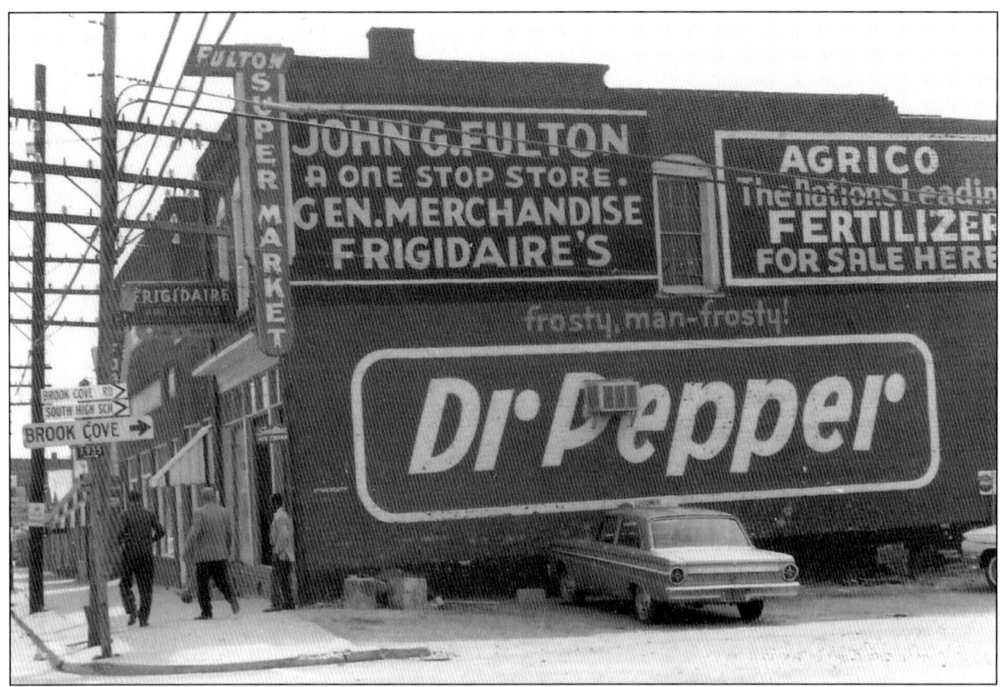

Taken in the 1960s, this photograph highlights the Dr. Pepper sign painted on the side of John G. Fulton's store. Also captured in this photograph is the right side view of Main Street from the present-day stoplight. (Courtesy of Barbara Fulton Tuttle.)

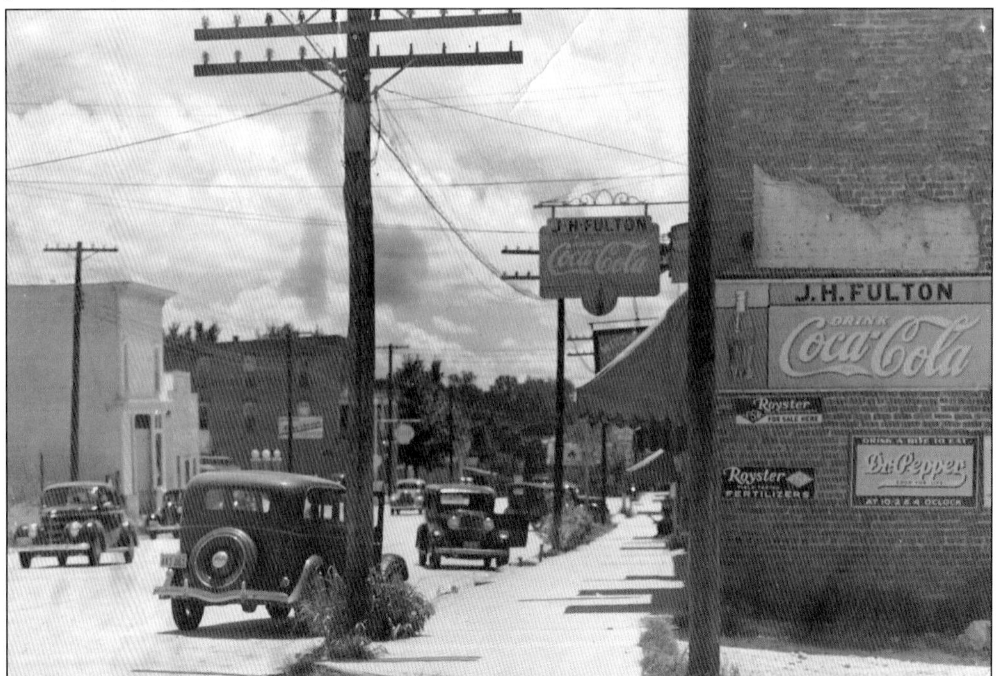

This view, taken from Fulton's store in 1937, highlights businesses on both sides of Main Street. Seen on the left side of the road are Manuel's Jewelry Store and the Dodson Hotel. (Courtesy of Barbara Fulton Tuttle.)

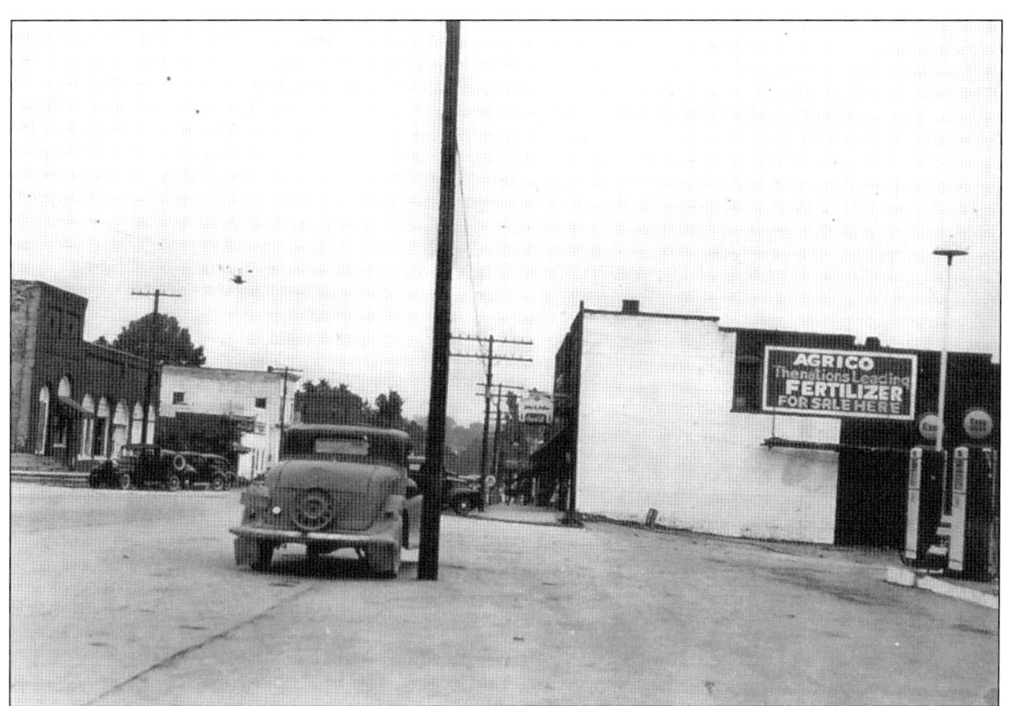

Found here is another street shot of the lower end of Walnut Cove. This photograph was taken from Tuttle Hardware. The gas pumps on the right stood where the vacant lot beside Tuttle Hardware is today. The station was later run by Buddy Boles. (Courtesy of Barbara Fulton Tuttle.)

J. WESLEY MOREFIELD & CO.
DEALERS IN
GENERAL MERCHANDISE
AND REAL ESTATE DEALERS

Walnut Cove, N. C., 4/19 1914

Elder S. A. Thompson
Steward
V. A.

Very Dear Bro. & Family
This Morning I am a lone
thing of my Dear Baptize
Friend and you darop in
my Mind and I felt a dutie
before me to write you althoug
felt two unworthy to try to address
such a good Man as I feel
you to be a god sent Man
to Preach the unserchable Riches
of Jesus. We have always thoug
so much of you and your Family
Ever since we had the Pleasure
of meeting you all.
I will try to help you on your
Church House when you Come
to the assosation if you get to
Come and I Want you and

This letterhead was from the general store operated by J. Wesley Morefield in Walnut Cove. (Author's collection.)

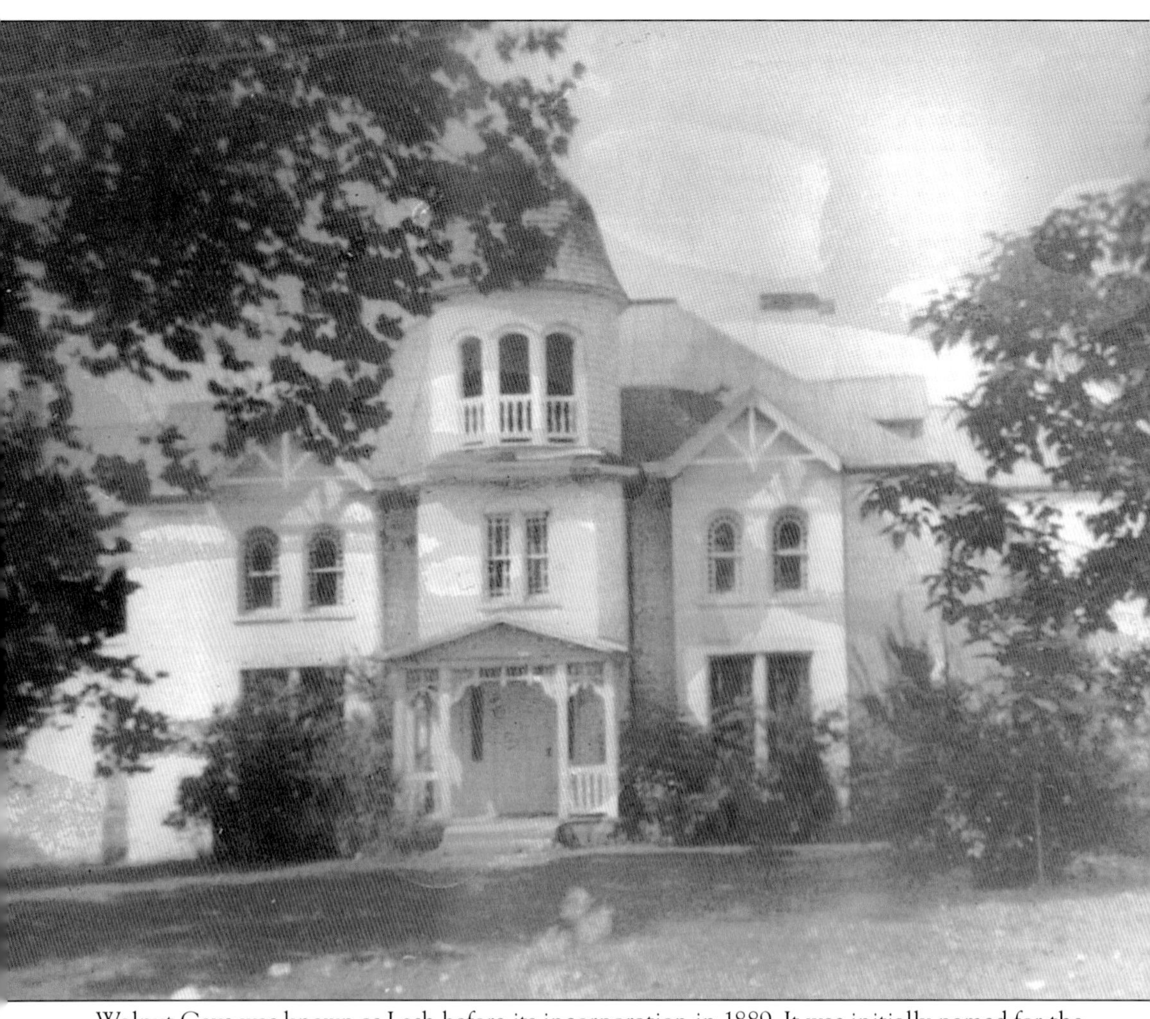

Walnut Cove was known as Lash before its incorporation in 1889. It was initially named for the large plantation owned by the Lash family in the area. Pictured here is the Lash house, which was later known as the Mitchell home place. (Courtesy of Hannah Mitchell Rothrock.)

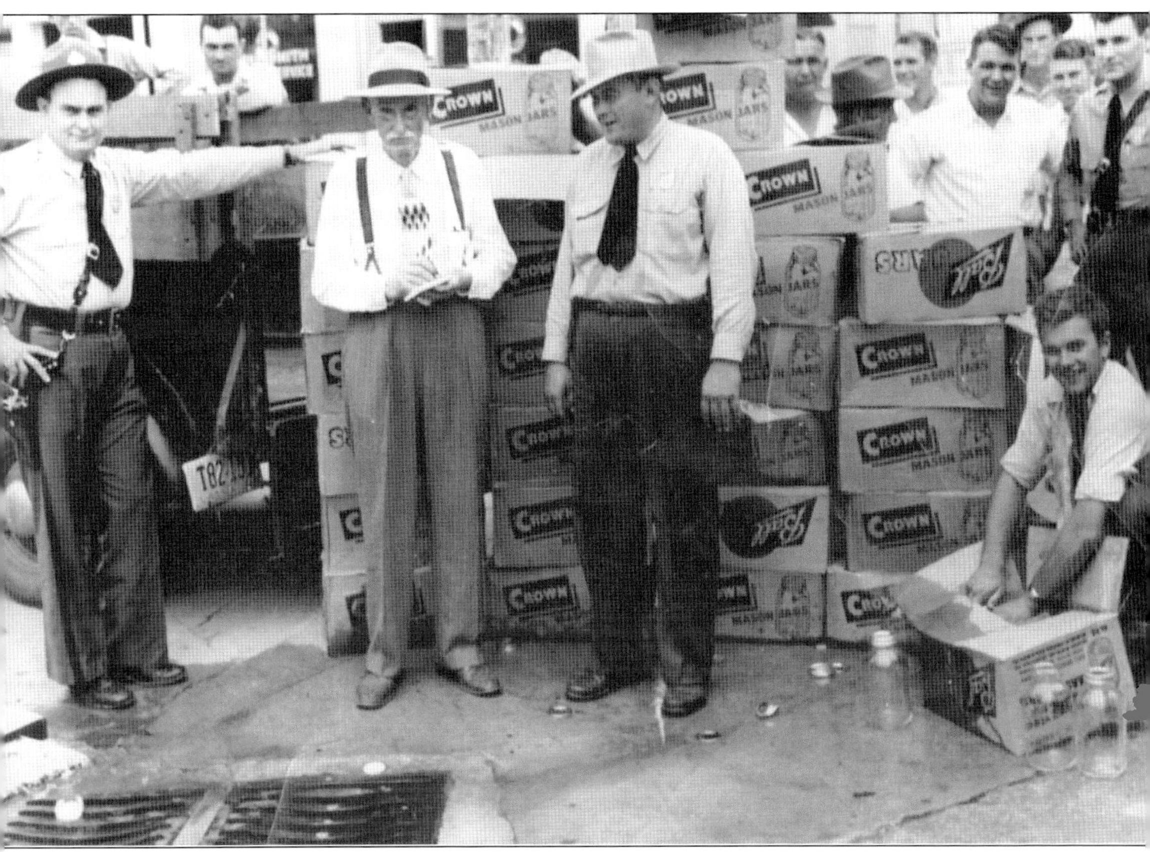

Pictured in 1945, (from left to right) W.C. Blaylock, Elkin Smith, and Luico Hill pour out white liquor they captured in Walnut Cove. (Courtesy Jerry and Sarah Stephens.)

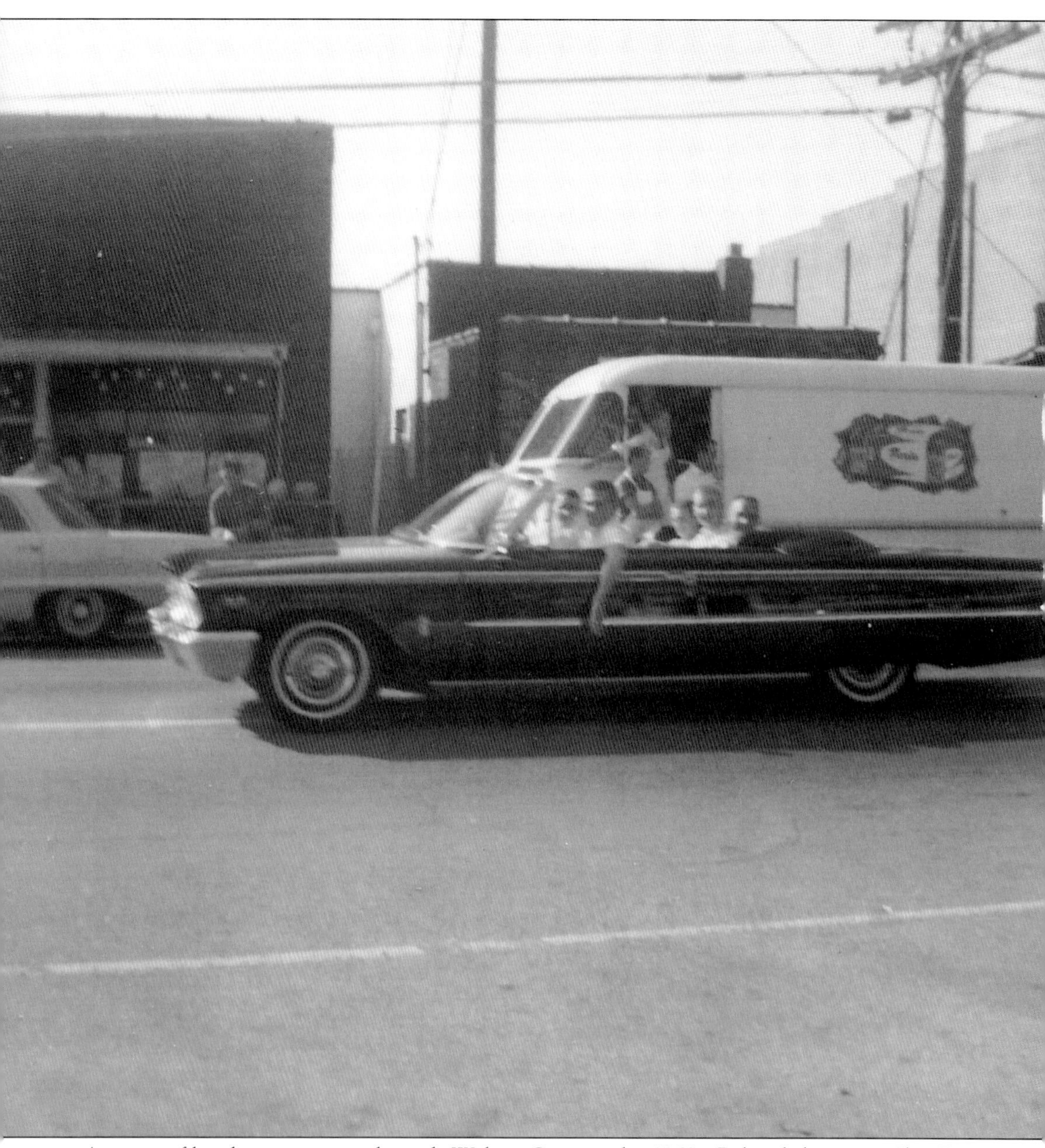

A group of local teens cruises through Walnut Cove in the 1960s. Behind them was ShopRite grocery store and the telephone company building. The ShopRite was later renovated and became Family Pharmacy. (Courtesy of Margie Dunlap.)

Clarence Wilson stands in the doorway of Western Auto, enticing customers to make a purchase. Later, the doorway was moved to make room for a vehicle bay. (Courtesy of Margie Dunlap.)

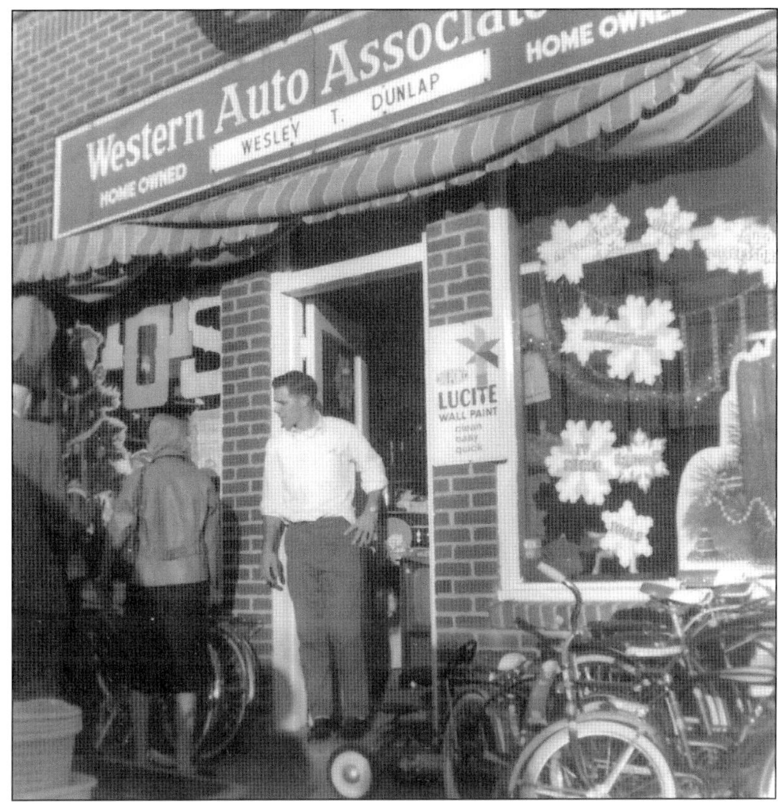

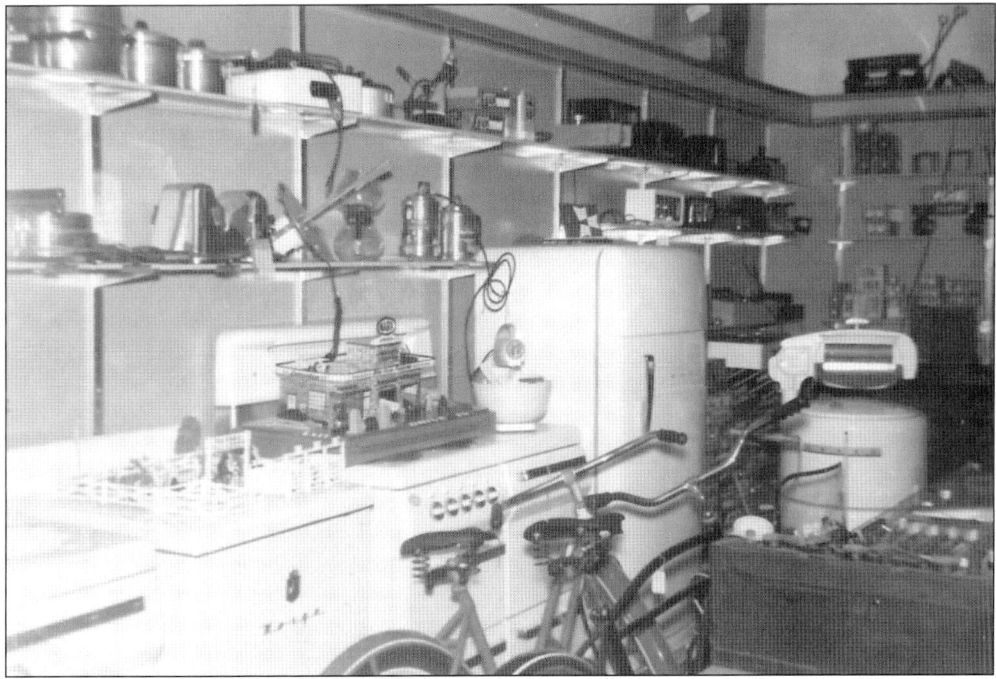

The shelves inside of Western Auto in Walnut Cove were stocked in this mid-century photograph. Merchandise typically ranged from toys to large appliances. (Courtesy of Margie Dunlap.)

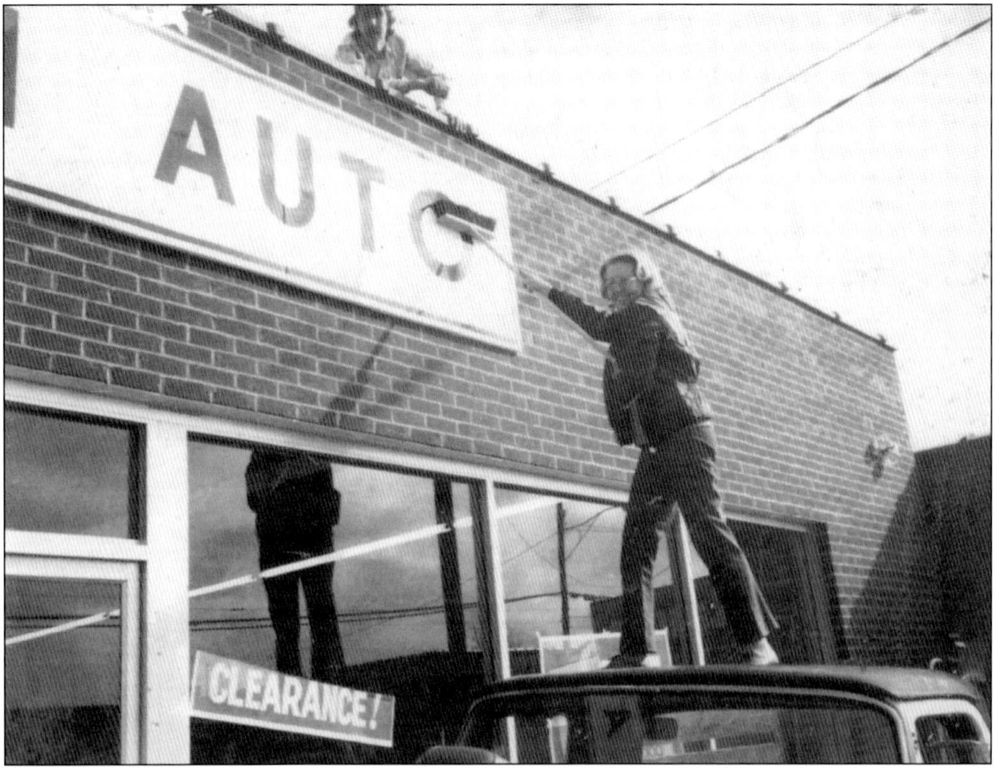

Margie Dunlap and her son Durwood install a new sign at Western Auto in 1974. Western Auto is still run by Durwood Dunlap. (Courtesy of Margie Dunlap.)

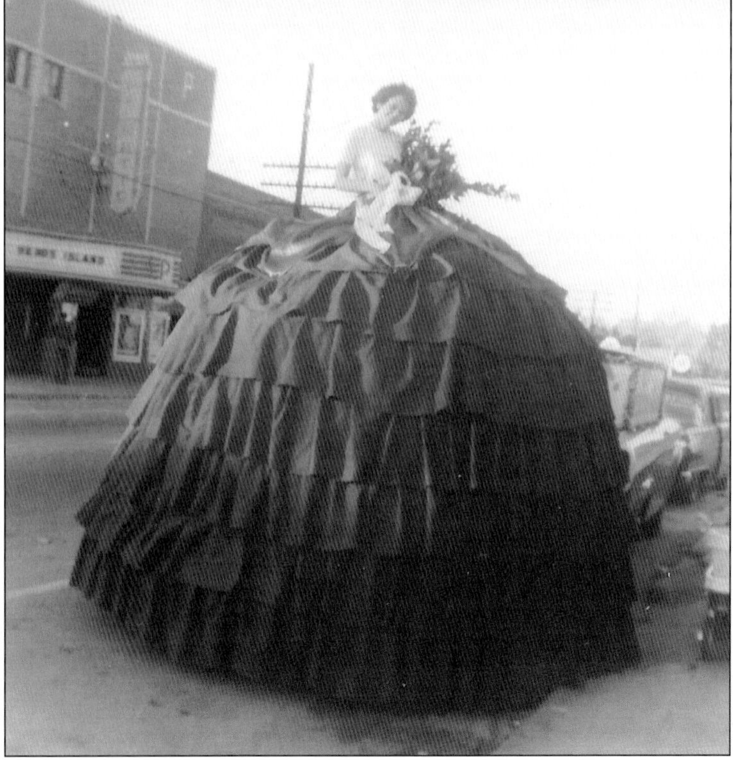

This parade in the 1960s shows Jackie Dunlap wearing a costume made by her aunt Margie Dunlap to advertise Dunlap's Western Auto. A man in the background can be seen contemplating seeing a movie at the Palmetto Theatre. (Courtesy of Margie Dunlap.)

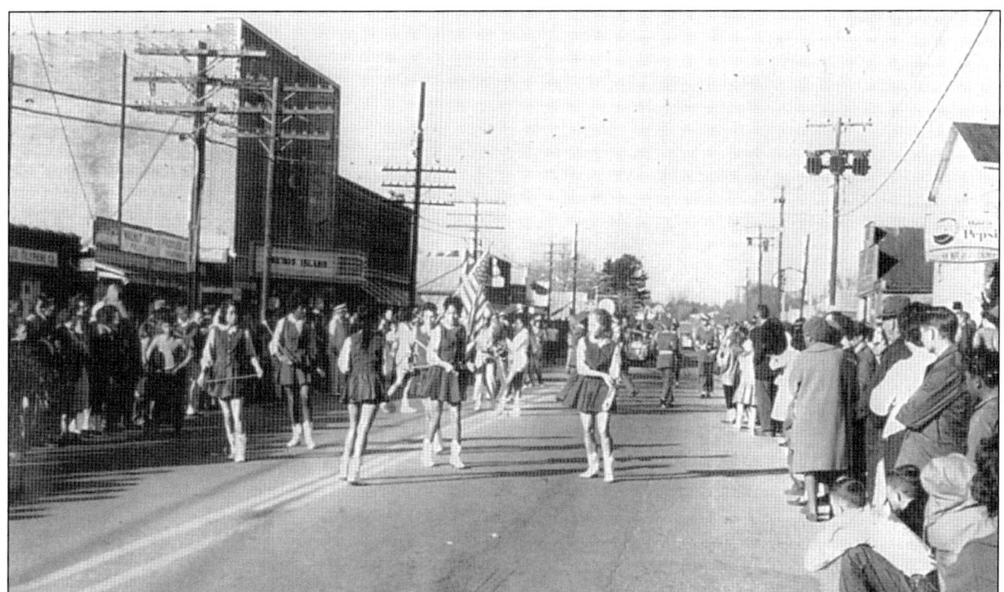

The London High School participates in the Walnut Cove Christmas Parade in the early 1960s. On the left, the Palmetto Theatre can be seen which still adorns Main Street today. (Courtesy of Don Richardson.)

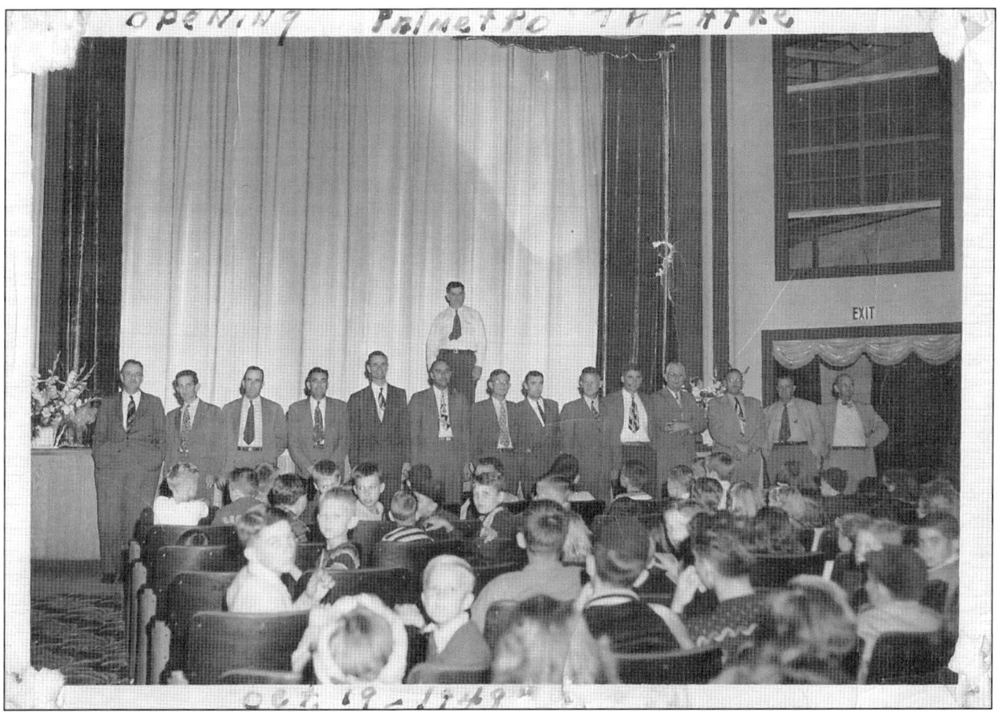

October 19, 1949, brought excitement to Walnut Cove's youngsters and adults alike. Walnut Cove's Rotary Club poses here proudly as the Palmetto Theatre prepares to show its first film of many. Some rotary members include Carlos Davis, R.G. Thomas, R.M. Greene, Dr. V.L. Dehart, and William Marshall. On the stage is Alex Booth, who ran the projector and was the son of the owner, Jesse Booth. (Courtesy of Barbara Fulton Tuttle.)

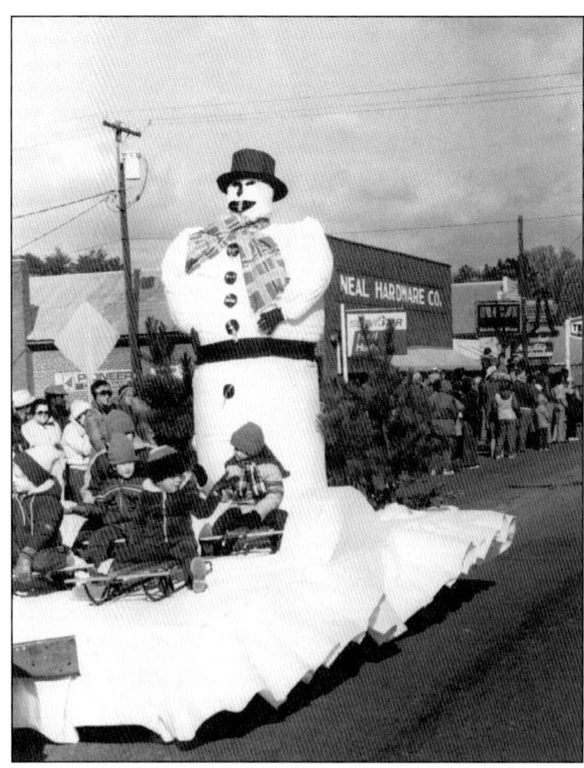

A float for Western Auto is seen here in 1981 with young riders (from left to right) Tatum Smith, Alexander Rutledge, Ryan Dunlap, and Joey Beck. Neal Hardware can be seen in the background. (Courtesy of Durwood and Patti Dunlap.)

This is the first business of George Neal Sr. It was located in a community of Stokes County known as Campbell. Situated to the rear of the store was the Neal family home. Neal Sr.'s children can be seen to the right. (Courtesy of Linda Neal Alcott.)

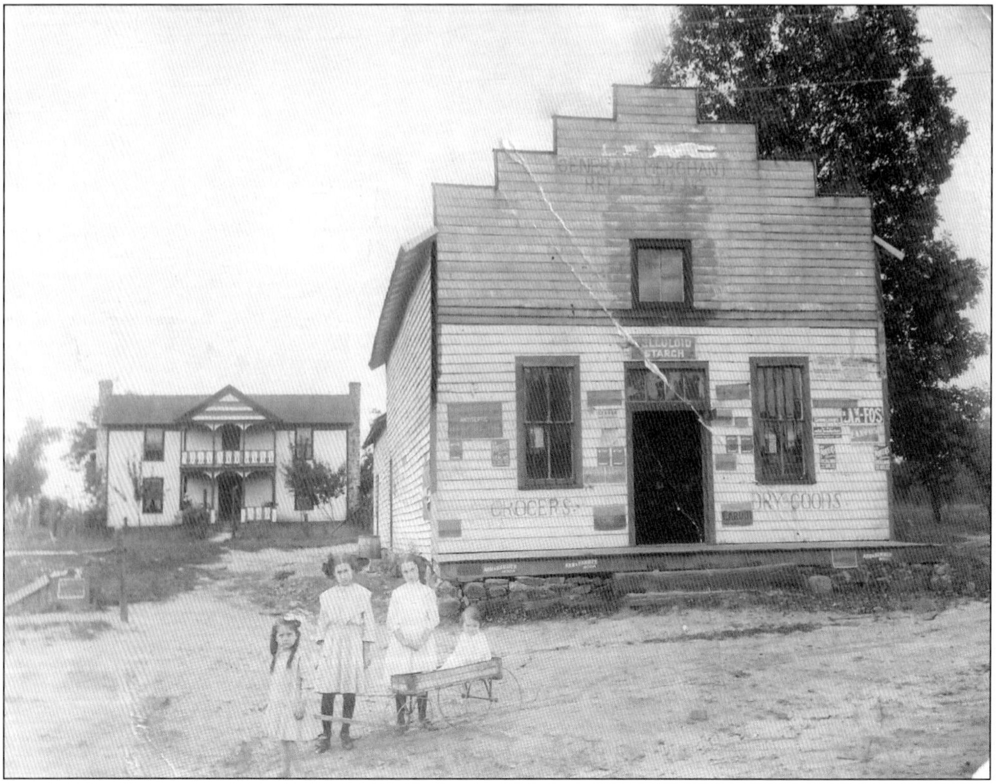

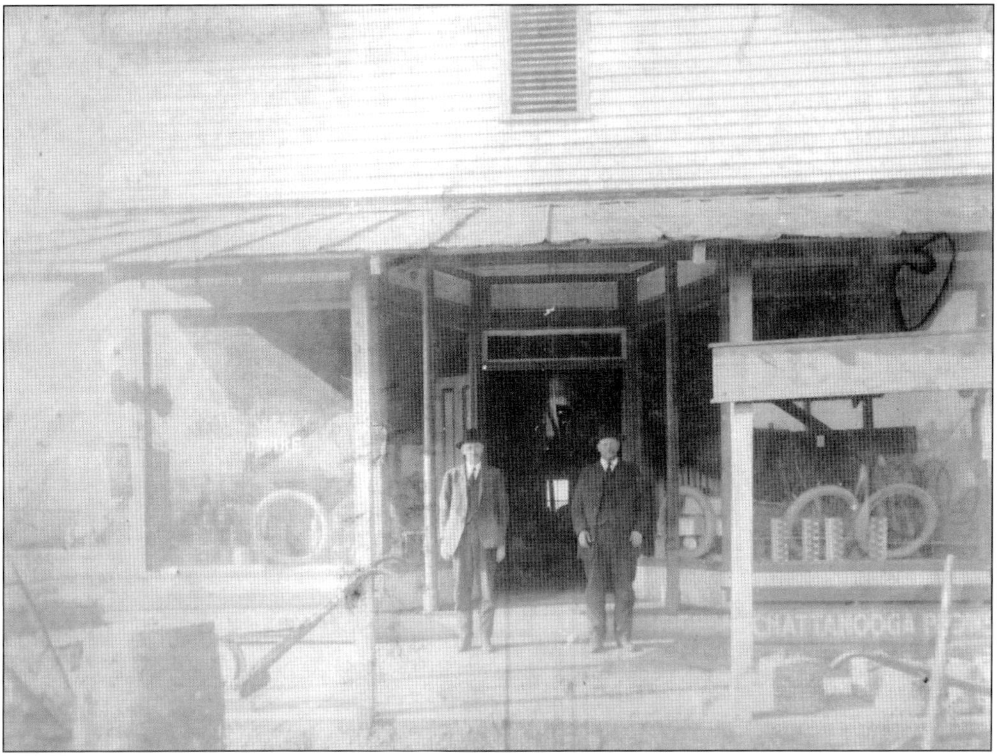

After Neal Sr. moved to Walnut Cove, he partnered in business with Mr. Spencer to form Neal and Spencer Hardware. It is thought to have been located in the old Alley's Maytag building, which still stands today as Alley's Vintage Shoppe. Though it is not known which they are, the two individuals pictured are George Neal and Mr. Hutchins. (Courtesy of Linda Neal Alcott.)

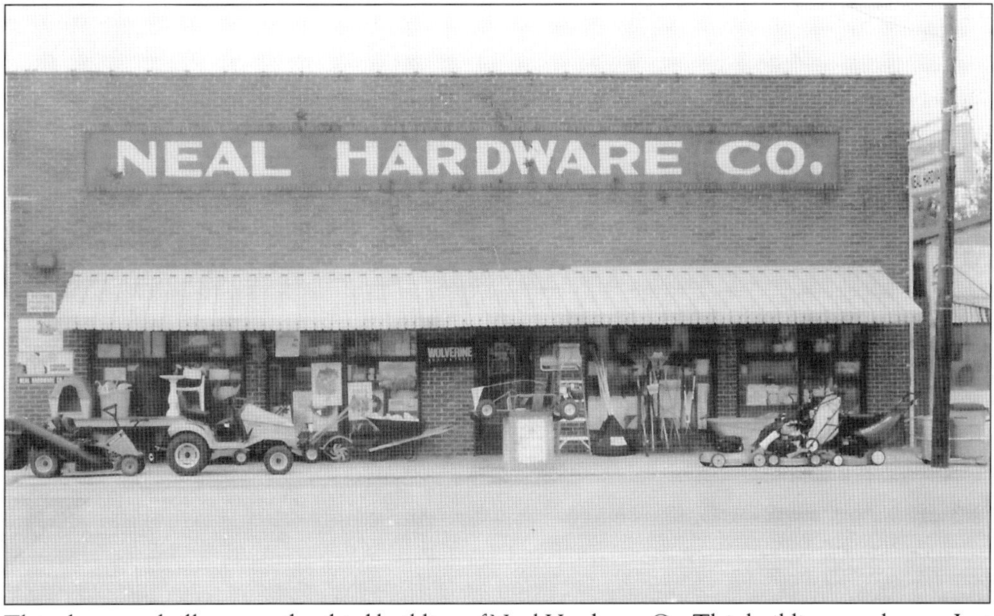

This photograph illustrates the third building of Neal Hardware Co. This building now houses Just Plain Country antiques and craft mall owned by Kathy Dix. (Courtesy of Don Richardson.)

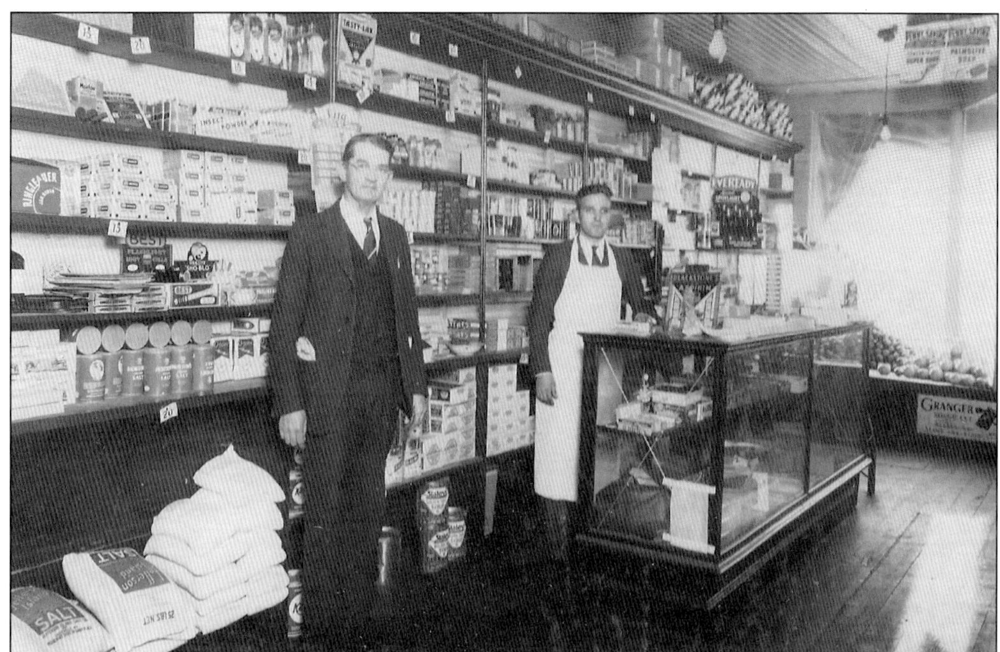

Located in Walnut Cove, Arbrey Tuttle (left) and Harry Davis (right) ran a general store during the first quarter of the 20th century on Main Street, located diagonally across from Neal Hardware. This photograph captured the interior view in 1922. This building was originally Lash's Store, located on the corner of Fourth and Main Streets. It was later moved to the location in the photograph. (Courtesy of Barbara Fulton Tuttle.)

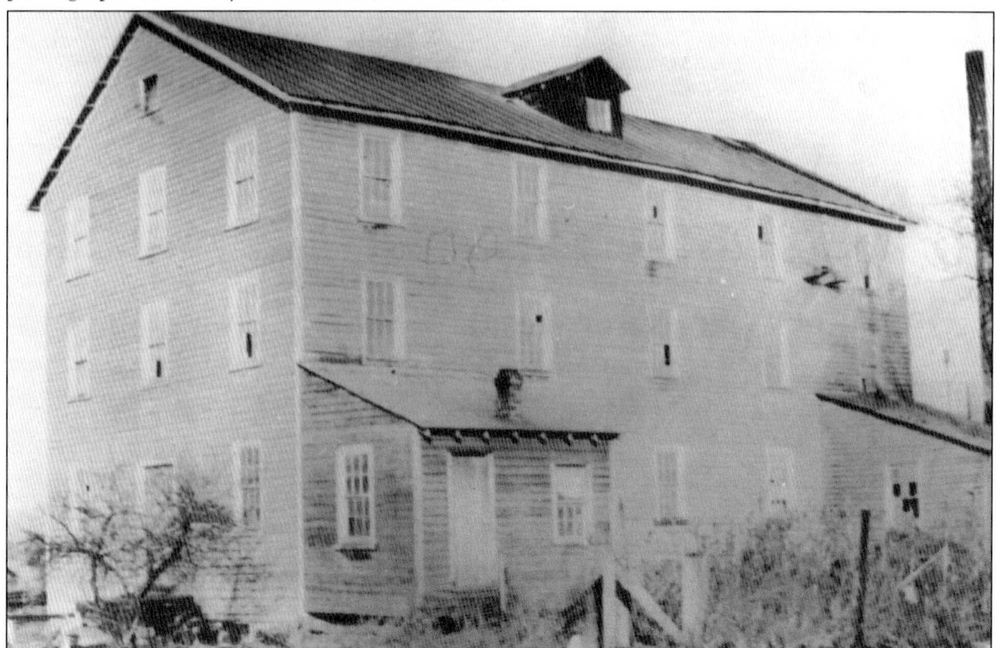

Monitor Roller Mills was photographed during the early part of the 20th century. First established by Andrew Jackson Fair, this mill has continued to operate for over 100 years, presently by the Southern family. (Courtesy of Ronnie Southern.)

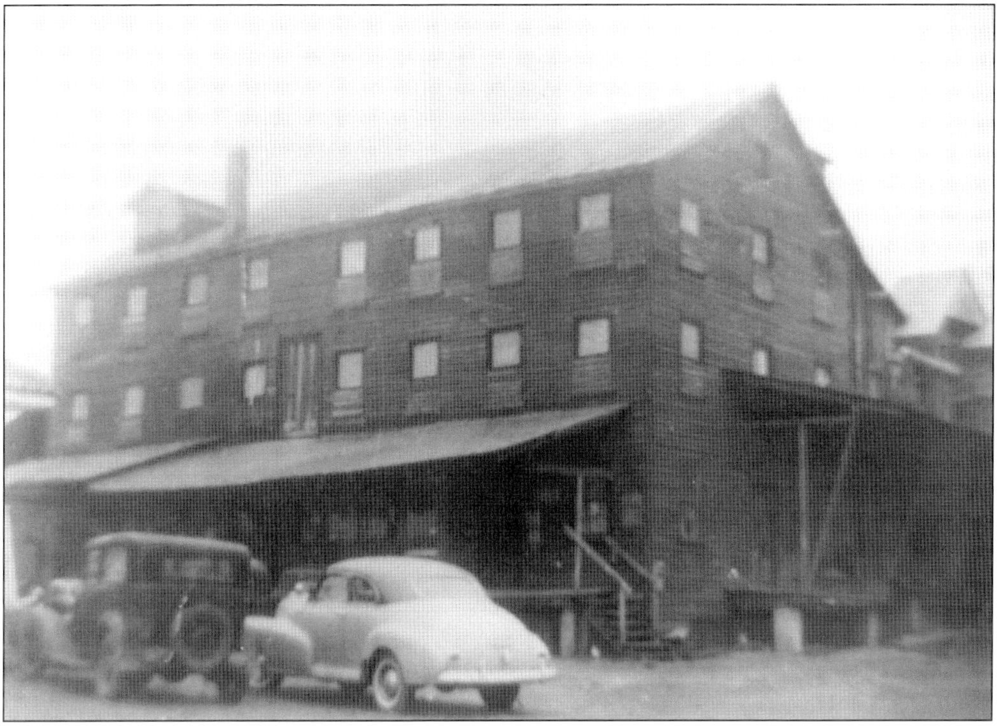

A later view of Monitor Roller Mills was captured in this c. 1945 photograph. It burned in 1959. (Courtesy of Ronnie Southern.)

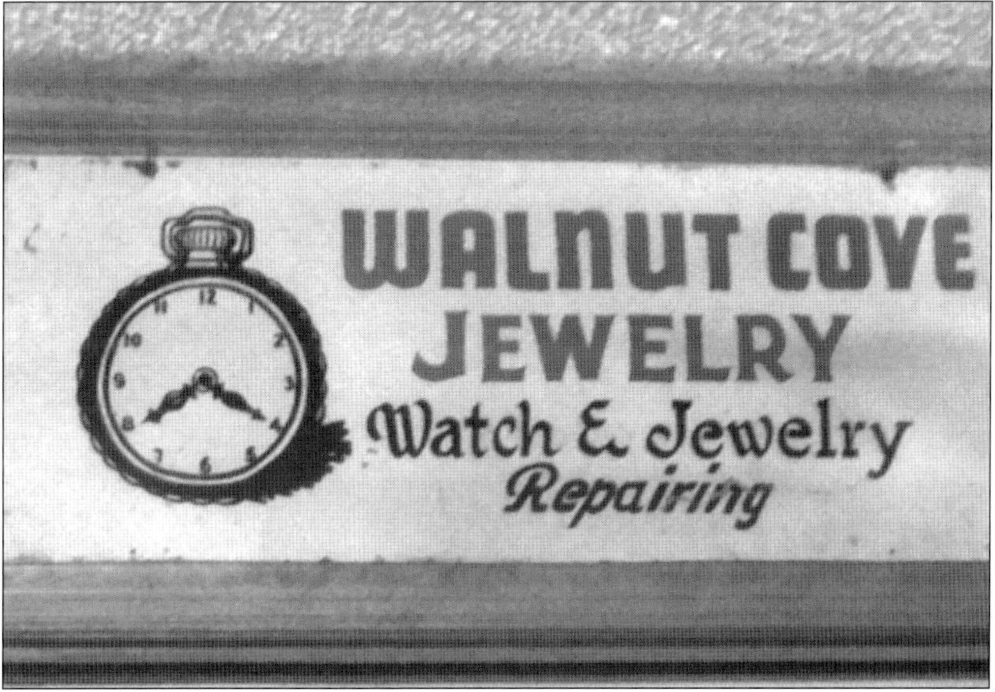

This sign hung outside of the Walnut Cove Jewelry store on Main Street for many years. It was operated by the King family in the 1950s. (Author's collection.)

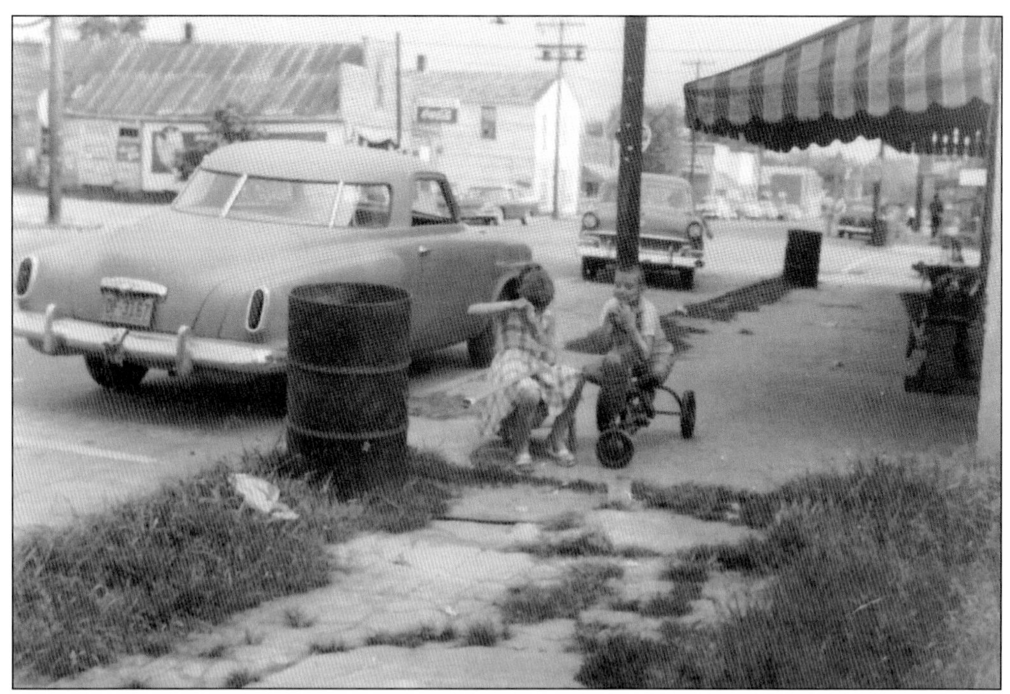

Kimbyl Alley Ferrell (left), daughter of Lester and Dorothy Alley, owners of Alley's Maytag, plays with Terry King, whose parents owned Walnut Cove Jewelry. (Courtesy Richard and Kimbyl Alley Ferrell.)

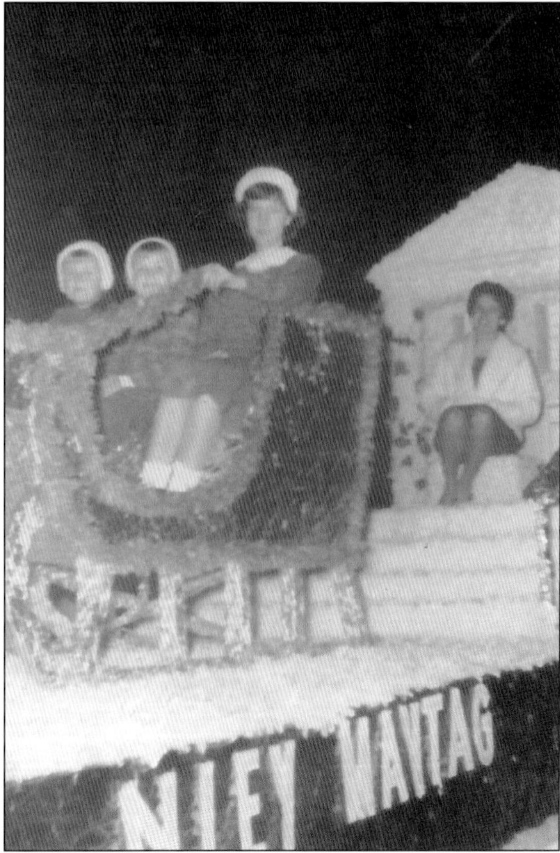

Kimbyl Alley Ferrell is seen here during a Christmas parade in the 1950s. This float advertised Alley's Maytag, which was operated by her parents, Lester and Dorothy Alley. (Courtesy Richard and Kimbyl Alley Ferrell.)

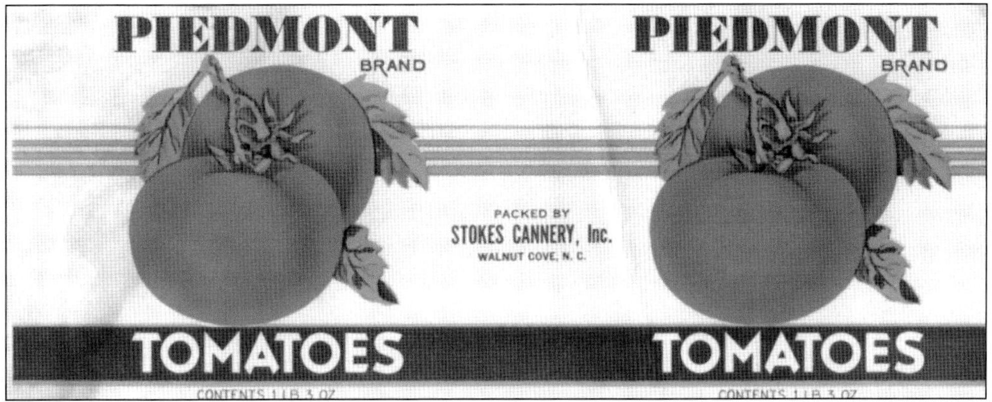

The Stokes Cannery was located on Windmill Street in Walnut Cove. Food was saved for families who could not help with the tobacco crop and save food simultaneously. This label was for a can of tomatoes at the cannery. (Author's collection.)

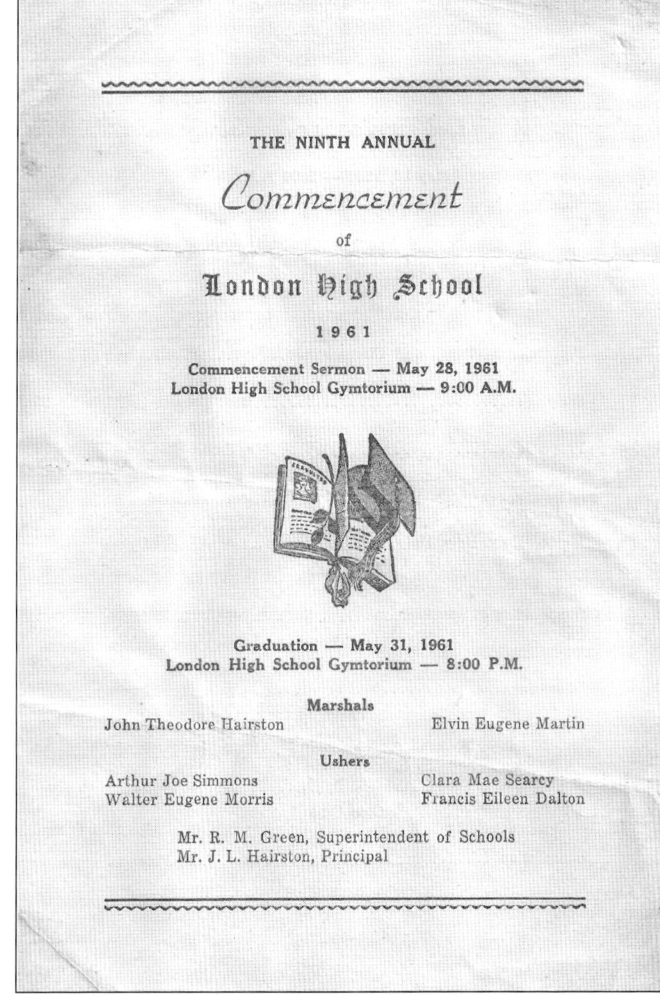

THE NINTH ANNUAL

Commencement

of

London High School

1961

Commencement Sermon — May 28, 1961
London High School Gymtorium — 9:00 A.M.

Graduation — May 31, 1961
London High School Gymtorium — 8:00 P.M.

Marshals

John Theodore Hairston — Elvin Eugene Martin

Ushers

Arthur Joe Simmons — Clara Mae Searcy
Walter Eugene Morris — Francis Eileen Dalton

Mr. R. M. Green, Superintendent of Schools
Mr. J. L. Hairston, Principal

This program was from a graduation at London High School in 1961. This school was built for the African American population of Walnut Cove. The school was closed in later years, but eventually it reopened and is still in operation today as an elementary school. (Author's collection.)

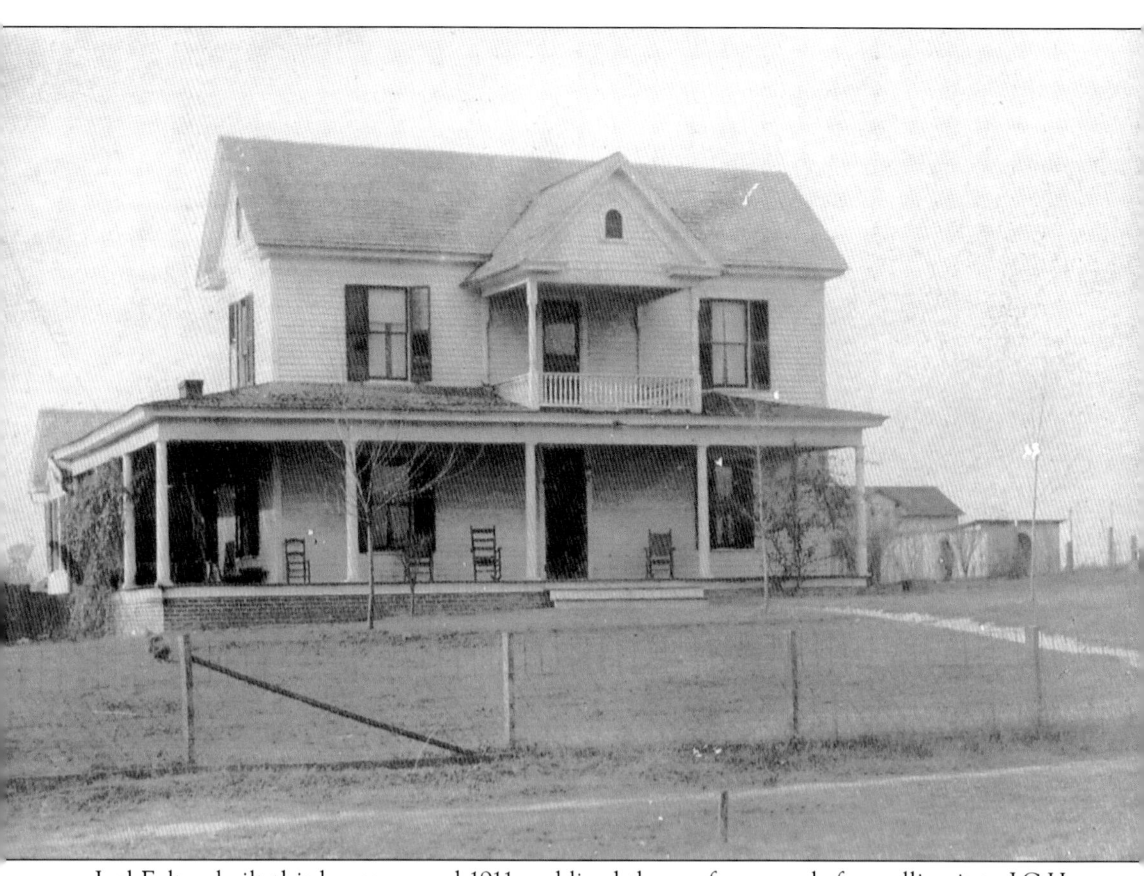

Joel Fulton built this house around 1911 and lived there a few years before selling it to J.G.H. Mitchell in 1913. Mitchell went on to hold several prestigious offices, such as register of deeds, clerk of superior court and state legislator. (Courtesy of Davis Chapel Historical Association, Inc.)

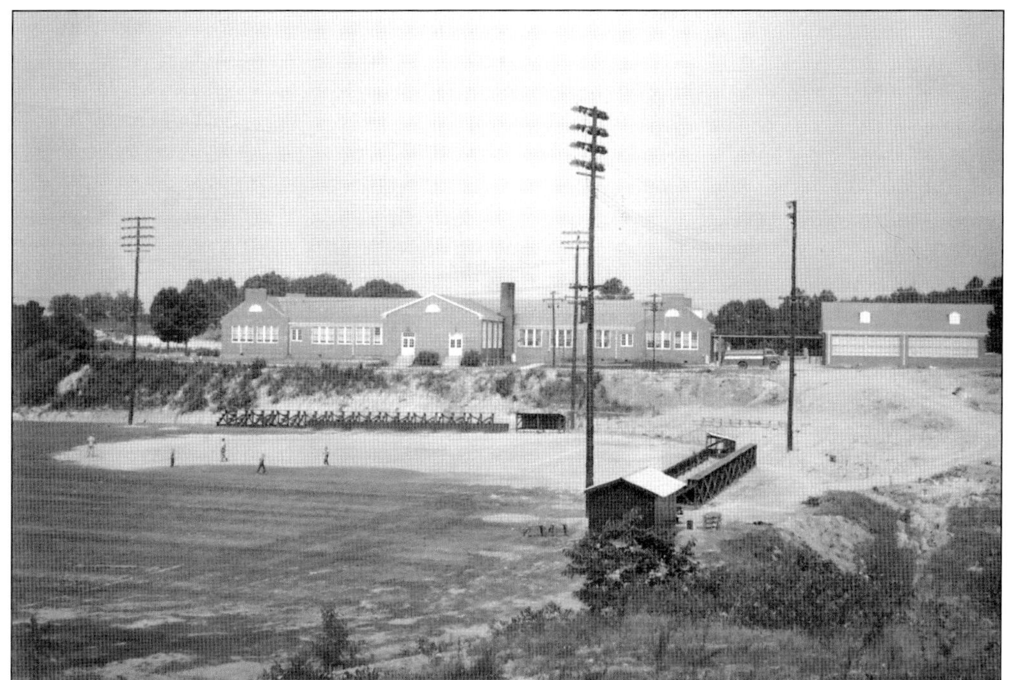

In this 1960s photograph, individuals practice a game of baseball at Walnut Cove High School. Today, the school is known as Southeastern Stokes Middle School. The building seen in this photograph houses the cafeteria and offices. (Courtesy of Barbara Fulton Tuttle.)

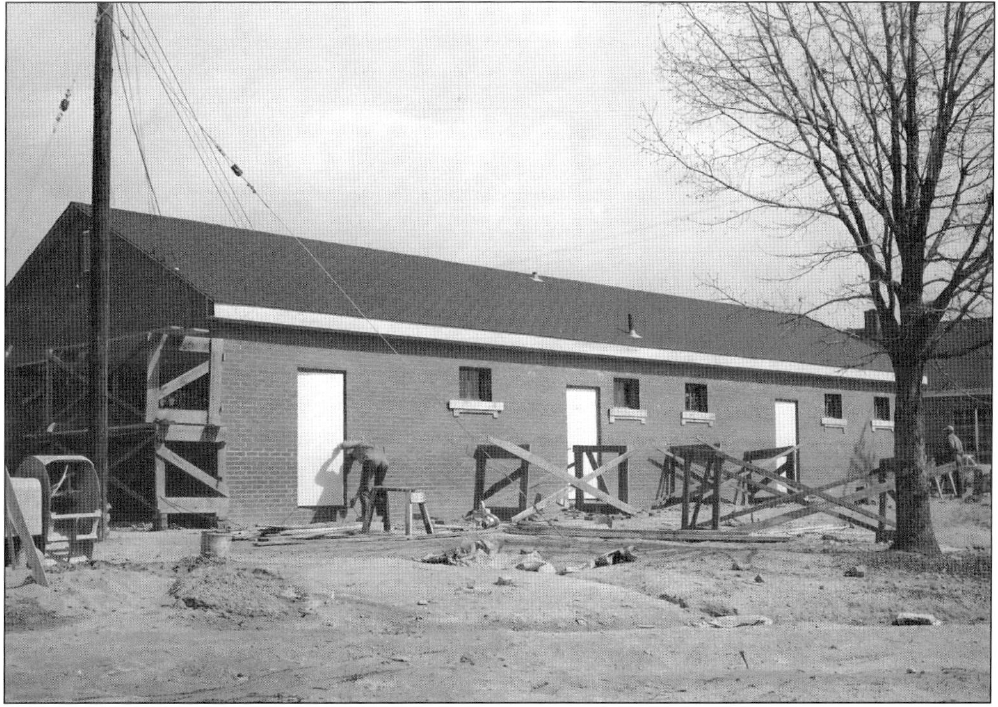

The 1956 construction of the field house is pictured here at Walnut Cove High School. (Courtesy of Barbara Fulton Tuttle.)

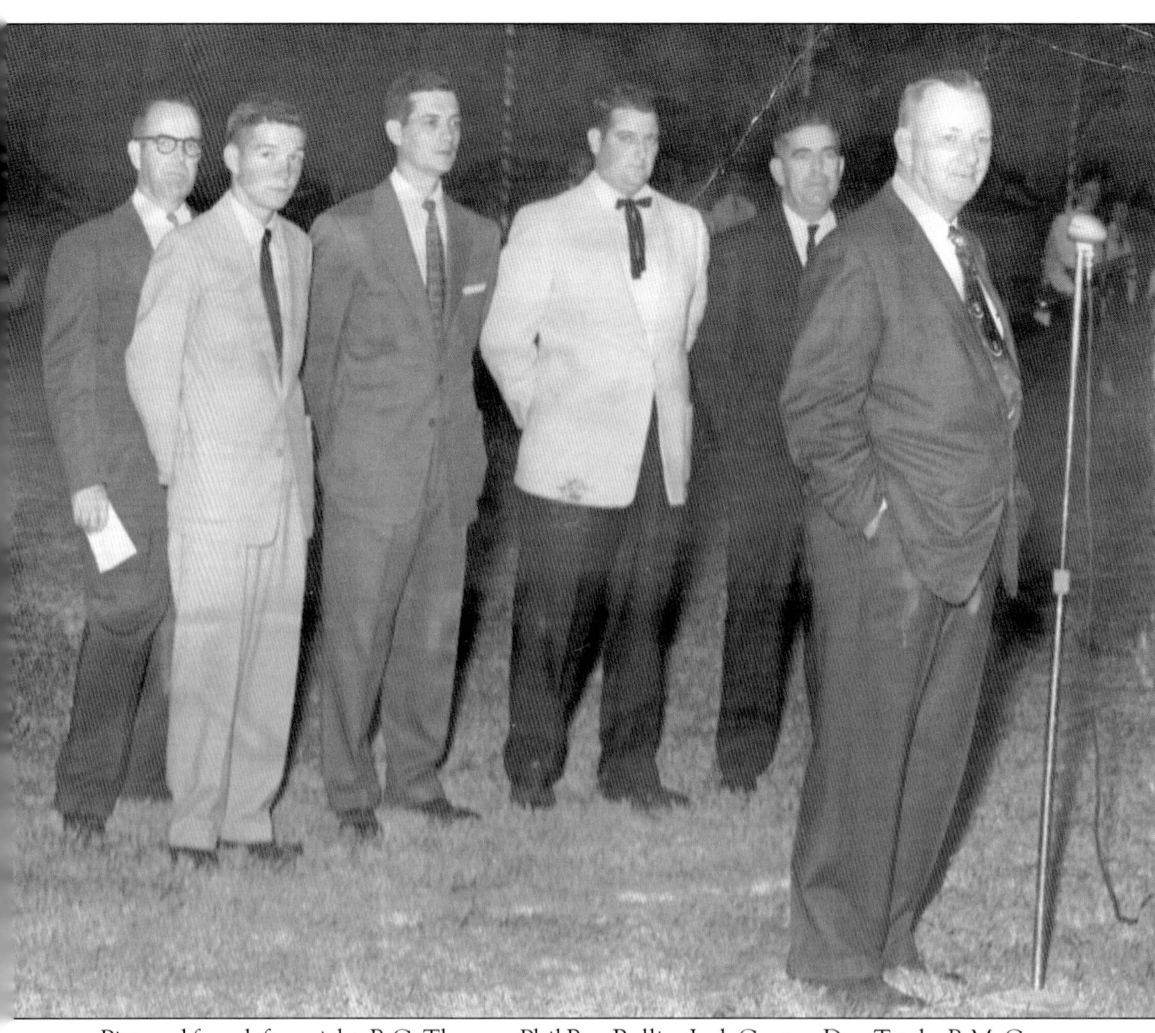

Pictured from left to right, R.G. Thomas, Phil Ray Bullin, Jack Gentry, Don Tuttle, R.M. Greene, and John G. Fulton attend the dedication of the Walnut Cove High School Stadium. (Courtesy of Barbara Fulton Tuttle.)

Sporting events have been popular in Stokes County for many years. They were seen as a time of fellowship and fun. Seen here is a young boy dressed in his Walnut Cove baseball uniform sometime in the 1940s. (Courtesy of Dr. Jack and Nancy Helsabeck Fowler.)

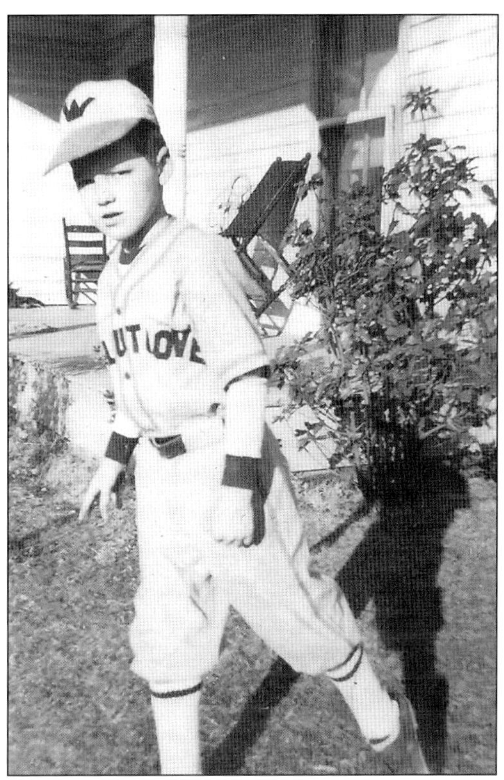

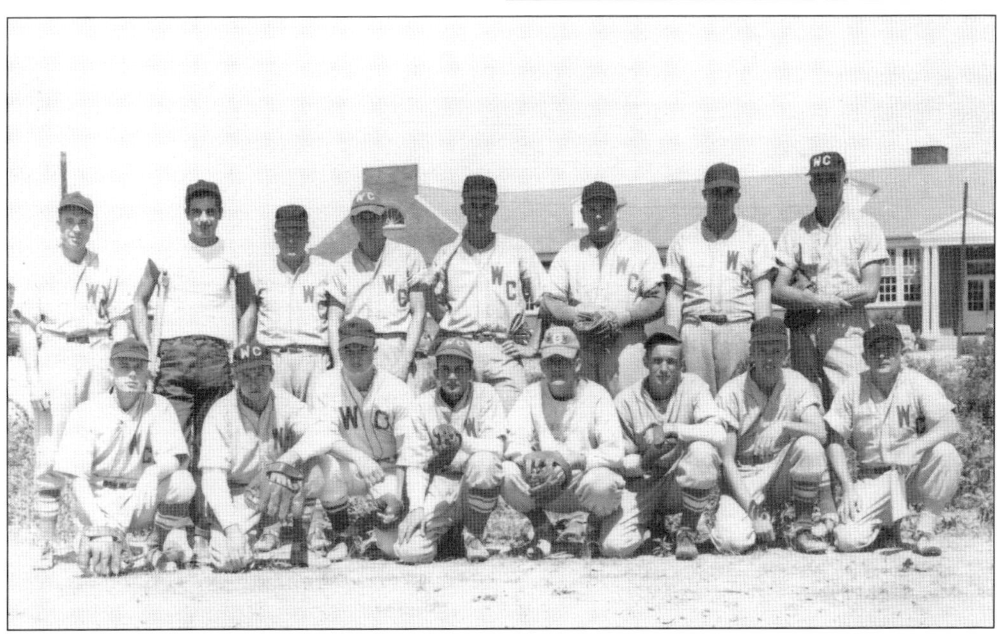

The Walnut Cove baseball team of 1948 poses for this photograph on May 22, 1948. The team members are (first row) Richard Vernon, Billy Nelson, Don Boles, Richard Vernon, Bobby Heath, Roy Dunlap, Harold Tuttle, and Musk Johnson; (second row) Elwood Young, Paul Smith, Mr. Tedder, Fred Young, Dunk Dunlap, Alex Booth, Rob Miller, and Elwood Richardson. (Courtesy Tommy Young.)

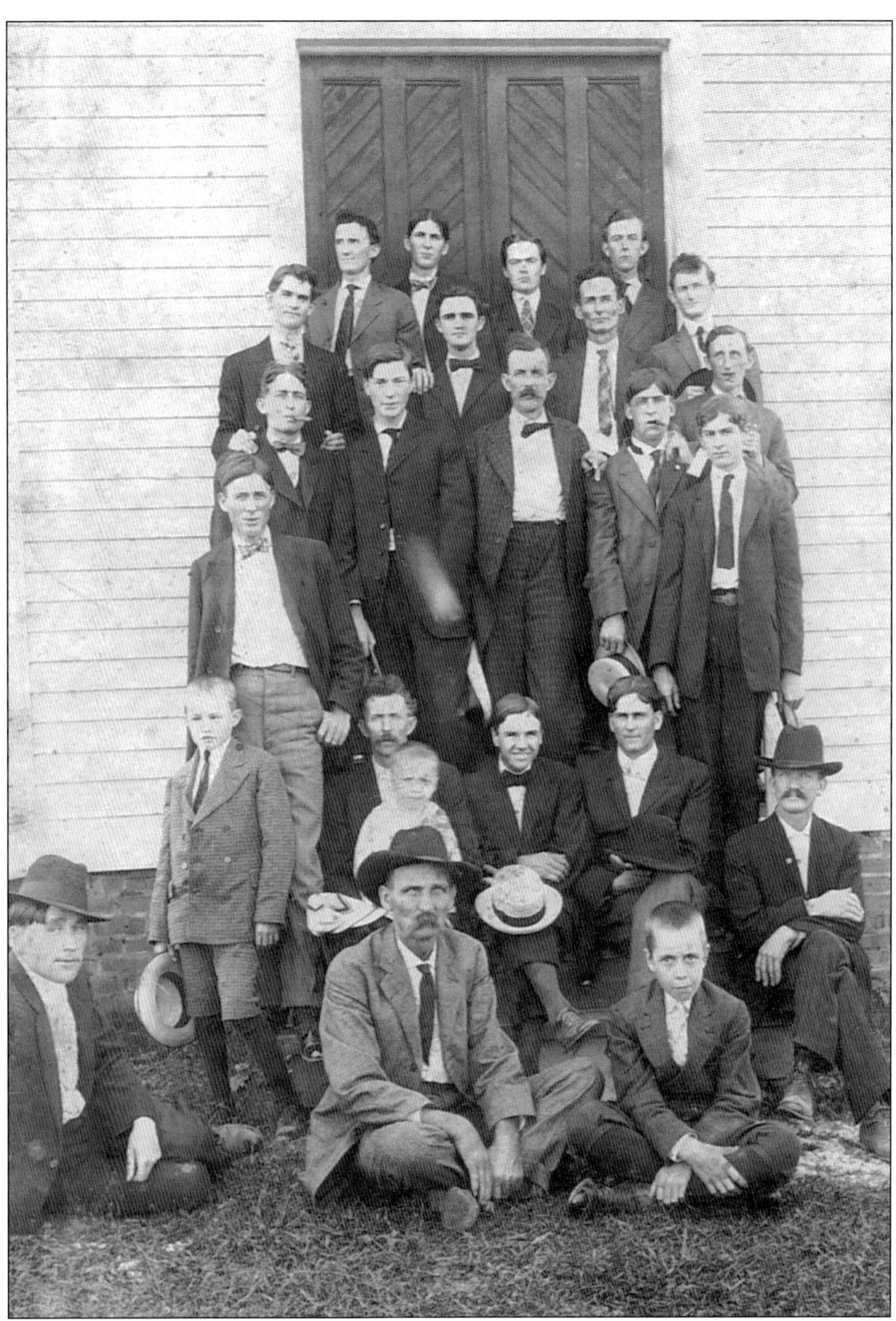

Pictured in the early 1900s are some of Walnut Cove's citizens around the turn of the century. Some individuals here are Walter Joyce, Jacob Fulton, Roy Vaughn, Will Wheeler, J.L. Mitchell, Harry Davis, Jim Voss, Oscar Petree, Will East, and Will Rierson. (Courtesy of Barbara Fulton Tuttle.)

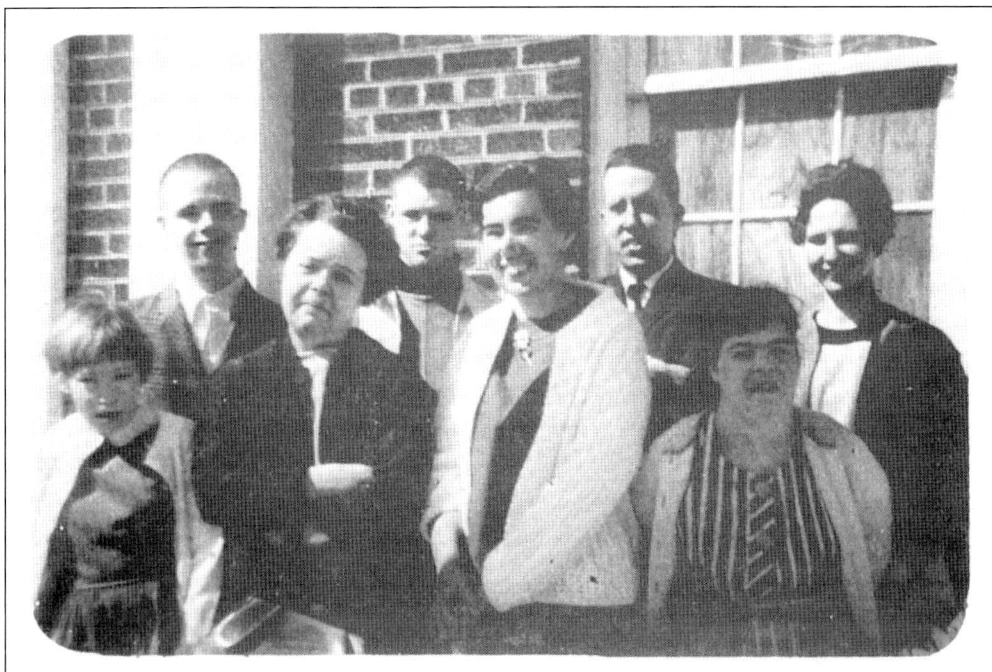

Captured here is a class at Pine Crest School during the 1960s. (Courtesy of Lois Dodson Smith.)

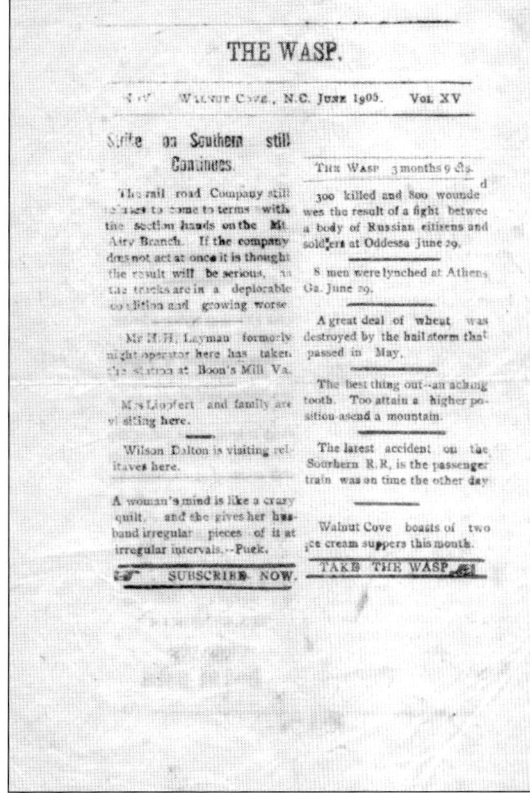

THE WASP.

WALNUT COVE, N.C. JUNE 1905. VOL XV

Strike on Southern still Continues.

The rail road Company still refuses to come to terms with the section hands on the Mt. Airy Branch. If the company does not act at once it is thought the result will be serious, as the tracks are in a deplorable condition and growing worse.

Mr H.H. Layman formerly night operator here has taken the station at Boon's Mill Va.

Mrs Liopfert and family are visiting here.

Wilson Dalton is visiting relitaves here.

A woman's mind is like a crazy quilt, and she gives her husband irregular pieces of it at irregular intervals.--Puck.

SUBSCRIBE NOW.

THE WASP 3 months 9 cts.

300 killed and 800 wounded wes the result of a fight betwee a body of Russian citizens and soldiers at Oddessa June 29.

8 men were lynched at Athens Ga. June 29.

A great deal of wheat was destroyed by the hail storm that passed in May.

The best thing out--an aching tooth. Too attain a higher position-asend a mountain.

The latest accident on the Sourhern R.R, is the passenger train was on time the other day

Walnut Cove boasts of two ice cream suppers this month.

TAKE THE WASP

The *Wasp* newspaper was published by A.D. Jones in Walnut Cove. This is one of very few remaining copies. (Author's collection.)

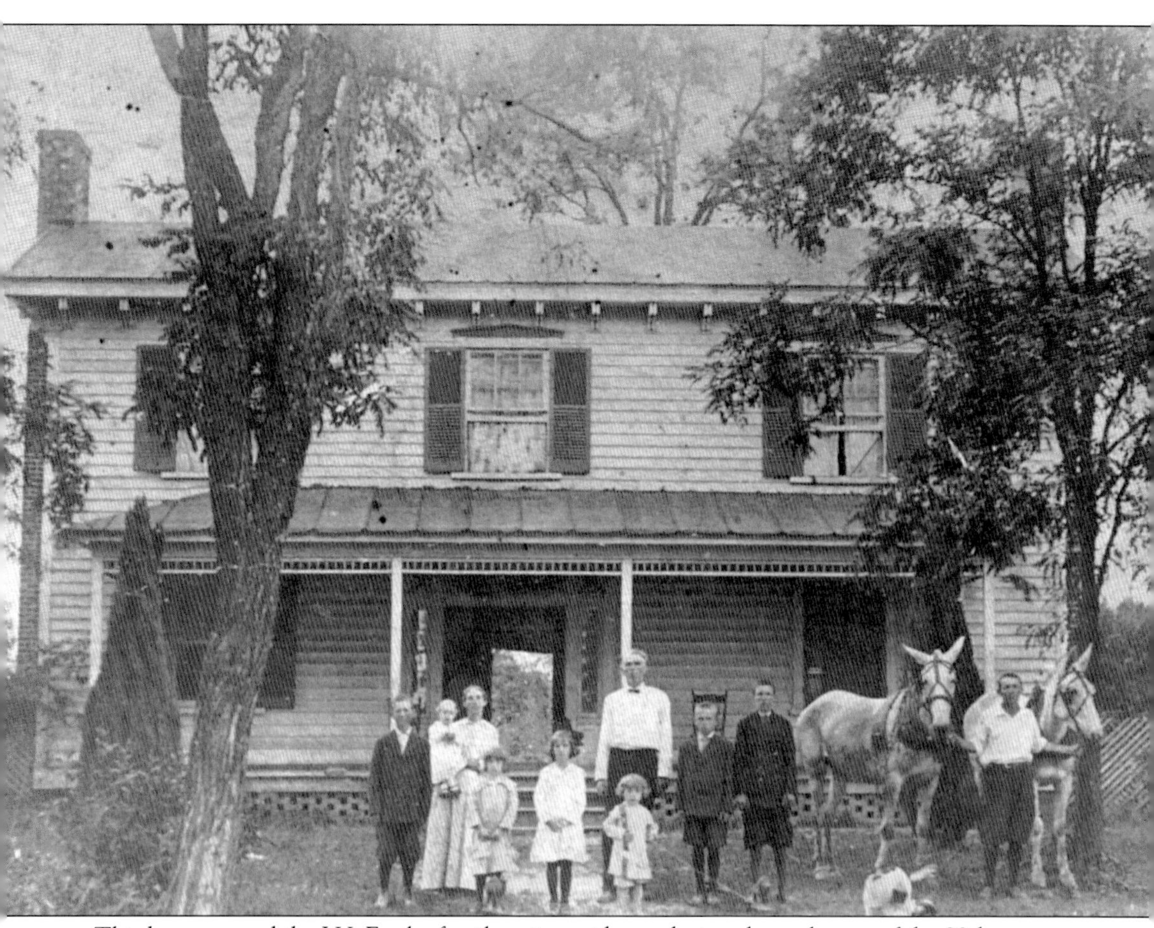

This house served the J.H. Fowler family as its residence during the early part of the 20th century. Later, it was sold and remodeled, and in 1945, it reopened as Pine Crest School, a home for the mentally handicapped. (Courtesy of Dr. Jack and Nancy Helsabeck Fowler.)

Two

The Outskirts of Town

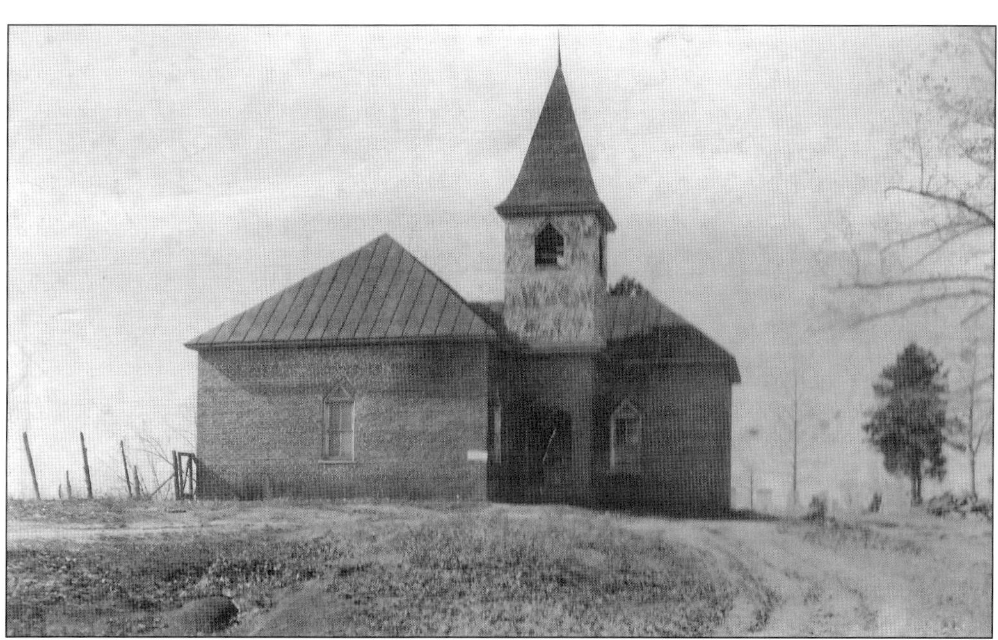

This structure is the third building of Stokesburg United Methodist Church, which was completed in 1907. The first was torn down to build a new church, and the second was destroyed by fire in 1906 during preparation for the Christmas Eve service. This photograph is believed to have been taken during completion of the 1907 church. Note the unfinished roof. (Courtesy of Dr. Jack and Nancy Helsabeck Fowler.)

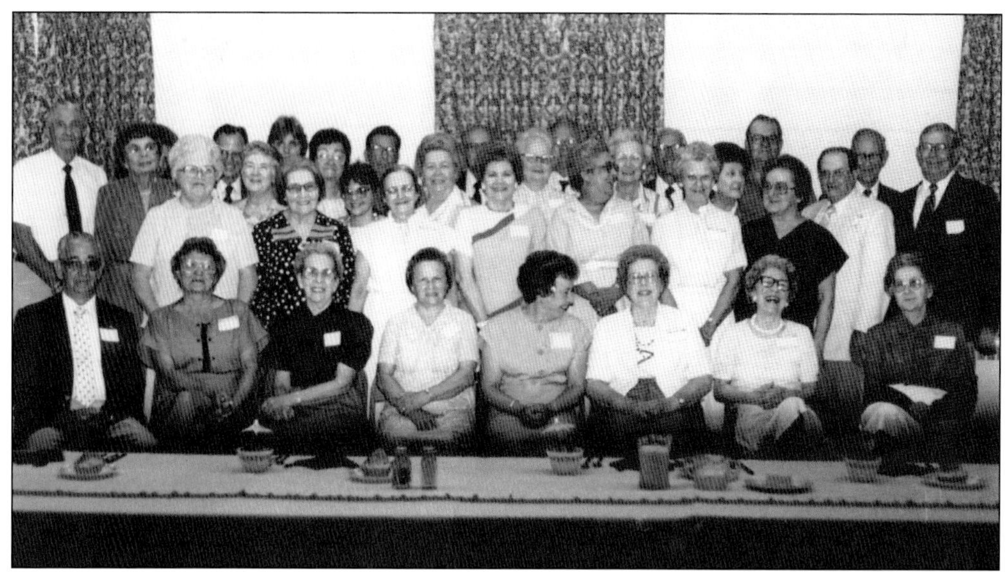

The 50th reunion of Walnut Cove School class of 1935 was held at Stokesburg United Methodist Church on August 8, 1985. Some members present were Ida Valentine, Evelyn Smith Mitchell, and Lois Dodson Smith. (Author's collection.)

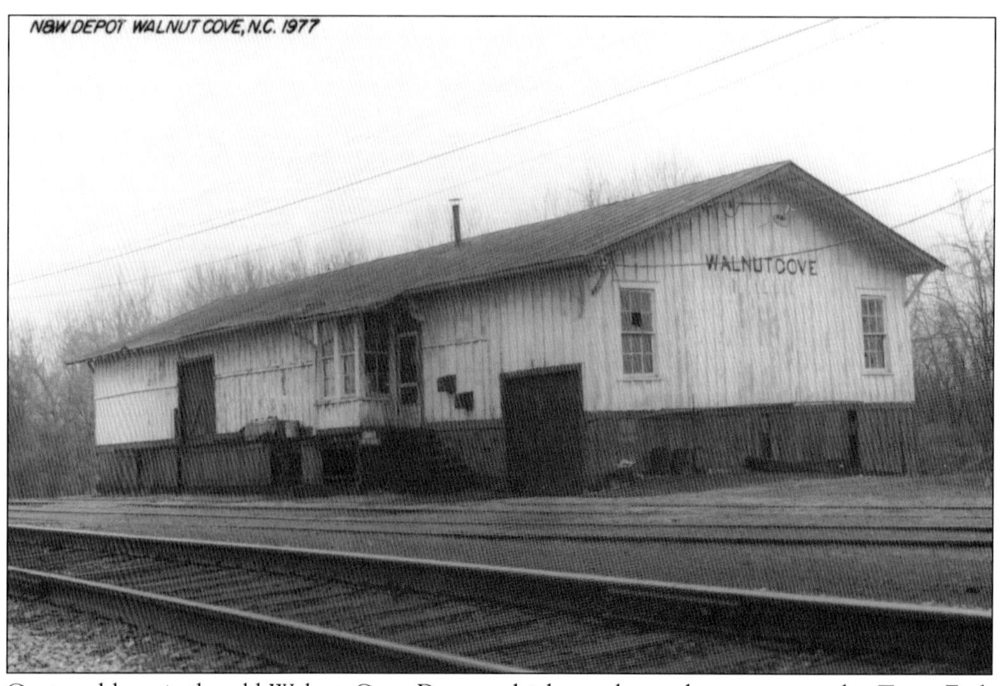

Captured here is the old Walnut Cove Depot, which was located near present-day Town Fork Produce. This building was later moved to a private residence after many years of vacancy. (Courtesy of Wayne and Louise Biby.)

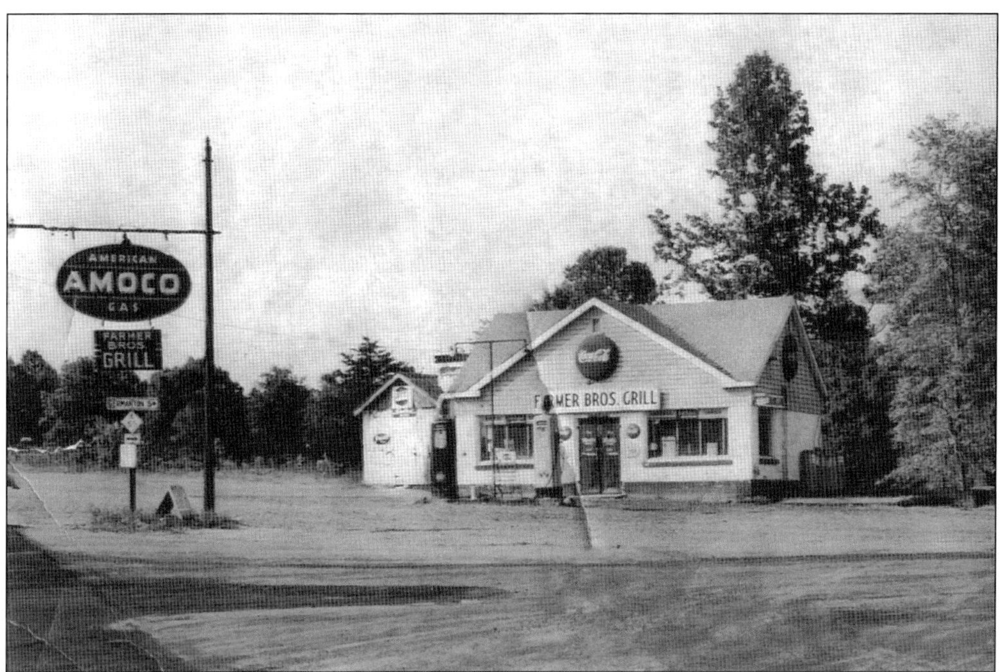

Farmers Grill, located near present-day Ingles grocery store, is shown here around 1940. It was a very popular hangout in its time. (Courtesy of Don Richardson.)

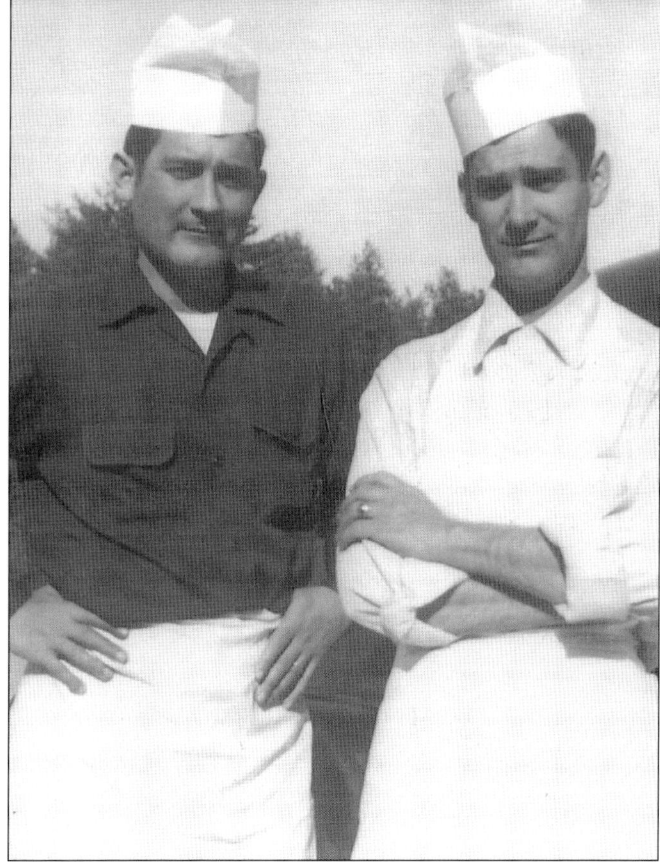

Shown here are the proud owners of Farmers Grill in Walnut Cove, Russell (left) and Raymond Farmer. (Courtesy of Don Richardson.)

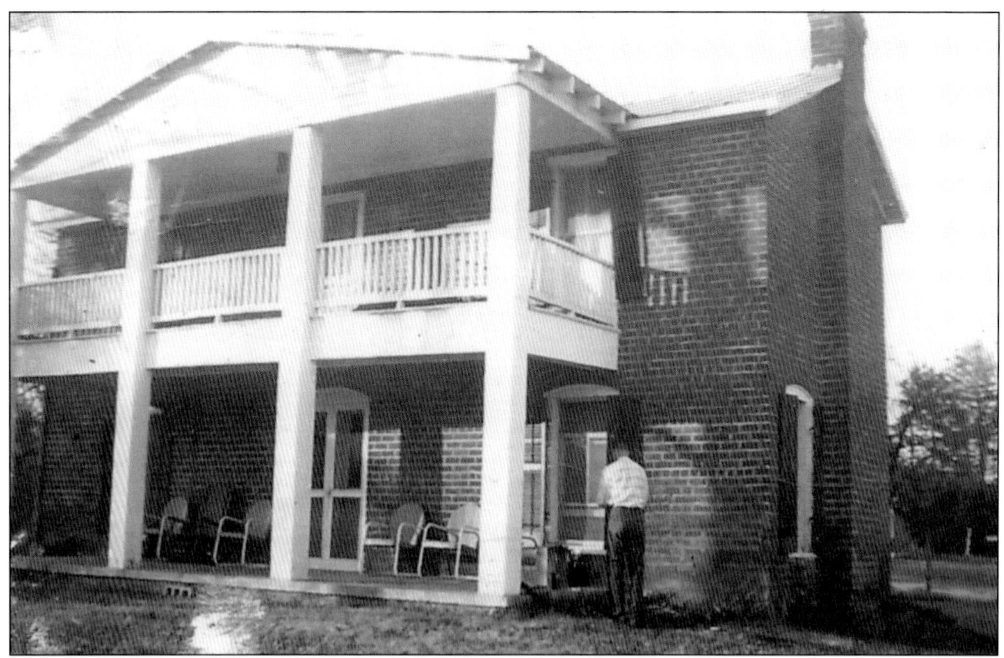

The Barker family was responsible for the construction of this beautiful home. In the 1950s, it was sold to the Edward Freas family. Freas was an avid rock collector and was well known by school-aged children for his rock exhibitions at the elementary schools. (Courtesy James Harbuck.)

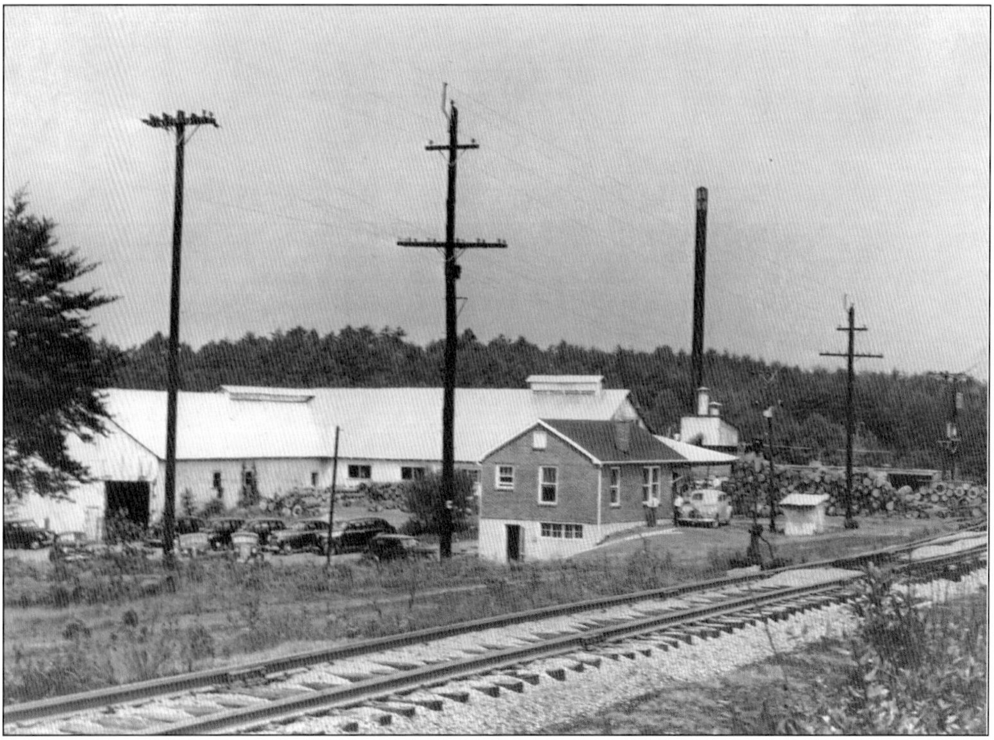

The Walnut Cove Veneer Plant, located near the present-day Olympic Family Restaurant, was photographed here in the early 1950s. (Courtesy of Jerry and Yvonne Rutledge.)

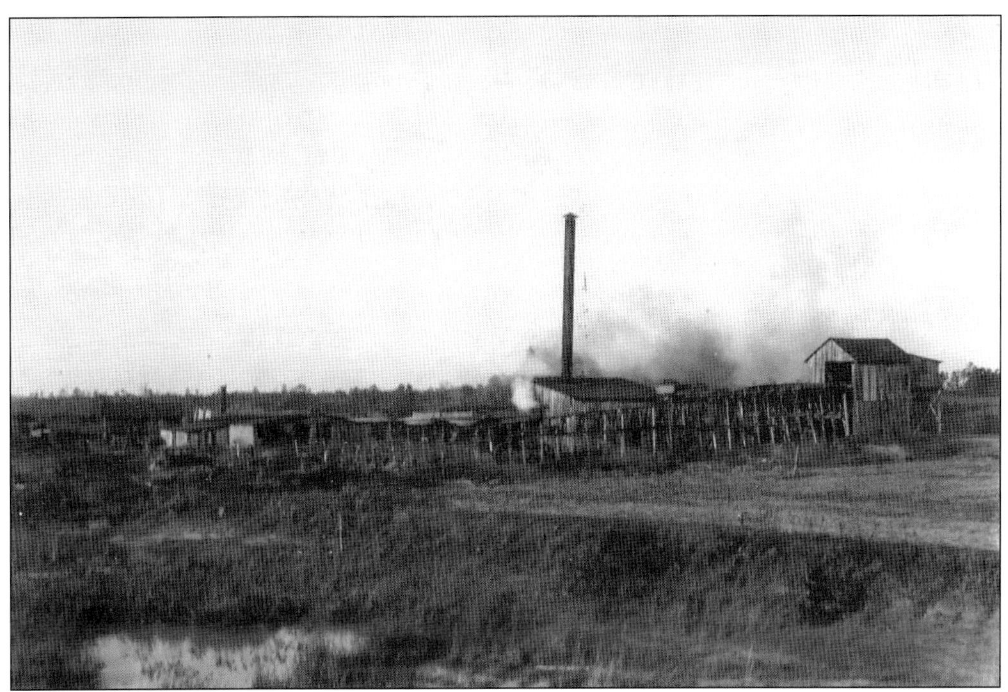

Another common business in the early 20th century was that of brick-making. Captured here in 1922 is Walker's Brickyard, located in Walnut Cove. This brickyard produced many bricks for area construction, as did other area brickyards. (Courtesy of Barbara Fulton Tuttle.)

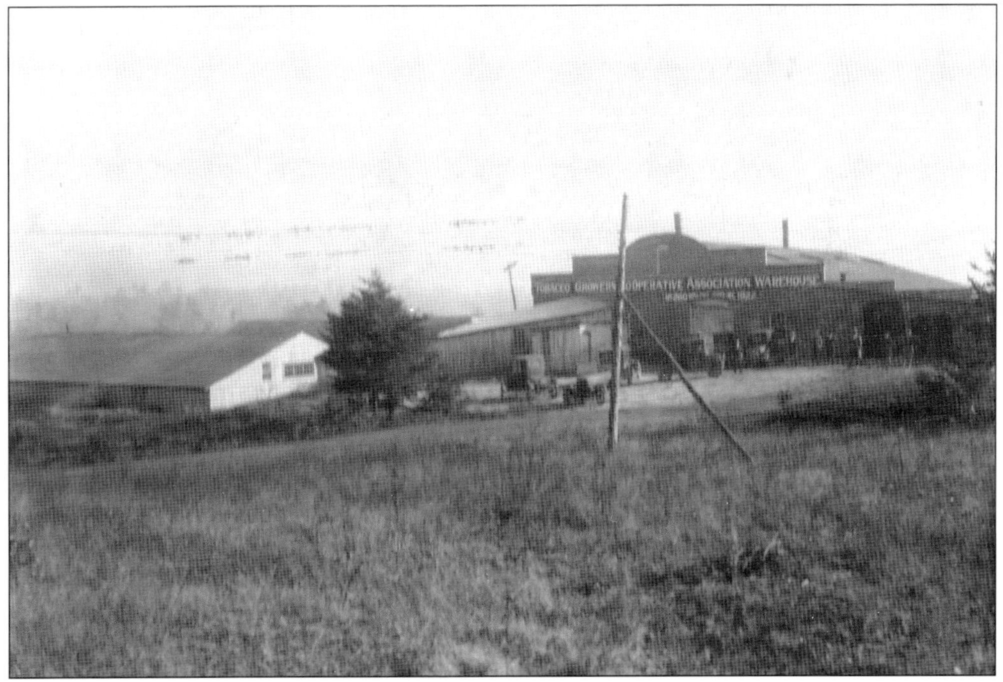

The Tobacco Growers Association Warehouse is pictured here in 1922. Tobacco sellers were either paid in scrip or in installments, much of the reason it did not last very long. This structure stood where present-day Hedgecock Builders Supply is. (Courtesy of Barbara Fulton Tuttle.)

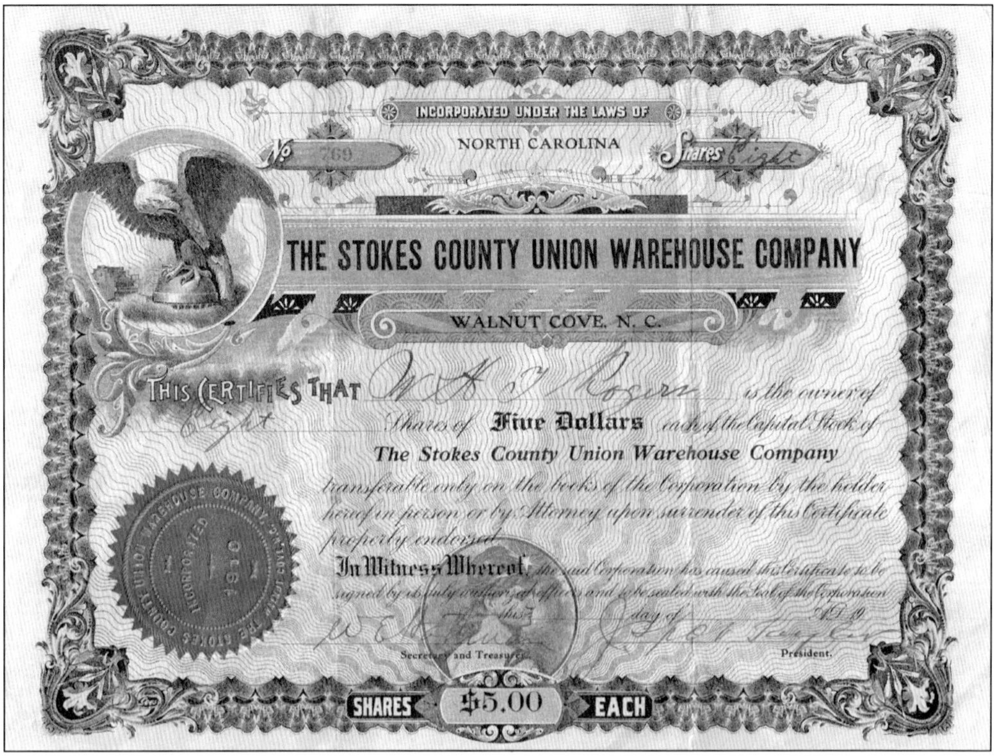

INCORPORATED UNDER THE LAWS OF

NORTH CAROLINA

No 769 Shares Eight

THE STOKES COUNTY UNION WAREHOUSE COMPANY

WALNUT COVE, N. C.

This Certifies That W. A. J. Rogers is the owner of Eight Shares of **Five Dollars** each of the Capital Stock of *The Stokes County Union Warehouse Company* transferable only on the books of the Corporation by the holder hereof in person or by Attorney upon surrender of this Certificate properly endorsed.

In Witness Whereof, the said Corporation has caused this Certificate to be signed by its duly authorized officers and to be sealed with the Seal of the Corporation this day of A.D. 19

Secretary and Treasurer — President.

SHARES $5.00 EACH

This stock certificate was issued to W.A. Rogers by J. Spot Taylor for five shares in the Stokes County Union Warehouse Company. This was one of several tobacco warehouses located in Walnut Cove during the early portion of the 20th century. (Courtesy of Stokes County Historical Society.)

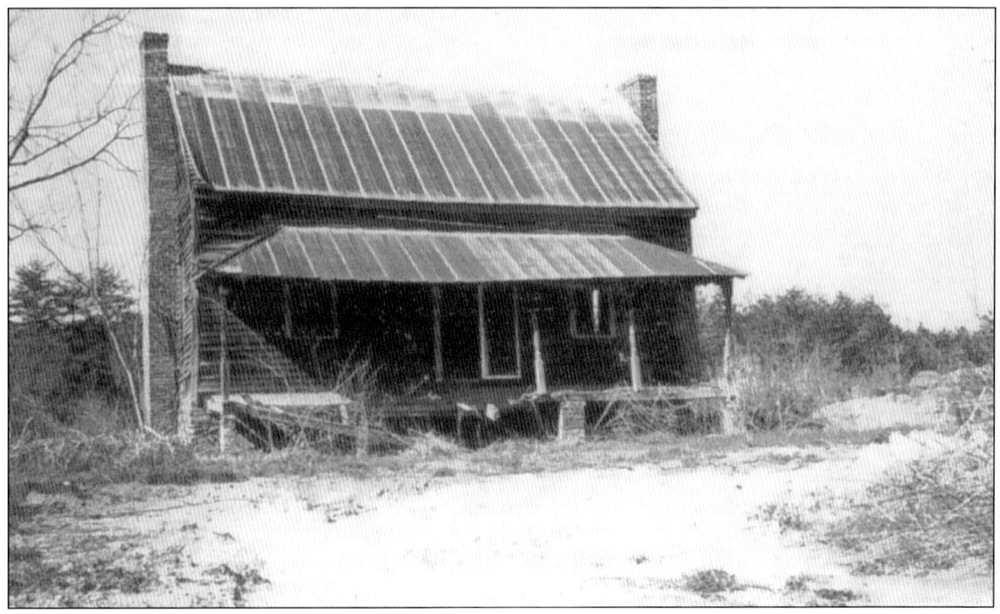

Peter Hairston was the owner of Sauratown Plantation in the Oldtown area of Walnut Cove. This particular house, located in the Dry Hollow area, was one of many tenant homes belonging to the family. (Author's collection.)

This steam tractor was one of the firsts of its time at Walnut Cove. It arrived on the Norfolk and Western Railway in the 1930s. (Courtesy of Dr. Jack and Nancy Helsabeck Fowler.)

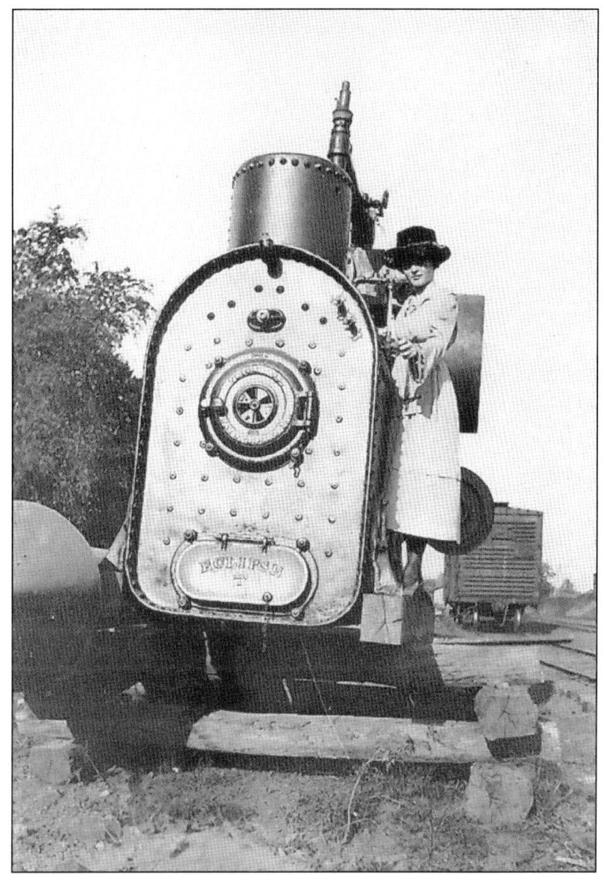

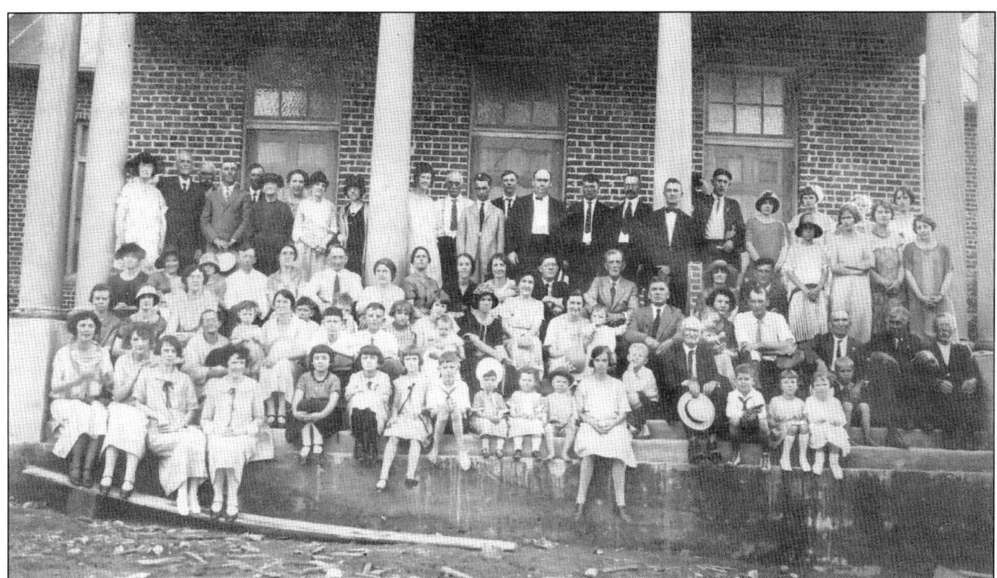

This photograph was taken in 1925 at the dedication of Leak Memorial Baptist Church. It was originally the Mount Tabor Baptist Church, which was built in 1886. The name changed on July 20, 1925. (Courtesy Jerry and Sarah Stephens.)

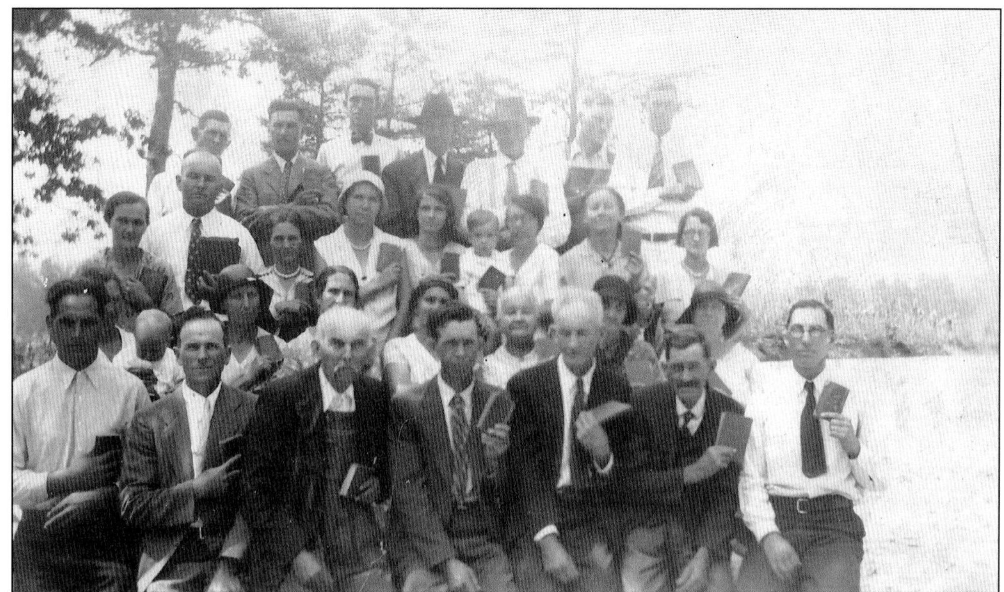

Rosebud Christian Church's adult class poses for this photograph in 1932. Pictured from left to right are, (first row) Oliver Smith, B.L. Tuttle, Charlie Smith, Frank Young, Bob Smith, Henry Kritz, and Albert Miller; (second row) Nannie Smith and son Franklin, Polly Newsome, Lily Wiles, Louzetta Mitchell, Jettie Smith, Mrs. T.D. Young, and Bessie Ring; (third row) Dora Smith, C.O. Smith, Minnie Smith, Nora Wooten, Nannie Mitchell, Pearl Miller, Tom Miller, Pauline Smith Kritz, and Joy Tuttle; (fourth row) Wade Mitchell, Elmer Tuttle, Dee Ring, Will Tuttle, Gideon Tuttle, Jim Wooten, and Leonard Mitchell.

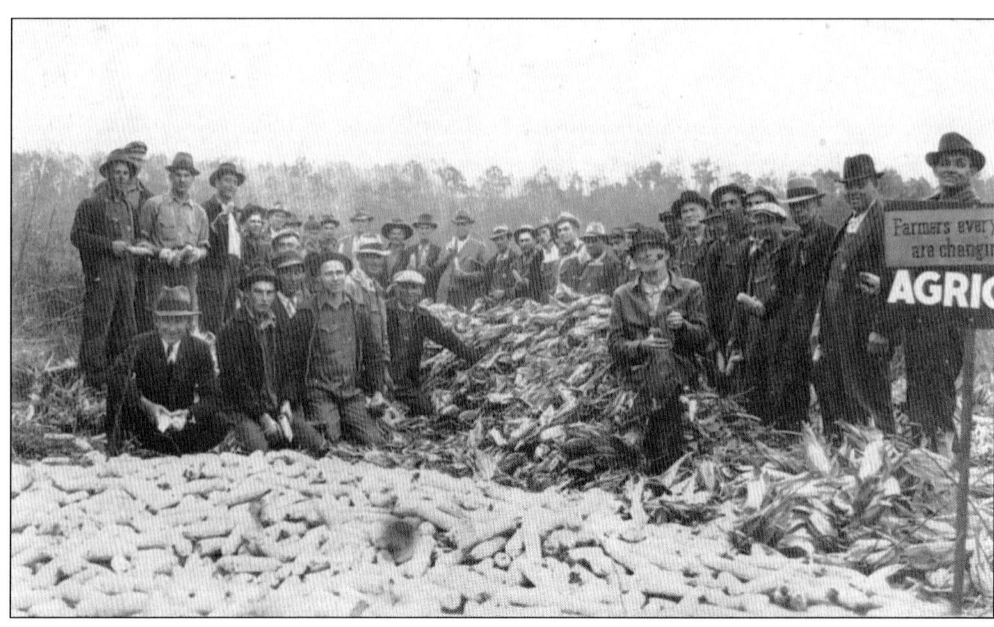

A corn shucking was considered a community event rather than a chore. This particular corn shucking took place on the Bailey Walker farm. (Courtesy of Barbara Fulton Tuttle.)

Charlie Lawson, a prominent member of the Walnut Cove and Germanton communities, murdered his wife and six of his seven children on Christmas Day 1929. To this day, it remains one of the most tragic events remembered in Stokes County. Visitors from across the country came to view the aftermath of the murder of the Lawson family. The mantel in this photograph portrays the signatures of visitors to the house sometime in the 1960s. (Author's collection.)

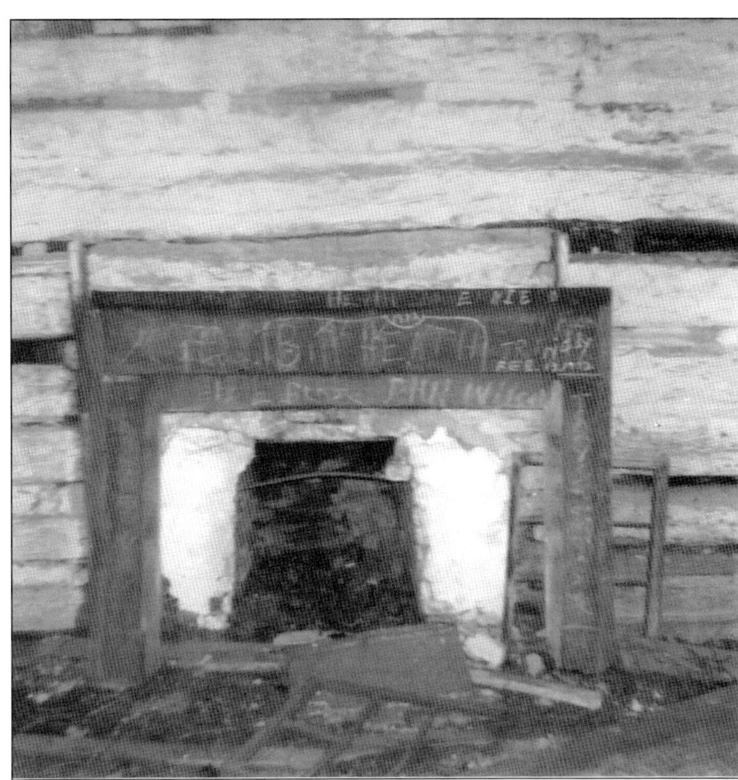

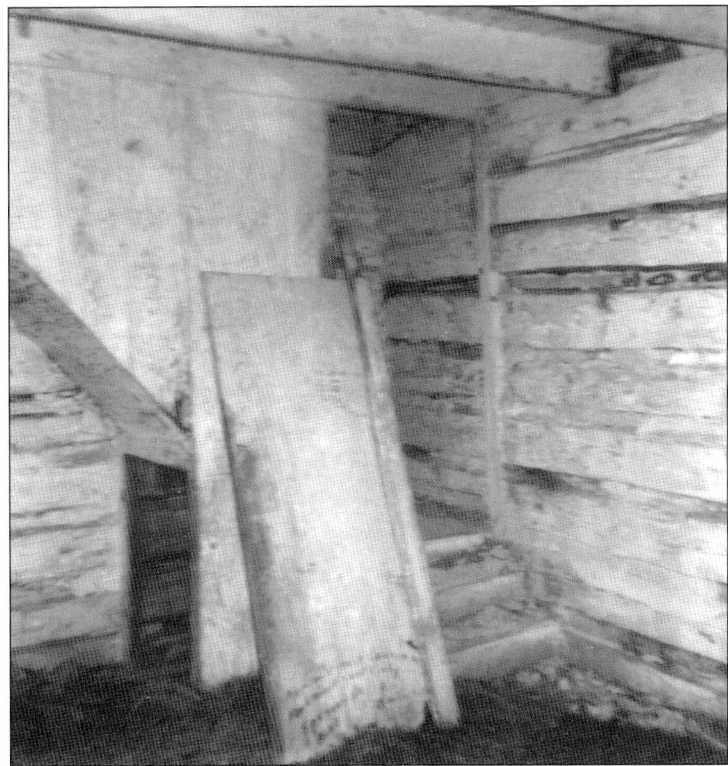

Another angle in the Lawson cabin shows the stairway to the upper bedroom of the cabin during the 1960s. By this time, the cabin had begun to fall into disrepair. (Author's collection.)

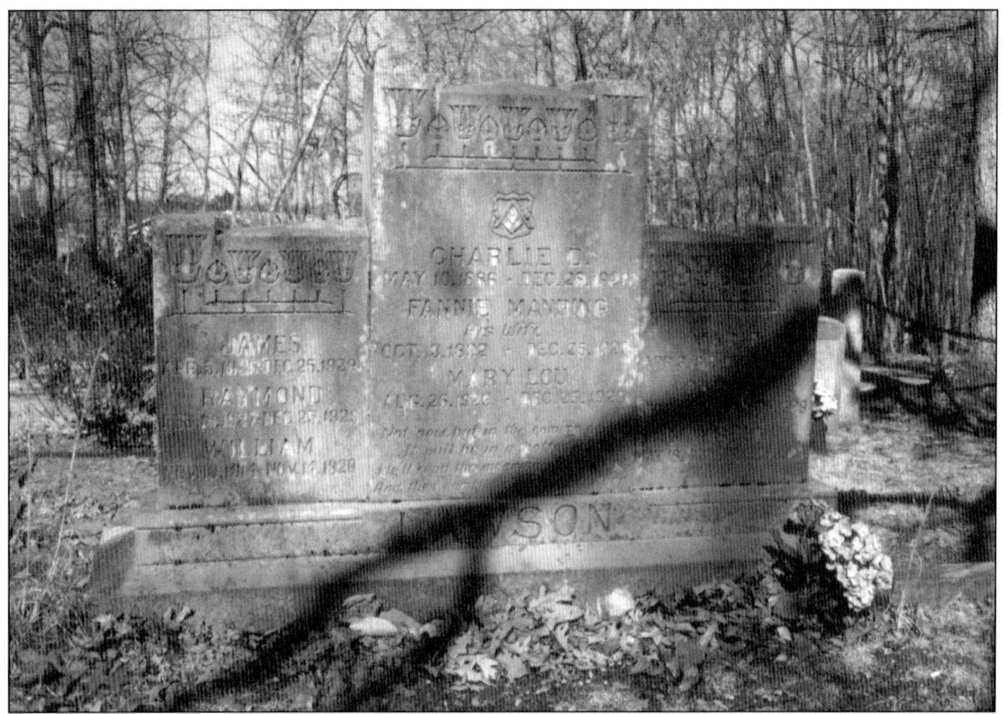

This photograph shows the mass grave in Browder Cemetery where the Lawson family is buried. (Author's collection.)

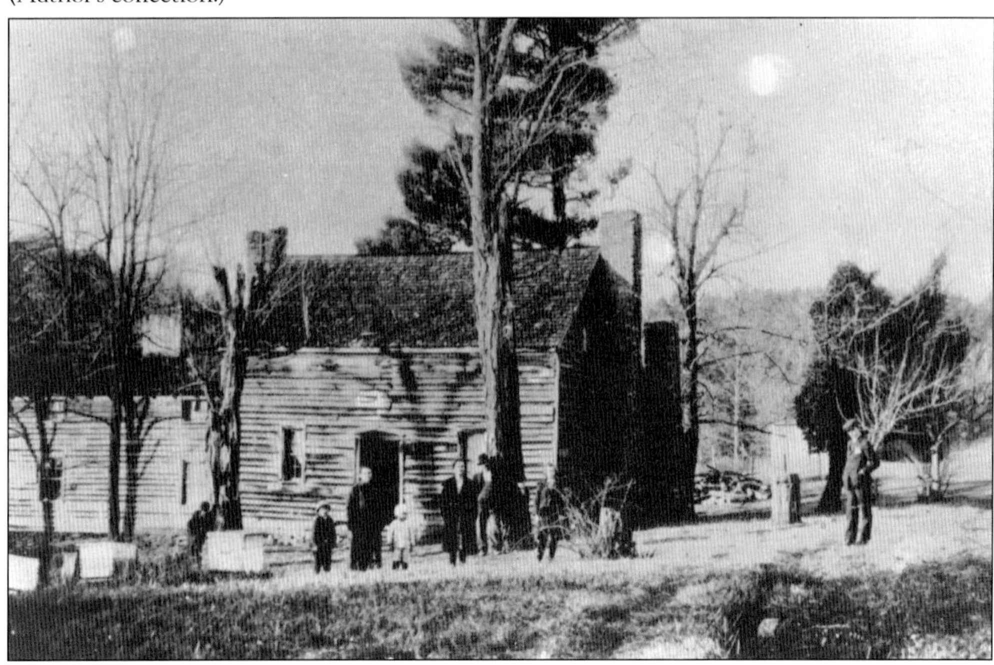
The Lewis Plantation house, seen here in the early 1900s, was home to the Lewis family for over 100 years, until they moved to their new home in the Meadows community during the mid-1920s. This house was located across the road from present-day South Stokes School until 1984. (Author's collection.)

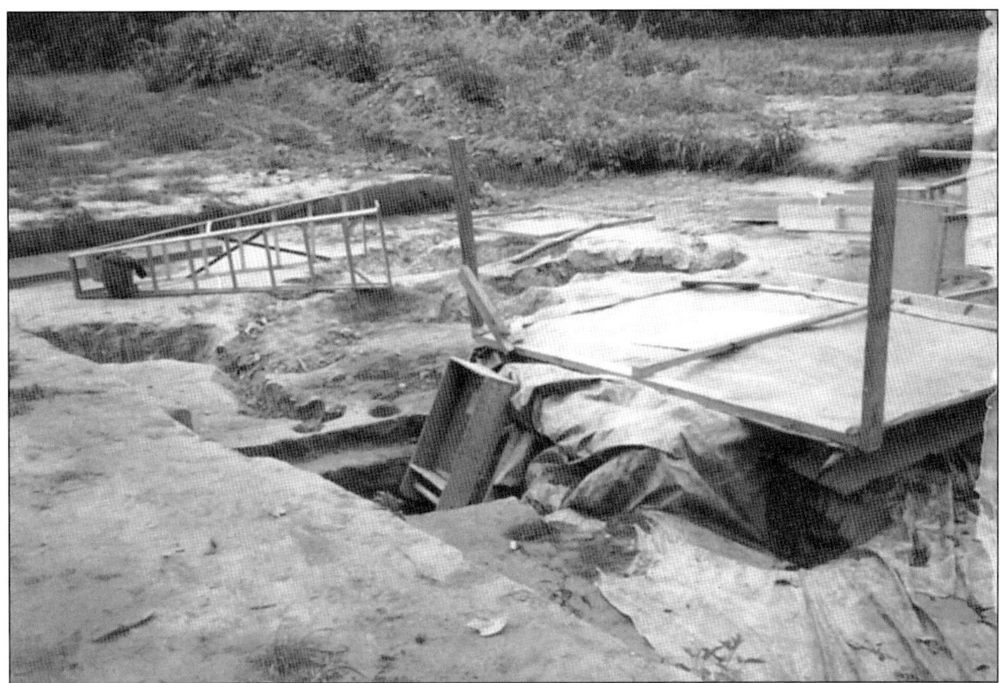

Indian artifacts have been found in Stokes County for many years. In 1973, a grave of an Indian princess was discovered. She would later be labeled as "the Sauratown Woman." This photograph was taken during the excavation of her burial site. (Author's collection.)

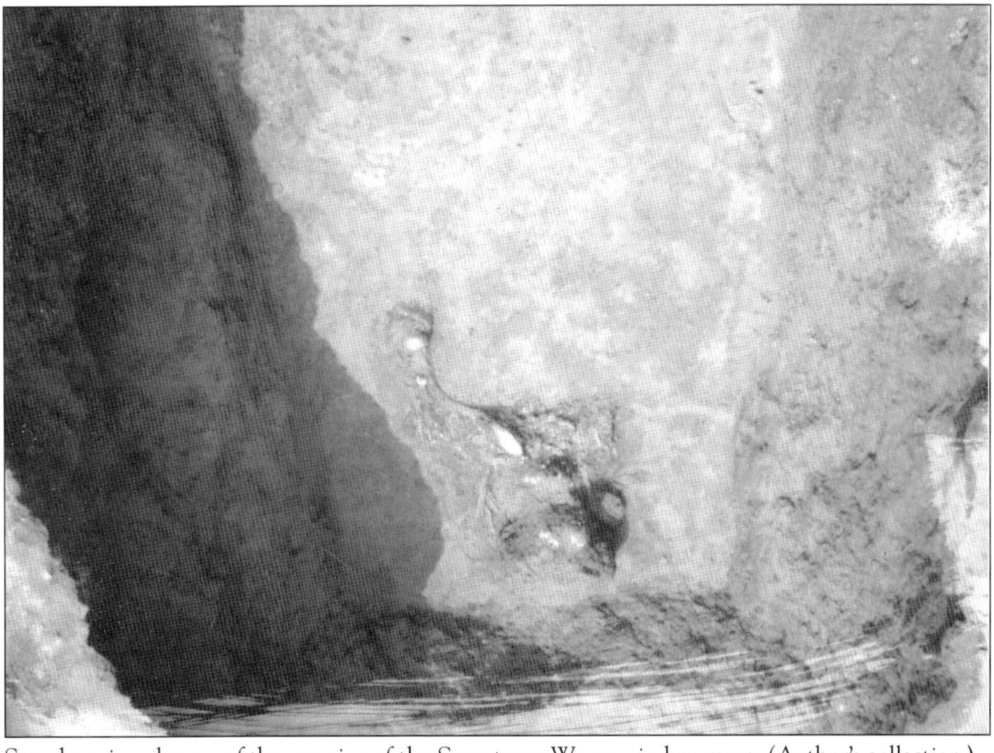

Seen here is a closeup of the remains of the Sauratown Woman in her grave. (Author's collection.)

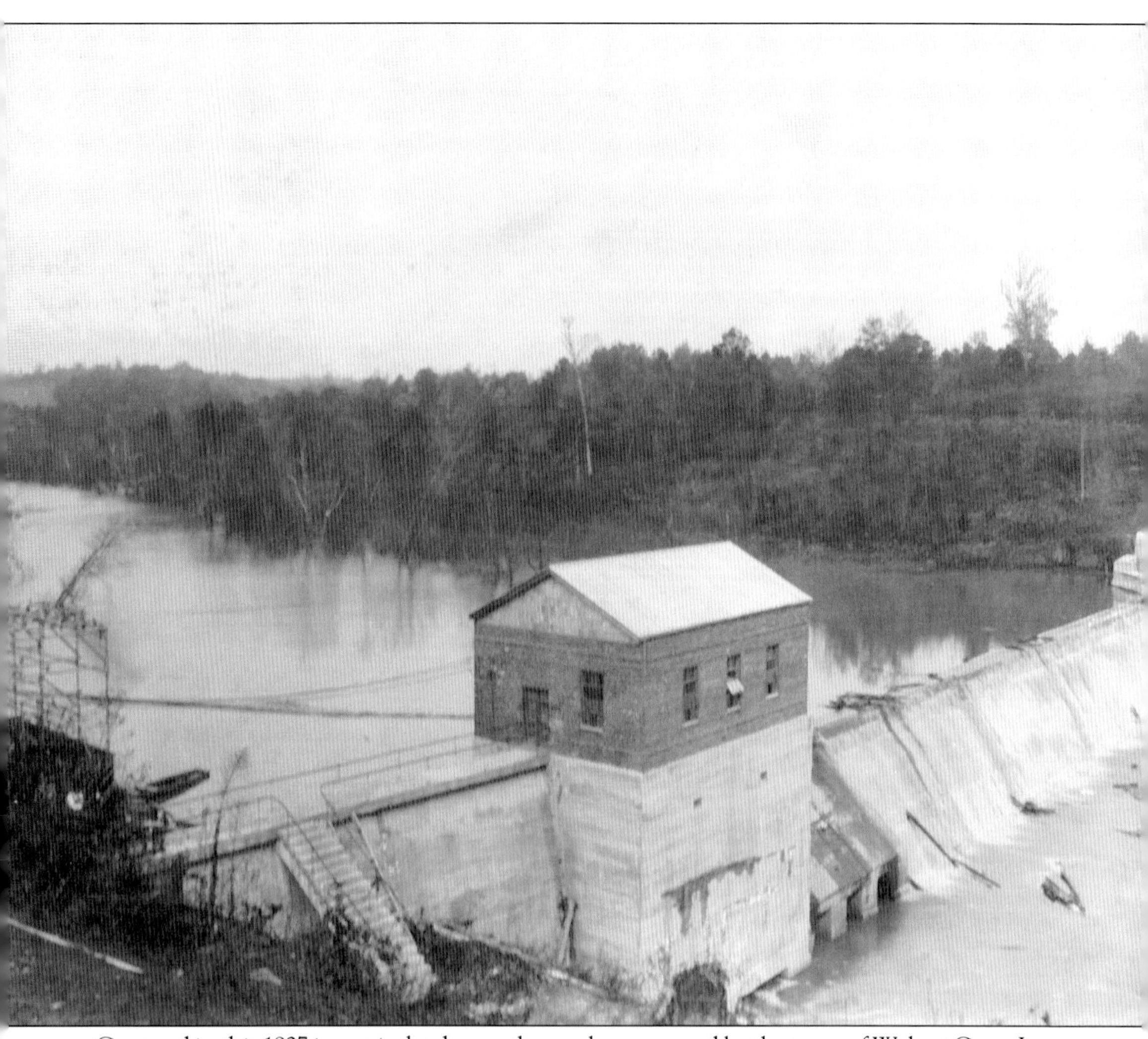

Captured in this 1927 image is the dam and powerhouse owned by the town of Walnut Cove. It was located on the Dan River but is no longer in operation. (Courtesy of Barbara Fulton Tuttle.)

Three

The Road to Danbury

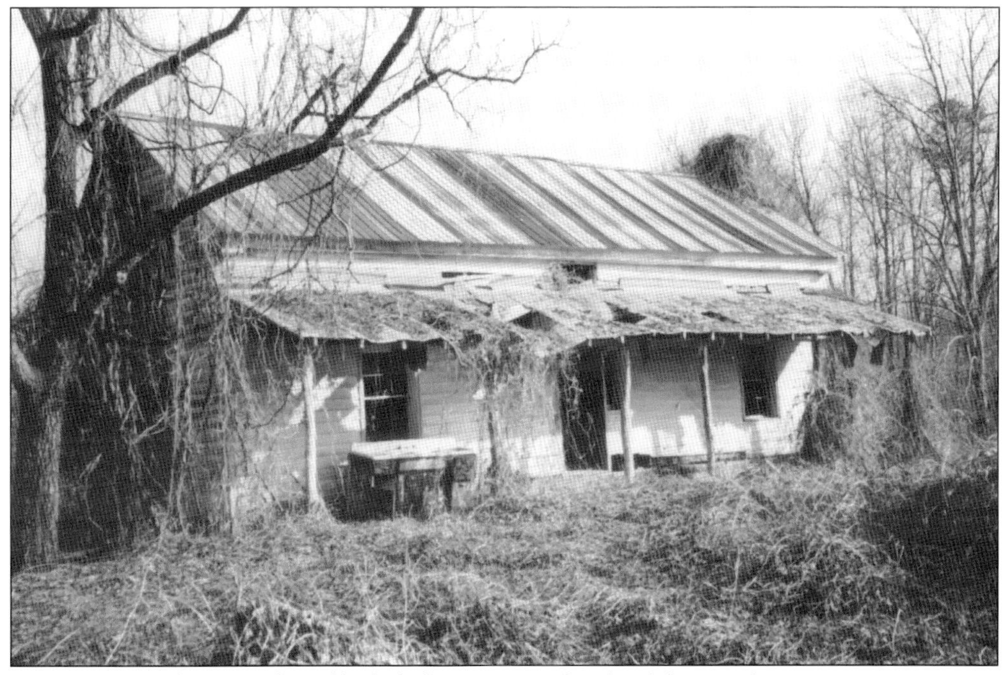

This house was home to the Alfred Shelton Stewart family of the Meadows area. Stewart was a primitive Baptist minister and farmer. He served in the Civil War with Company H of the 53rd Regiment, North Carolina Infantry. (Author's collection.)

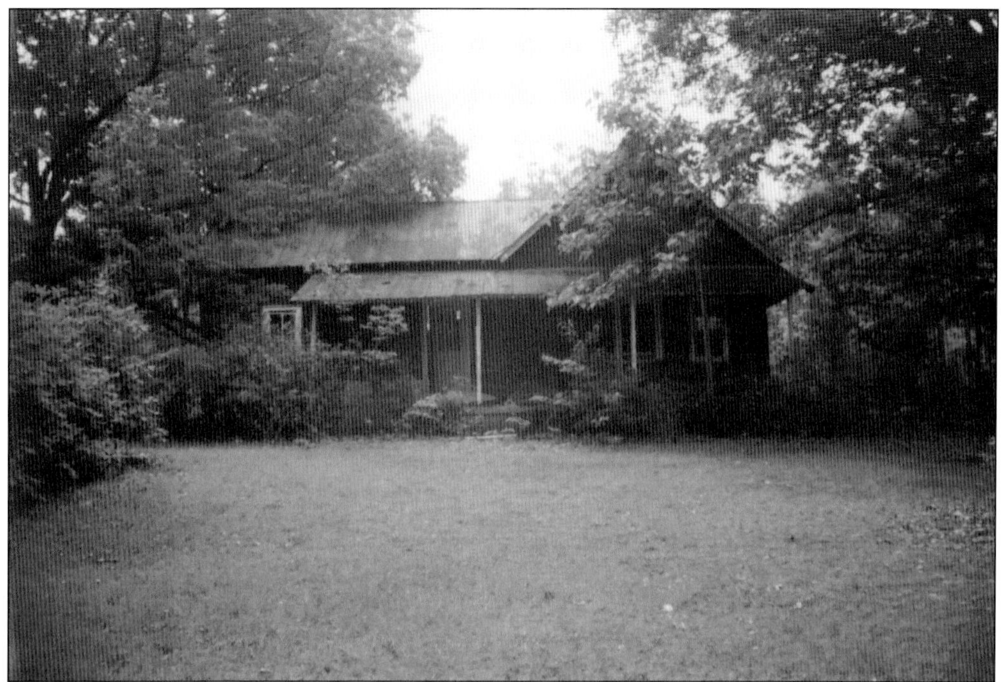

This building housed Stewart School on Stewart Road in Meadows many years ago. Land for the school was donated by Alfred Stewart. In 1932, the school closed to consolidate with Meadows School. (Author's collection.)

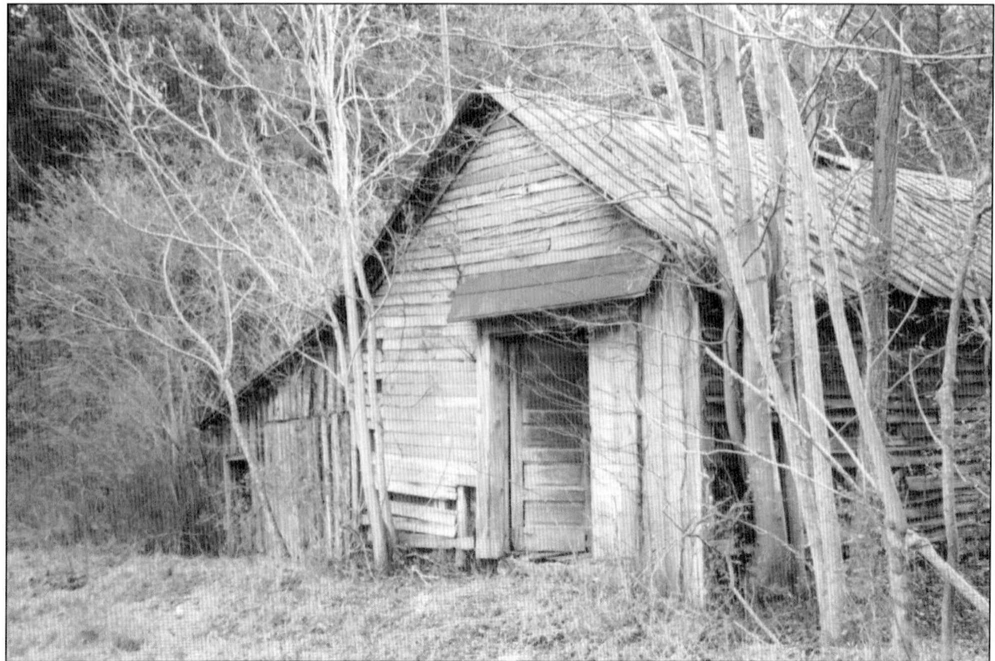

In 1915, this store building was used for the primary grades of the Stewart School. (Author's collection.)

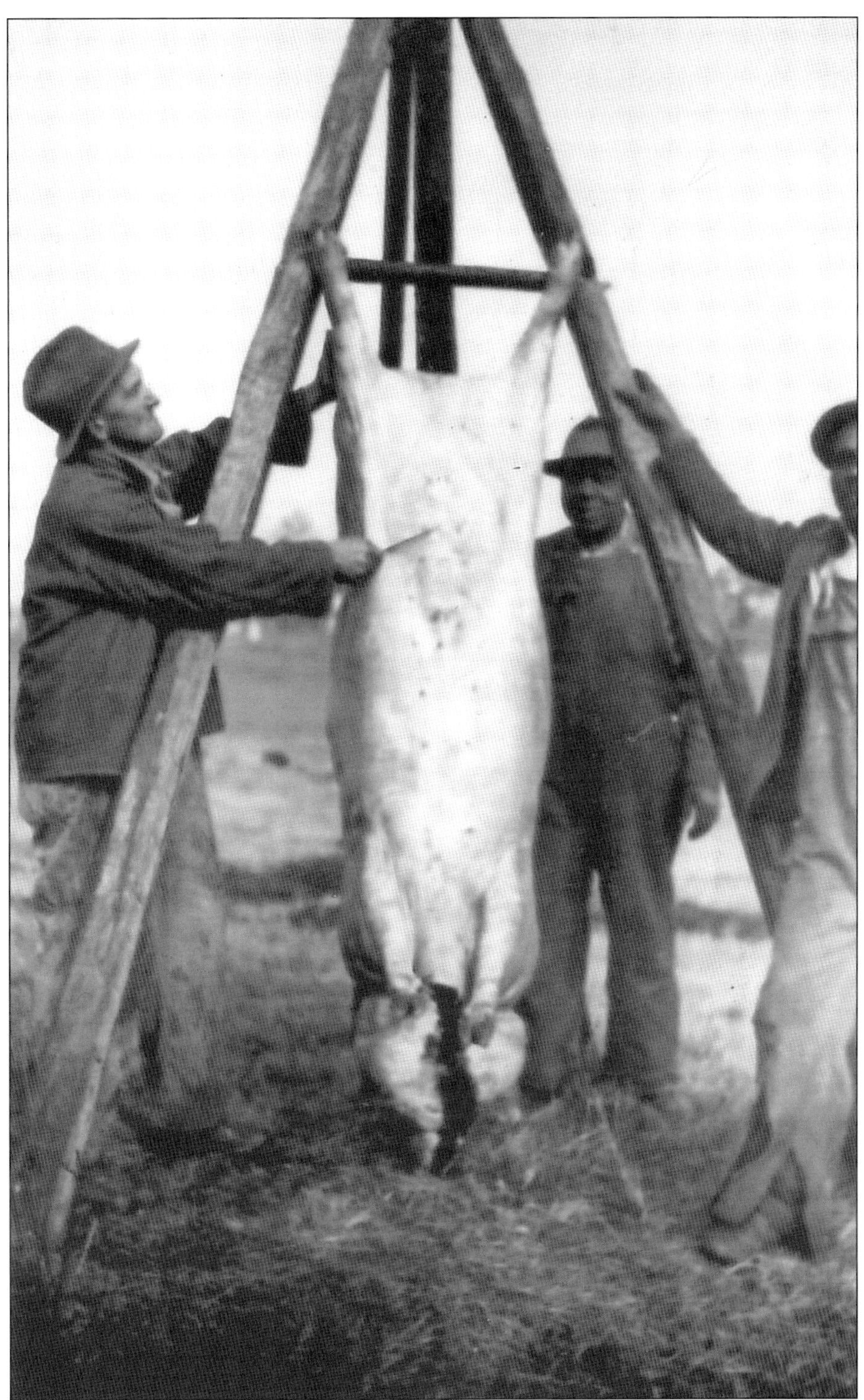

Many families raised hogs and livestock. When autumn came, it would be time to slaughter the hogs. This photograph depicts a hog slaughtering, which was a commonality in Stokes County. (Courtesy of Barbara Fulton Tuttle.)

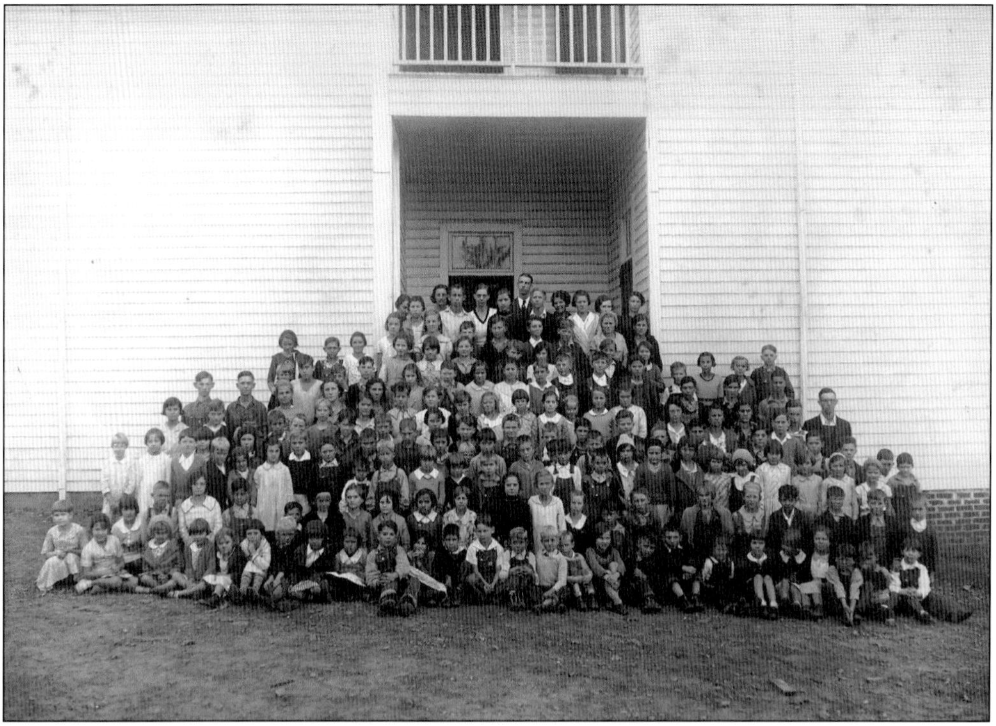

The entire student body of Meadows School gathers for this photograph in 1935. The school was built in 1922 and consolidated with Walnut Cove and Danbury in 1945. (Courtesy Richard and Kimbyl Alley Ferrell.)

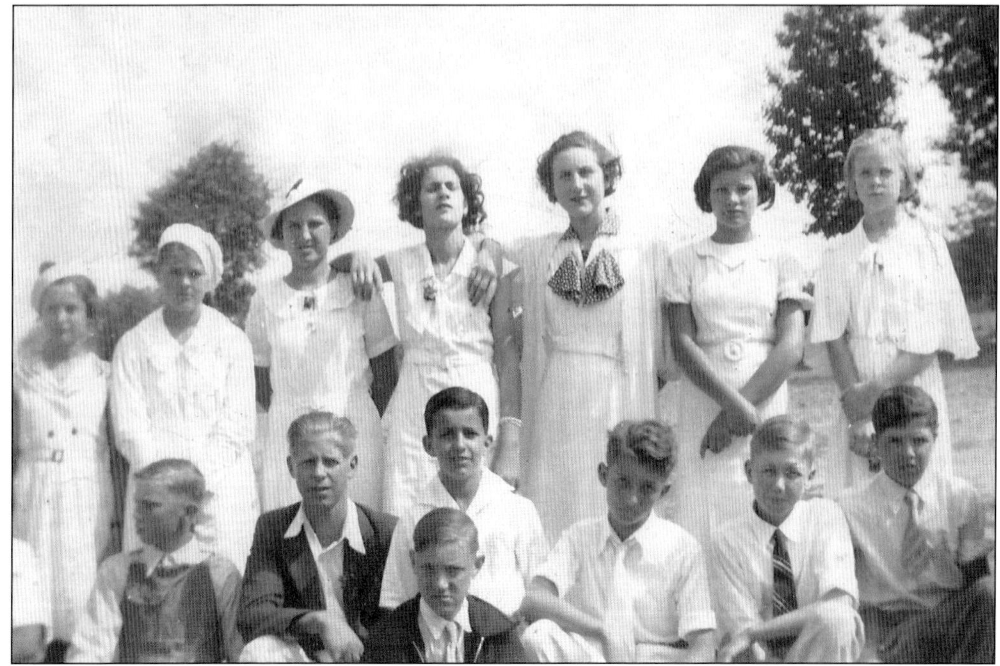

A class at Meadows School poses for this photograph in 1935. (Courtesy Richard and Kimbyl Alley Ferrell.)

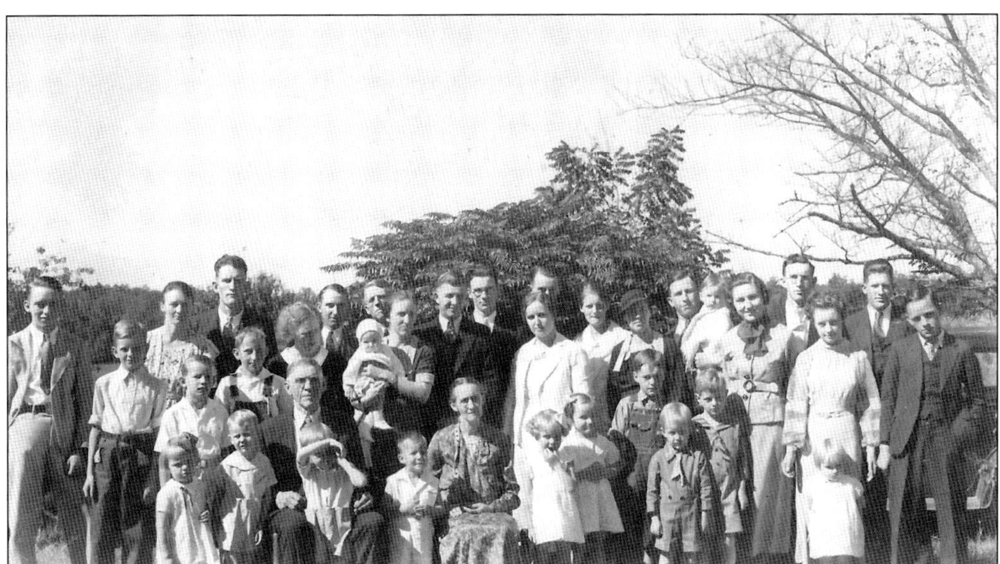

The J.W. Young family of the Meadows community poses for this photograph. Young was well known for his fine tobacco crops and allowed no mistakes in the manufacturing of his tobacco. (Courtesy of Richard and Kimbyl Alley Ferrell.)

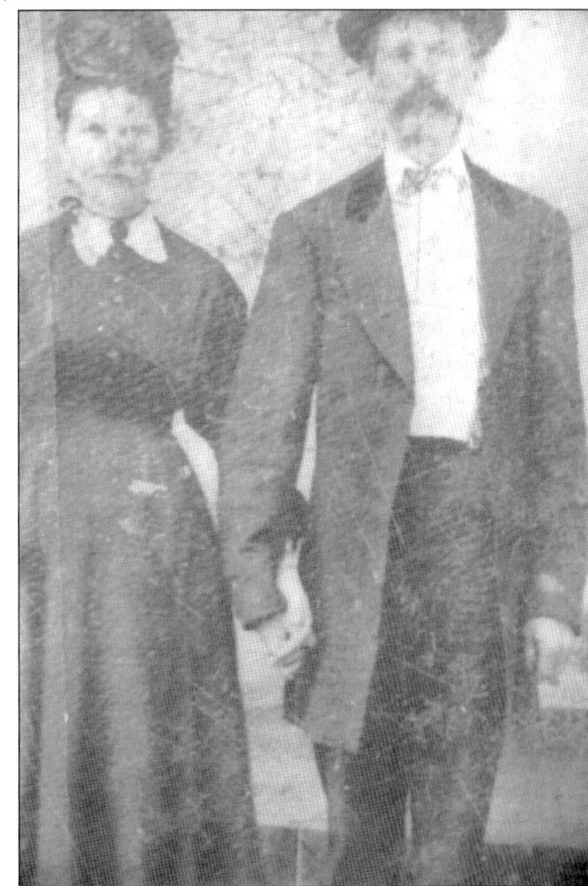

Family legend states that Calvin Young and his wife, Elmira Wall, both pictured here, were associates of R.J. Reynolds. When Reynolds decided to expand his tobacco manufacturing business, he asked the Youngs if they were interested in partnering with him in Winston-Salem. Calvin declined, stating that he would rather stay in Stokes County. (Courtesy Richard and Kimbyl Alley Ferrell.)

Auction Sale

32.4 acre farm of J. P. Lewis Estate, on Hwy No. 8,

near Flat Shoals Road, in Ross Store Community
Walnut Cove, N. C., On

September 5th, 1964

at 2:00 P. M.

This farm has good tobacco allotment with large road frontage, in a good community.

Has 8 room dwelling house, and other outbuildings.

Bid your judgment on this fine farm. A good investment or a good home.

SEE Paul Lewis, or C. A. Lewis, or any of heirs of J. P. Lewis.

L. H. van Noppen, Attorney,
Danbury, N. C.

This flyer advertised the sale of the J.P. Lewis farm, located in Ross' Store community, west of Meadows. Lewis was a known tobacco farmer of Stokes County. (Author's collection.)

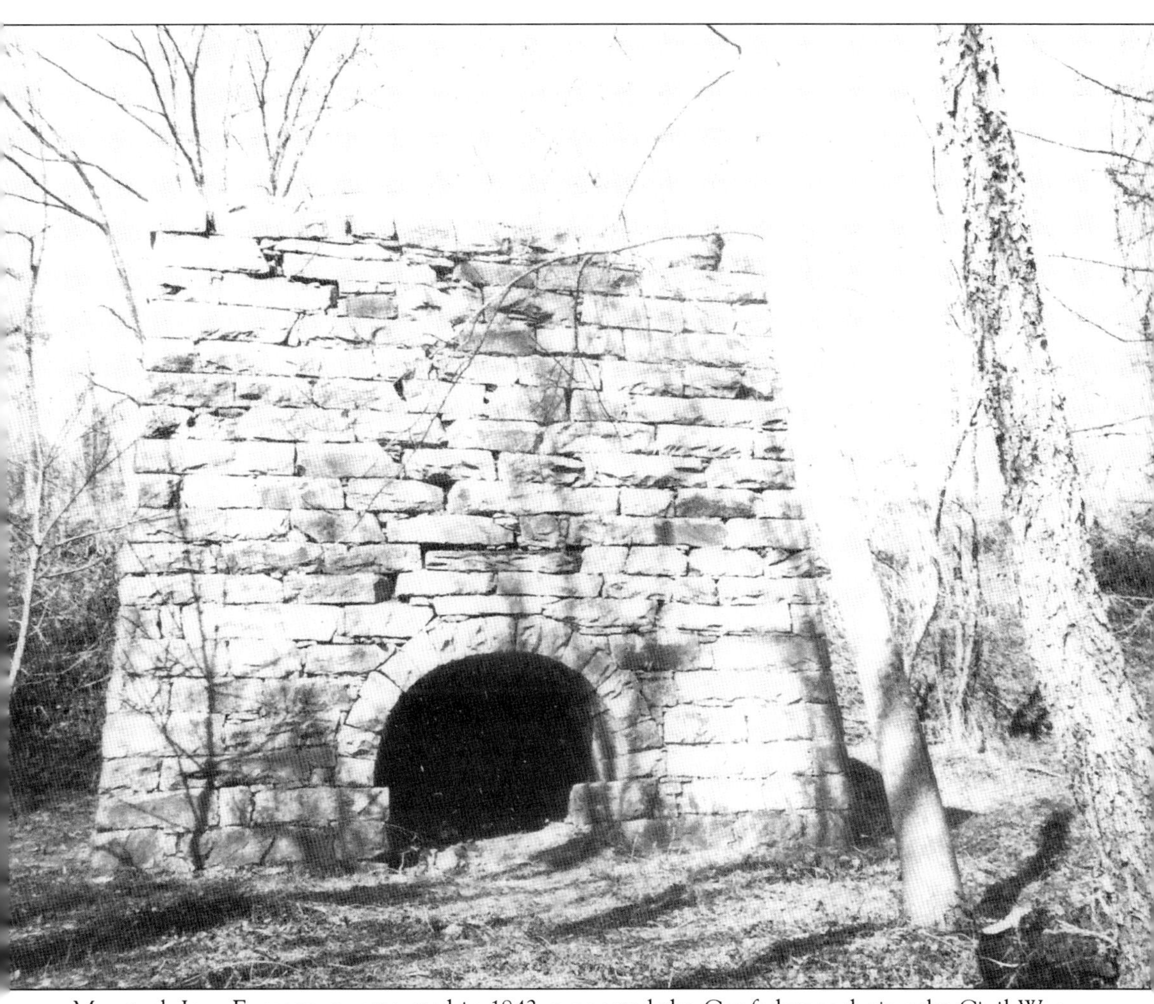

Moratock Iron Furnace, constructed in 1843, supported the Confederacy during the Civil War by the way of iron. It operated until April 1865, when Gen. George Stoneman of Union forces made his way into Danbury and destroyed its operation. The iron furnace still stands in Moratock Park. (Author's collection.)

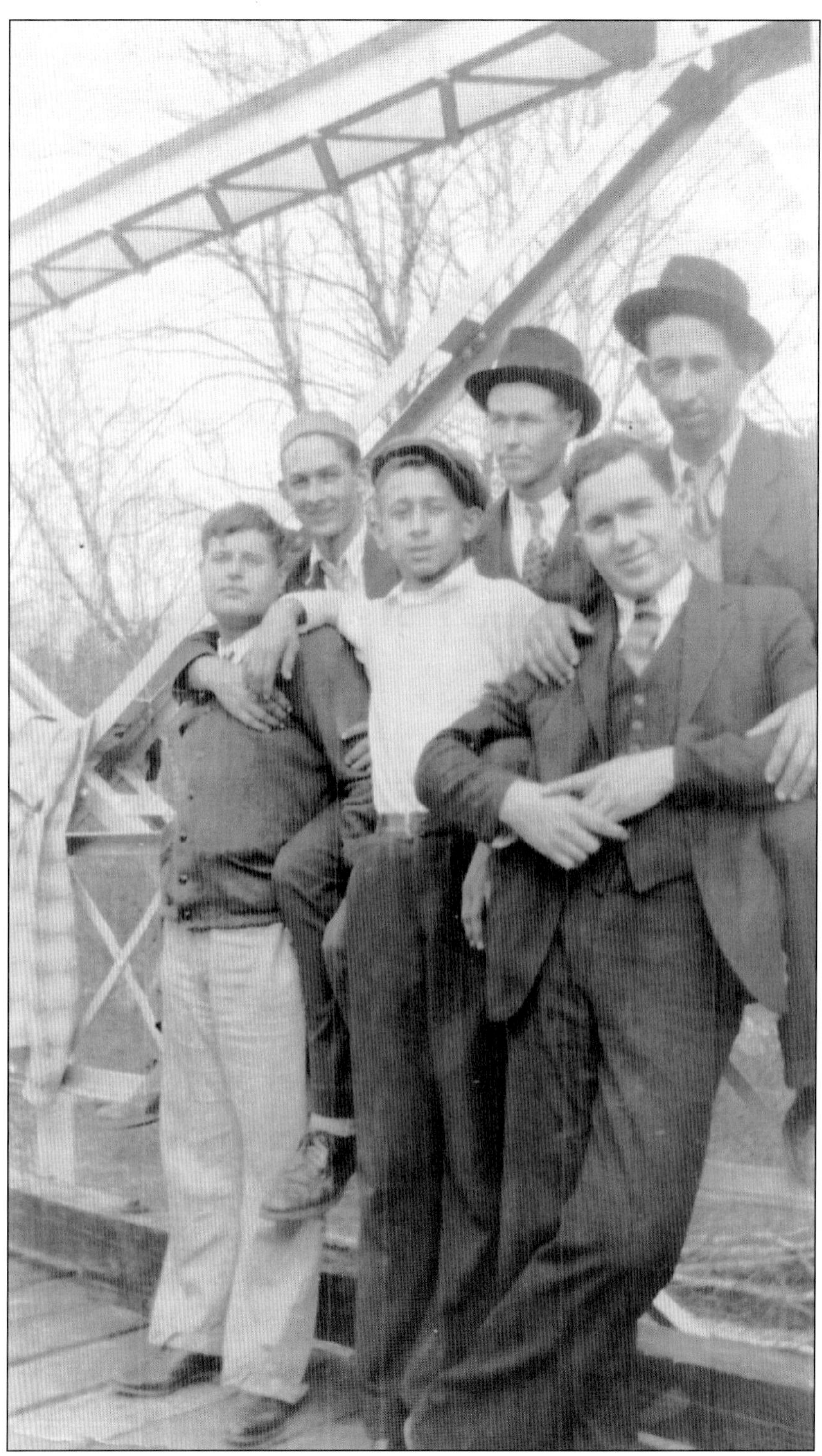

The Dunlap boys stopped to pose on the bridge located at Pitzer Road around 1934. The young man in the white shirt is Wesley Dunlap, who was later sheriff of Stokes County. (Courtesy of Durwood and Patti Dunlap.)

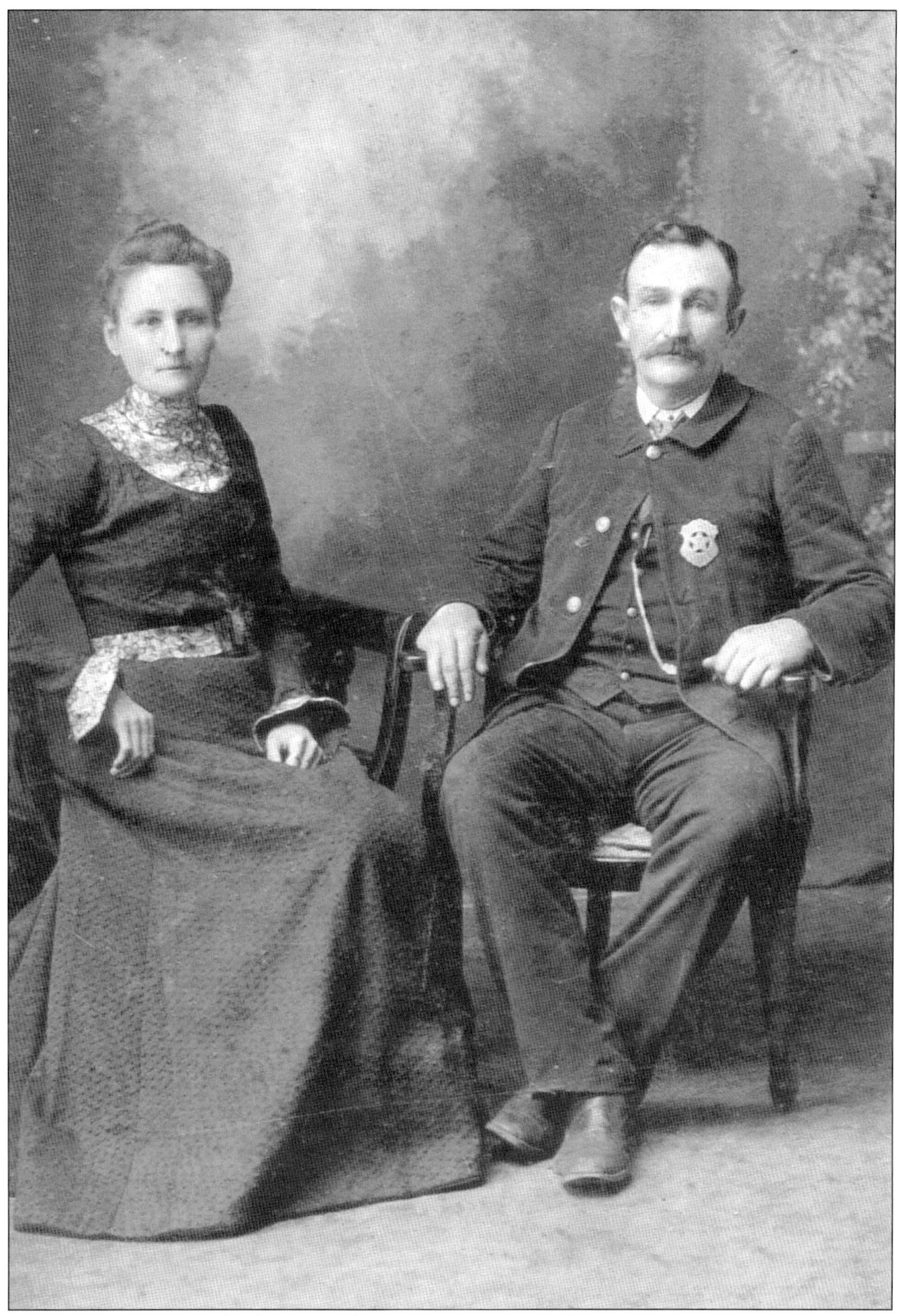

James Wesley Davis and Edna J. Smith are pictured here in the late 20th century. James's father, James Davis II, owned the Red Shoals Plantation on the Dan River. (Courtesy of Davis Chapel Historical Association, Inc.)

This c. 1780 chest is thought to have been built by an enslaved carpenter on the plantation of James Davis Sr. In his will, he left his illegitimate granddaughter a lot of furniture. This chest is believed to have been included in that lot of furniture. (Author's collection.)

Davis Chapel formed on the Davis Plantation during the last portion of the 18th century. This photograph shows Davis Chapel before the fire of 1922 that destroyed the church building. Although regular services aren't held, the church is still used for special functions. (Courtesy of Dr. Jack and Nancy Helsabeck Fowler.)

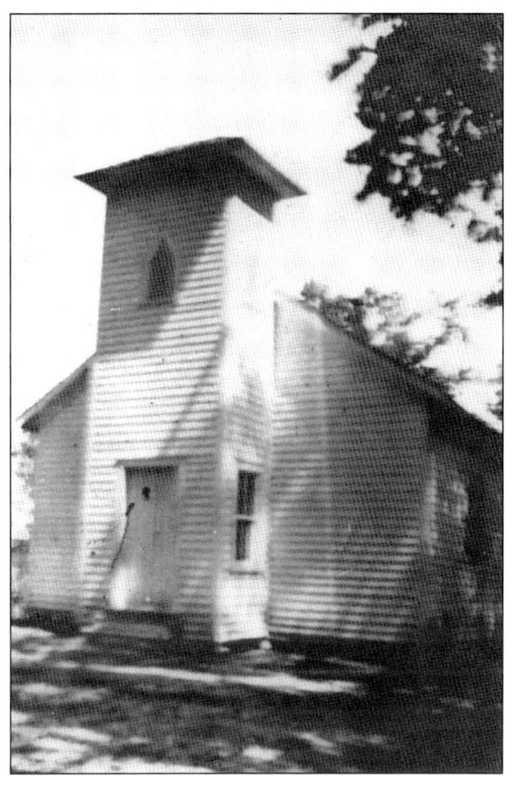

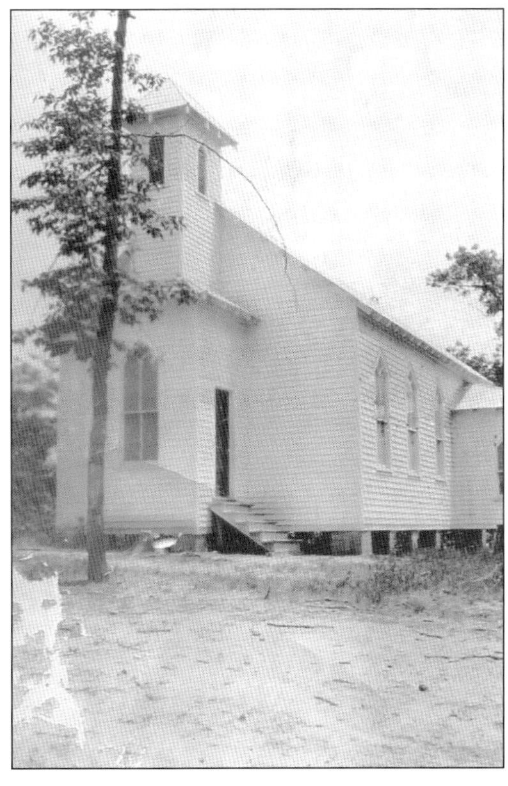

After the fire in 1922, Davis Chapel was rebuilt on its original foundation with minor changes. (Courtesy of Davis Chapel Historical Association, Inc.)

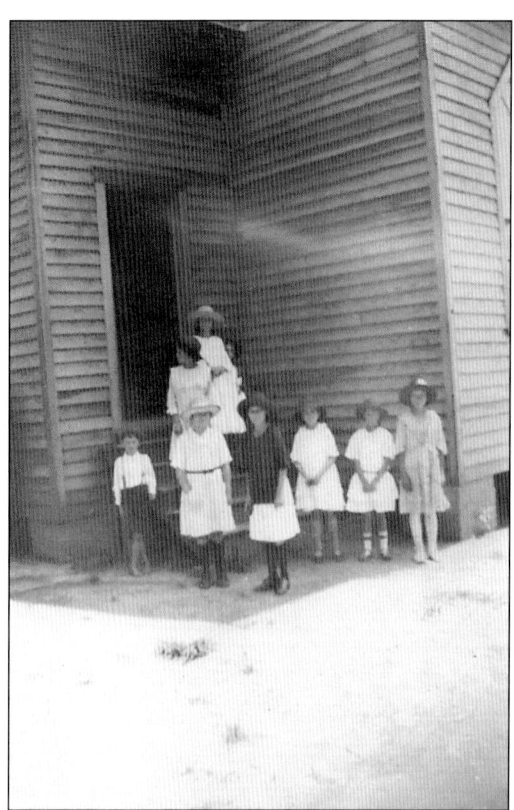

A Sunday school class is seen here at the new building for Davis Chapel. (Courtesy of Dr. Jack and Nancy Helsabeck Fowler.)

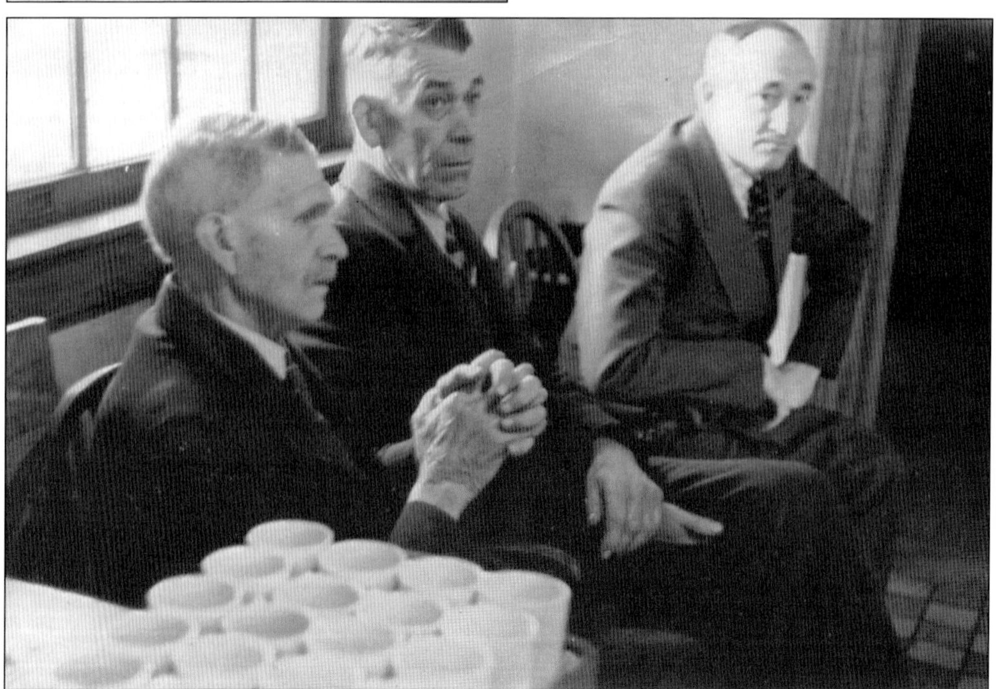

Pictured from left to right, J.P. Adkins, F. Flynt, and B.F. Evinridge talk in the kitchen of Davis Chapel during this 1937 love feast. (Courtesy of Davis Chapel Historical Association, Inc.)

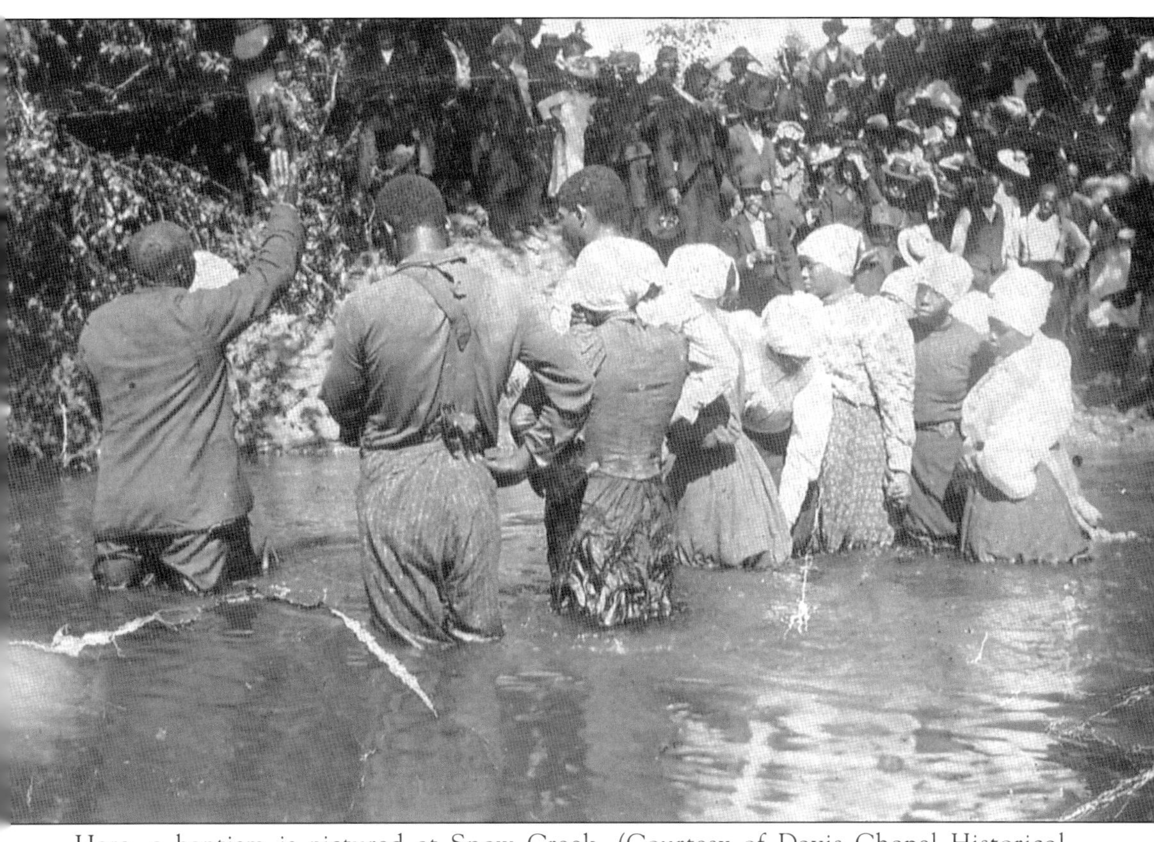

Here, a baptism is pictured at Snow Creek. (Courtesy of Davis Chapel Historical Association, Inc.)

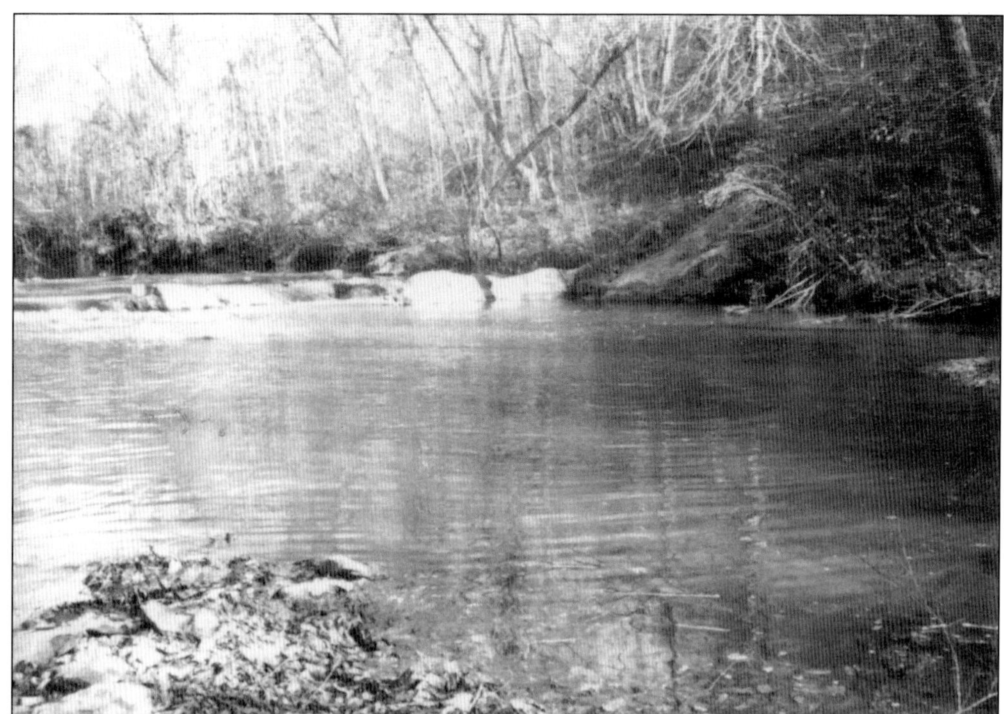

Shown is the site of Union Bloomery Forge on Snow Creek. It was built by Peter Perkins and James Martin. It had one fire and one hammer for forging iron, and it was powered by water. The forge produced about seven tons per year. (Author's collection.)

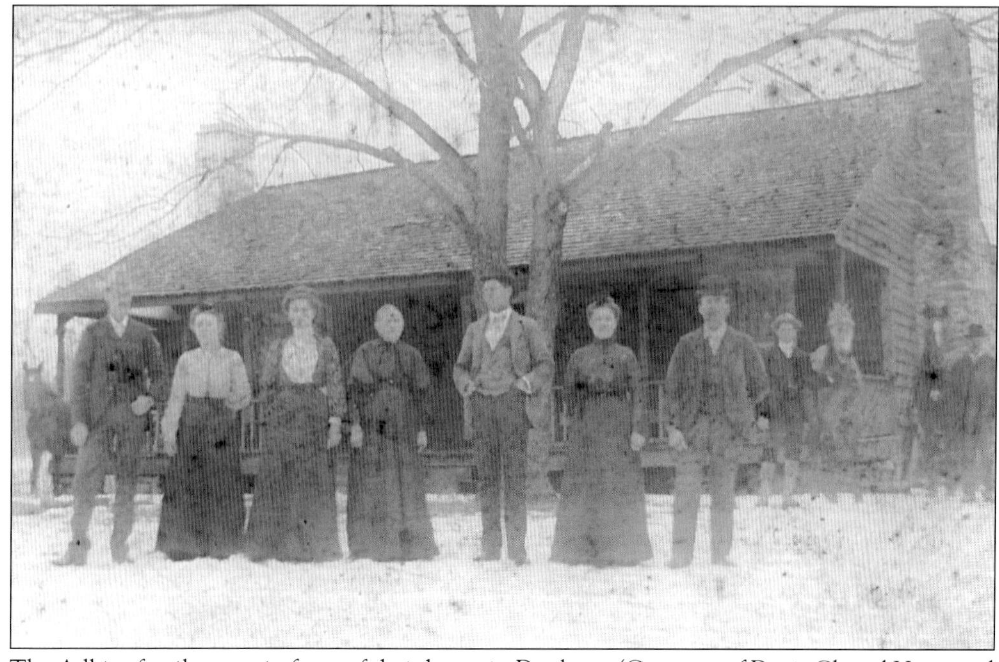

The Adkins family poses in front of their home in Danbury. (Courtesy of Davis Chapel Historical Association, Inc.)

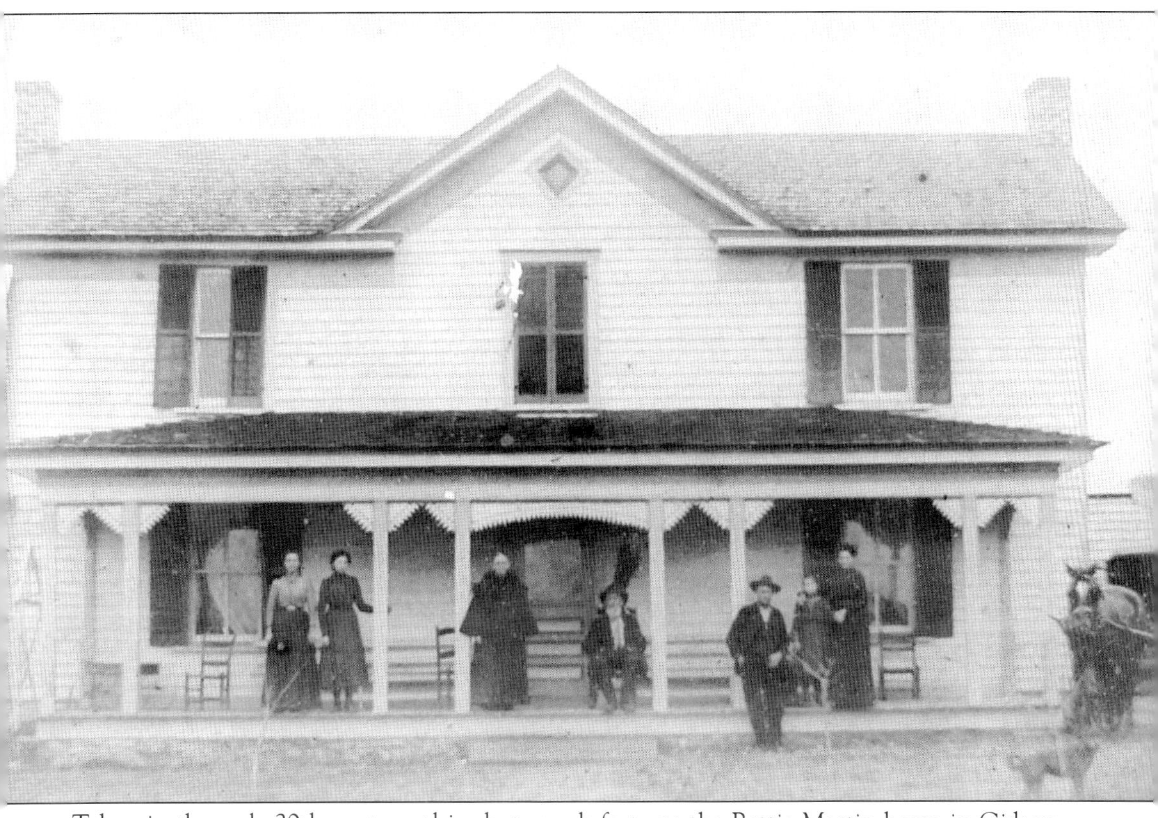

Taken in the early 20th century, this photograph features the Bettie Martin home in Gideon. (Courtesy of Davis Chapel Historical Association, Inc.)

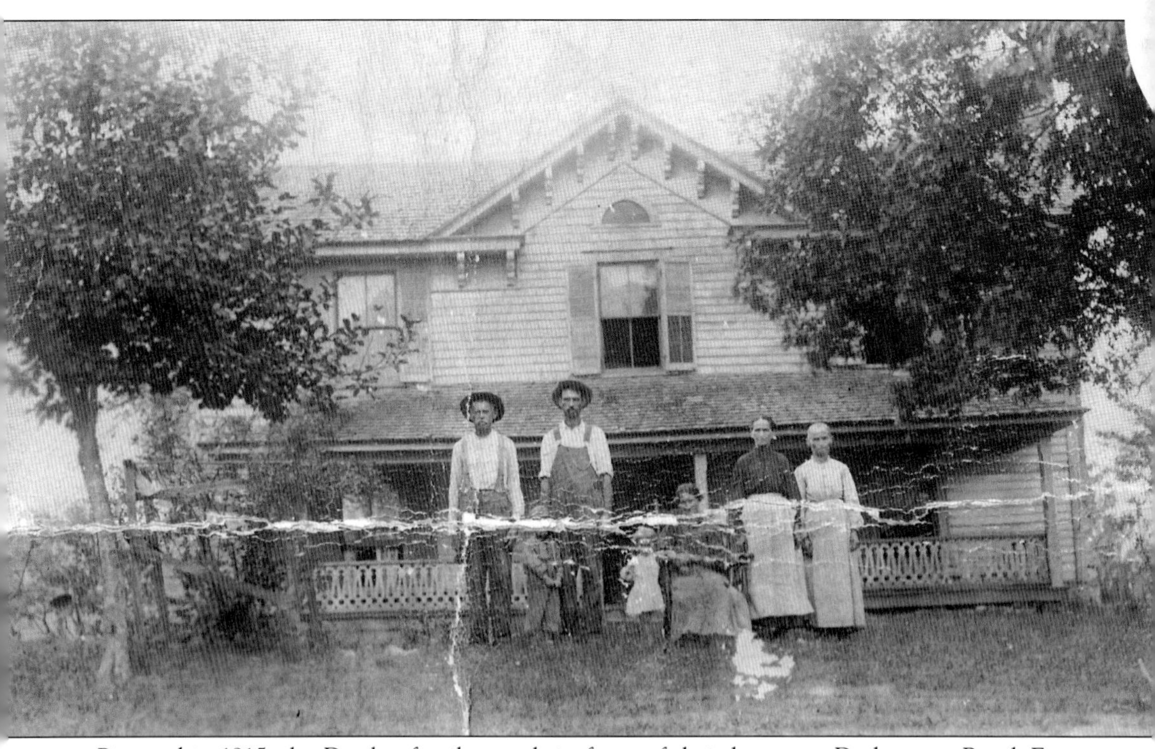

Pictured in 1915, the Dunlap family stands in front of their home on Dodgetown Road. From left to right, they are unidentified, William Taylor Dunlap, Lorene Dunlap (née Kirsch), Mollie Sapp Dunlap, Frances Reid Dunlap, and unidentified. The home was built sometime between 1870 and 1875 by George Taylor Dunlap and his wife, Mary Frances Reid Dunlap (the parents of William Taylor Dunlap). It was renovated in 2005 by present owners Durwood and Patti Dunlap. Durwood is the fourth generation of Dunlaps to live in this home and the seventh generation to live on this property. (Courtesy of Durwood and Patti Dunlap.)

Four

THE COUNTY SEAT

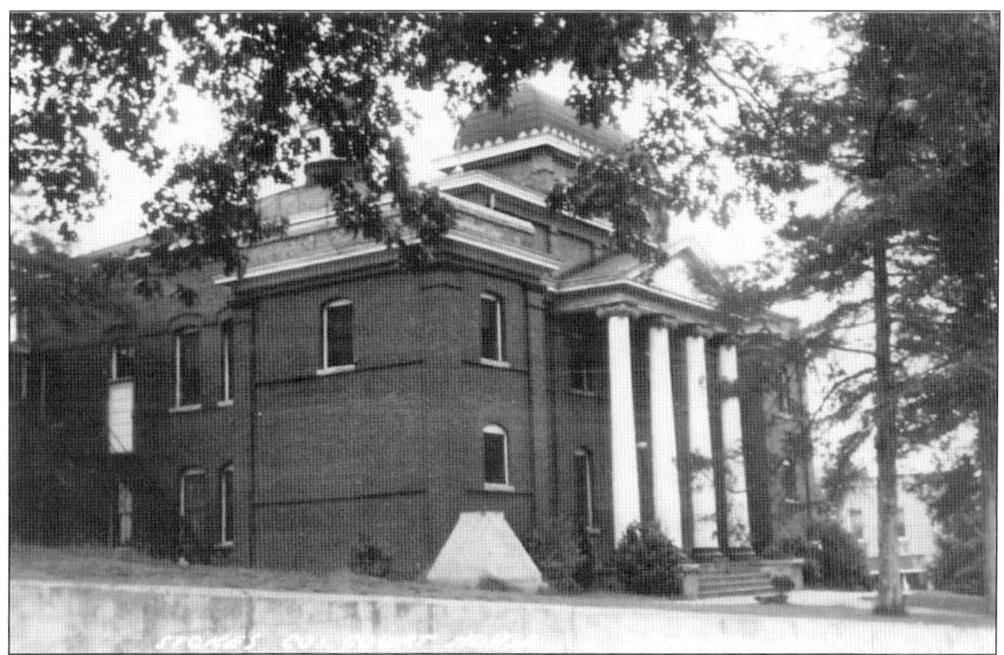

The Stokes County Courthouse was erected in 1904. It served the county seat as its courthouse from 1904 until 1982, when a new courthouse was erected about a mile west. This building now serves as offices for the board of education. (Author's collection.)

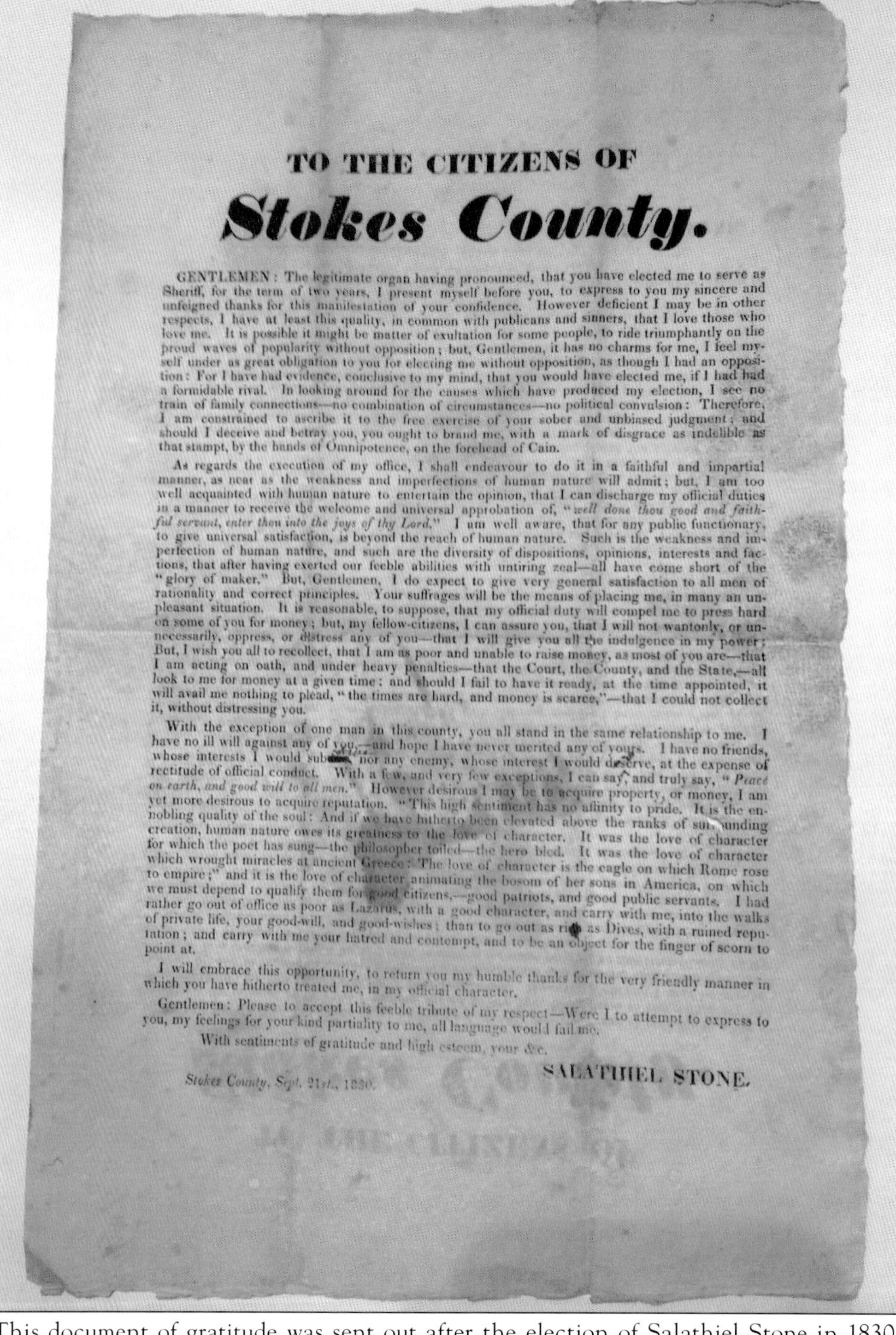

TO THE CITIZENS OF

Stokes County.

GENTLEMEN: The legitimate organ having pronounced, that you have elected me to serve as Sheriff, for the term of two years, I present myself before you, to express to you my sincere and unfeigned thanks for this manifestation of your confidence. However deficient I may be in other respects, I have at least this quality, in common with publicans and sinners, that I love those who love me. It is possible it might be matter of exultation for some people, to ride triumphantly on the proud waves of popularity without opposition; but, Gentlemen, it has no charms for me, I feel myself under as great obligation to you for electing me without opposition, as though I had an opposition: For I have had evidence, conclusive to my mind, that you would have elected me, if I had had a formidable rival. In looking around for the causes which have produced my election, I see no train of family connections—no combination of circumstances—no political convulsion: Therefore, I am constrained to ascribe it to the free exercise of your sober and unbiased judgment; and should I deceive and betray you, you ought to brand me, with a mark of disgrace as indelible as that stampt, by the hands of Omnipotence, on the forehead of Cain.

As regards the execution of my office, I shall endeavour to do it in a faithful and impartial manner, as near as the weakness and imperfections of human nature will admit; but, I am too well acquainted with human nature to entertain the opinion, that I can discharge my official duties in a manner to receive the welcome and universal approbation of, "*well done thou good and faithful servant, enter thou into the joys of thy Lord.*" I am well aware, that for any public functionary, to give universal satisfaction, is beyond the reach of human nature. Such is the weakness and imperfection of human nature, and such are the diversity of dispositions, opinions, interests and factions, that after having exerted our feeble abilities with untiring zeal—all have come short of the "glory of maker." But, Gentlemen, I do expect to give very general satisfaction to all men of rationality and correct principles. Your suffrages will be the means of placing me, in many an unpleasant situation. It is reasonable, to suppose, that my official duty will compel me to press hard on some of you for money; but, my fellow-citizens, I can assure you, that I will not wantonly, or unnecessarily, oppress, or distress any of you—that I will give you all the indulgence in my power; But, I wish you all to recollect, that I am as poor and unable to raise money, as most of you are—that I am acting on oath, and under heavy penalties—that the Court, the County, and the State,—all look to me for money at a given time: and should I fail to have it ready, at the time appointed, it will avail me nothing to plead, "the times are hard, and money is scarce,"—that I could not collect it, without distressing you.

With the exception of one man in this county, you all stand in the same relationship to me. I have no ill will against any of you,—and hope I have never merited any of yours. I have no friends, whose interests I would sub[illegible], nor any enemy, whose interest I would deserve, at the expense of rectitude of official conduct. With a few, and very few exceptions, I can say, and truly say, "*Peace on earth, and good will to all men.*" However desirous I may be to acquire property, or money, I am yet more desirous to acquire reputation. "This high sentiment has no affinity to pride. It is the ennobling quality of the soul: And if we have hitherto been elevated above the ranks of surrounding creation, human nature owes its greatness to the love of character. It was the love of character for which the poet has sung—the philosopher toiled—the hero bled. It was the love of character which wrought miracles at ancient Greece: The love of character is the eagle on which Rome rose to empire;" and it is the love of character animating the bosom of her sons in America, on which we must depend to qualify them for good citizens,—good patriots, and good public servants. I had rather go out of office as poor as Lazarus, with a good character, and carry with me, into the walks of private life, your good-will, and good-wishes; than to go out as rich as Dives, with a ruined reputation; and carry with me your hatred and contempt, and to be an object for the finger of scorn to point at.

I will embrace this opportunity, to return you my humble thanks for the very friendly manner in which you have hitherto treated me, in my official character.

Gentlemen: Please to accept this feeble tribute of my respect—Were I to attempt to express to you, my feelings for your kind partiality to me, all language would fail me.

With sentiments of gratitude and high esteem, your &c.

SALATHIEL STONE.

Stokes County, Sept. 21st., 1830.

This document of gratitude was sent out after the election of Salathiel Stone in 1830. (Author's collection.)

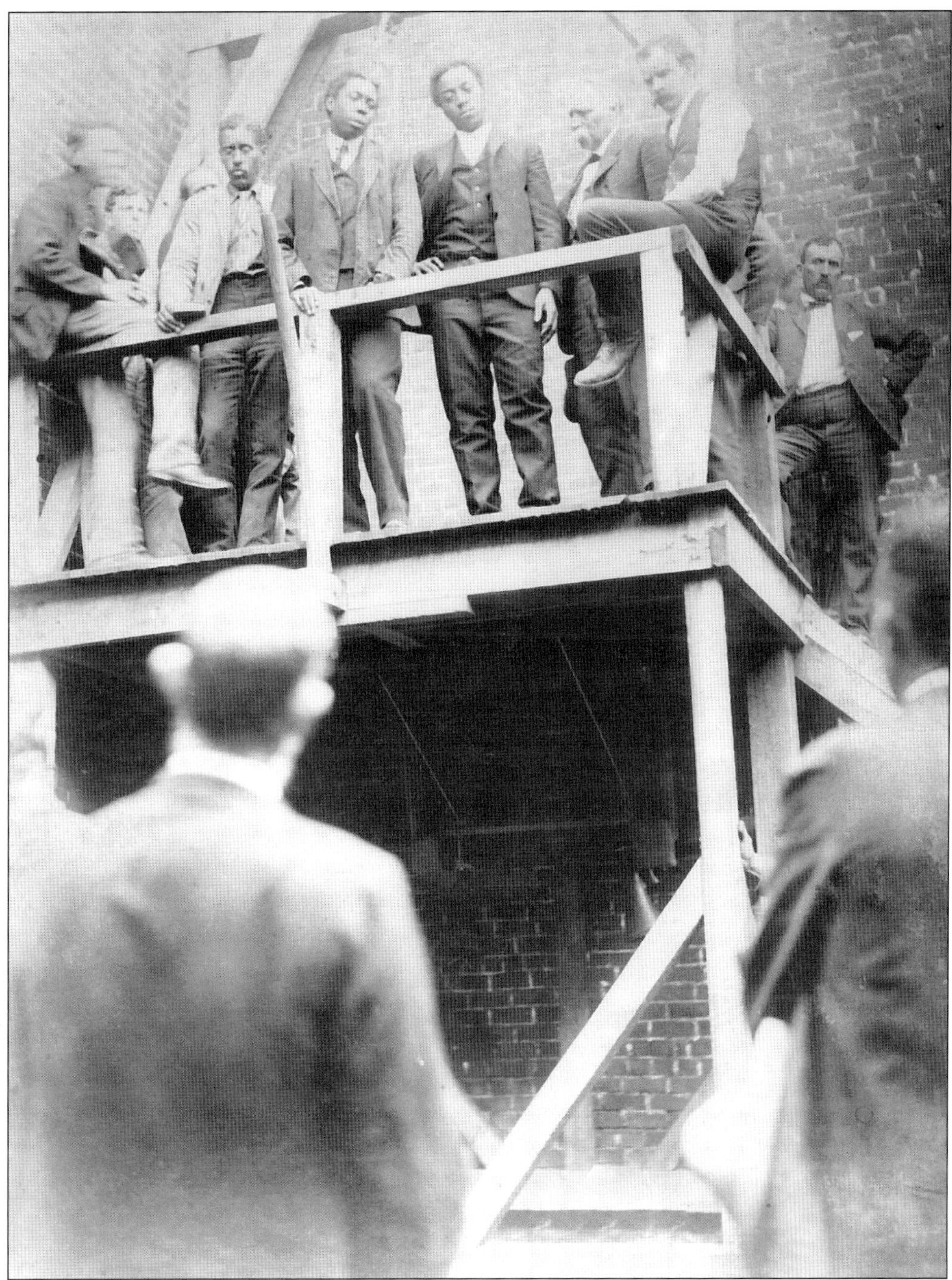

This hanging in the early 1900s was thought to have taken place in Stokes County around the turn of the century. Although it is undocumented, there are several stories of hangings in Stokes County. (Author's collection.)

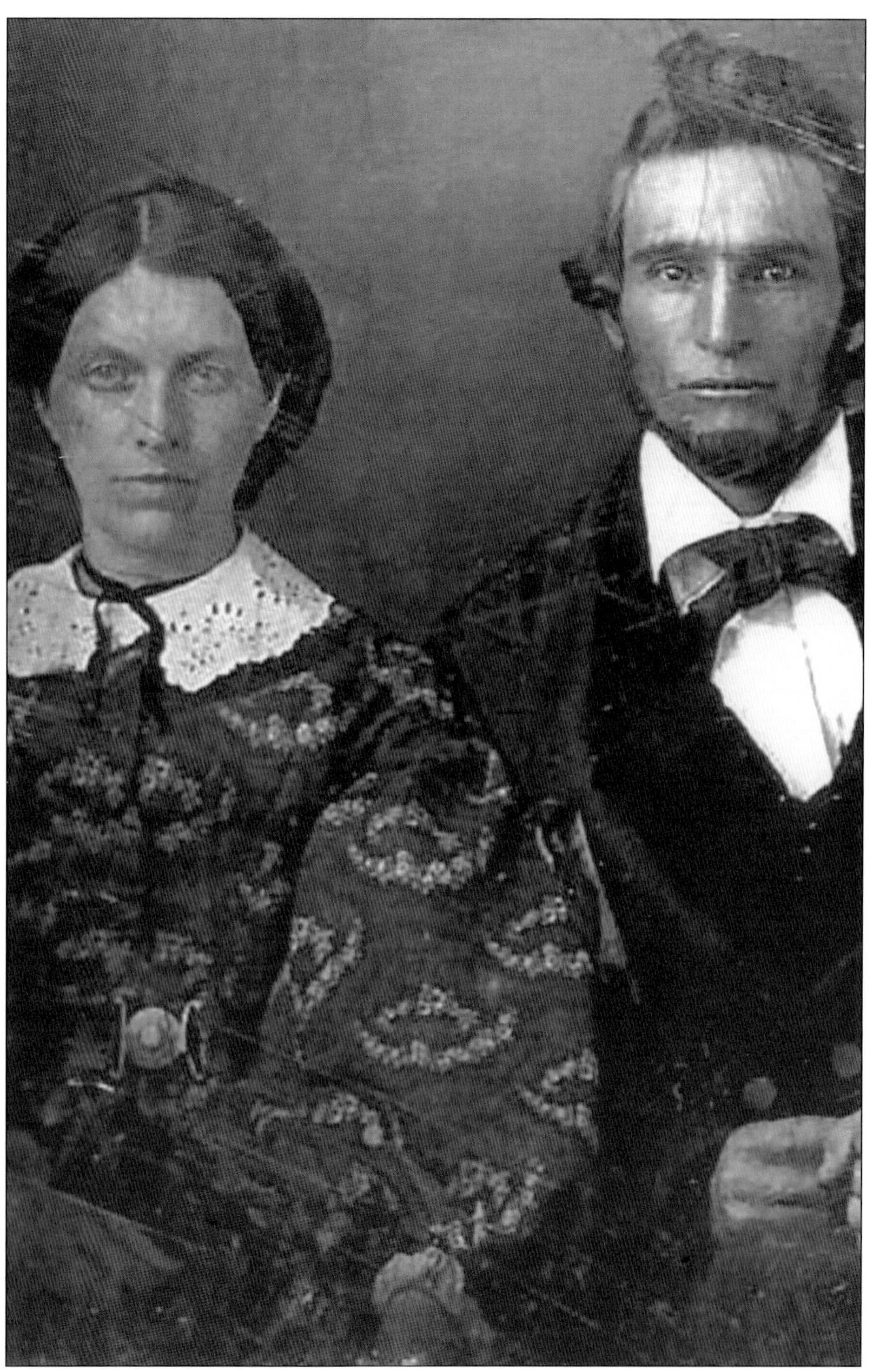

Spotswood Basset Taylor and his wife, Grace Ann McGhee, pose for this photograph sometime after the Civil War. Note that Grace wears the Civil War belt of her husband. (Courtesy of Charles Rodenbough.)

W. R. Bennett & Son

Dealers In

General Merchandise

Shipping Point: Walnut Cove, N. C.

Discarded Samples A Specialty.

Danbury, N. C., Route 1, Nov. 18 1915

Mr Thompson Rogers:

Birm[illegible] Mo

My Dear Sir: Some of my friends suggest that I be a Candidate for Register of Deeds of Stokes Co.

Learning of your prominence and influence in the Republican party I take this method to solicit your support your information as to the situation and should you approve of me I will appreciate anything you may do or say in my behalf.

Thanking you for a reply

Yours truly

M. B. Bennett

This is a letter from the W.R. Bennett & Son general merchandise store. The content of this letter is interesting, as it concerns M.B. Bennett applying as a candidate for Stokes County Register of Deeds. (Courtesy of Stokes County Historical Society.)

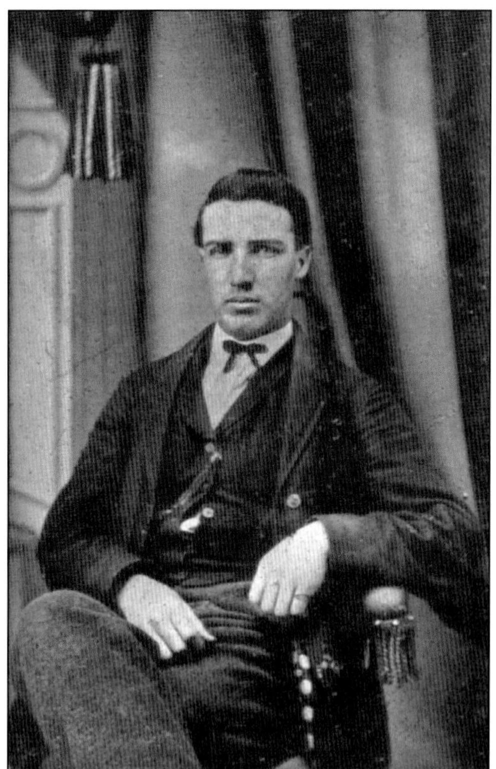

This early tintype photograph shows James Madison Tesh around 1870. Tesh was a photographer in Danbury and Madison during the early 1870s. (Courtesy Stokes County Historical Society.)

J. W. NEAL, Pres. N. E. PEPPER, Cashier.

OFFICE

Bank of Stokes County

Danbury, N.C.

June 23, 1921.

Mr. S. A. Thompson,
Stuart, Va.

Dear sir :

Please accept our thanks for your services in the matter of the J. B. Martin land. Mr. Lawson has spoken to us about your kind assistance while he was at Stuart, and we wish you to send your bill for services, and also for the telegram which you so thoughtfully sent us.

Yours truly,

Cashier.

This letter from the Bank of Stokes County branch in Danbury was sent out in 1921 by Nathaniel Eugene Pepper, who was cashier at that time. (Author's collection.)

Nannie Adkins Chilton and Mrs. A.J. Fagg pose for this photograph in Danbury. Moody's Tavern can be seen in the background. (Courtesy of Davis Chapel Historical Association, Inc.)

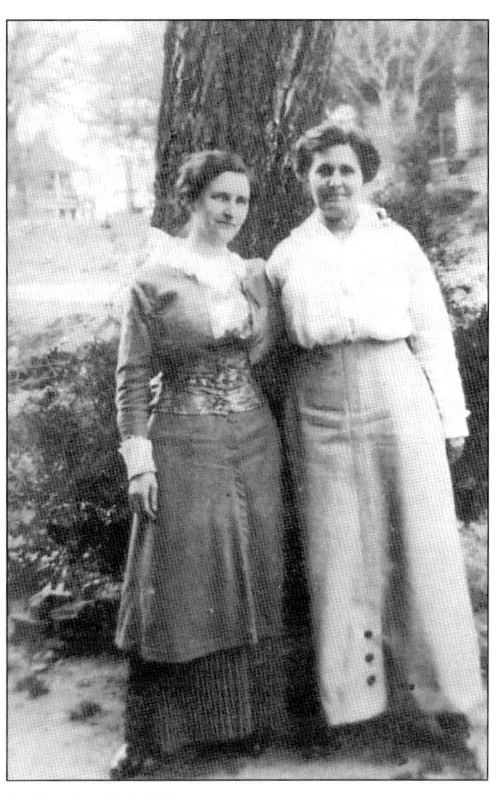

OFFICE OF CHAIRMAN

COUNTY BOARD OF ELECTIONS

STOKES COUNTY

Danbury, N.C. Aug. 1st,1913,
191

Messrs. Thompson & Burton, Attys,
Stuart, Va.,

Gentlemen:-

Your favor to hand relative to the claim of the Chattanooga Medicine Co. Vs. J.R.Hill. You enclosed letter from our clients stating that I could stand for the costs and by thus doing get a good contingent fee.It is unusual for me to pay the cost, but I believe I will risk it anyway,so I will try him.We will divide on what you and I think is an equitable basis in case I collect.I may lose but I will make him see a hard time in the losing,

Very Truly Yours,

J.D. Humphreys

This letter was sent out by the Stokes County Board of Elections in 1913. (Author's collection.)

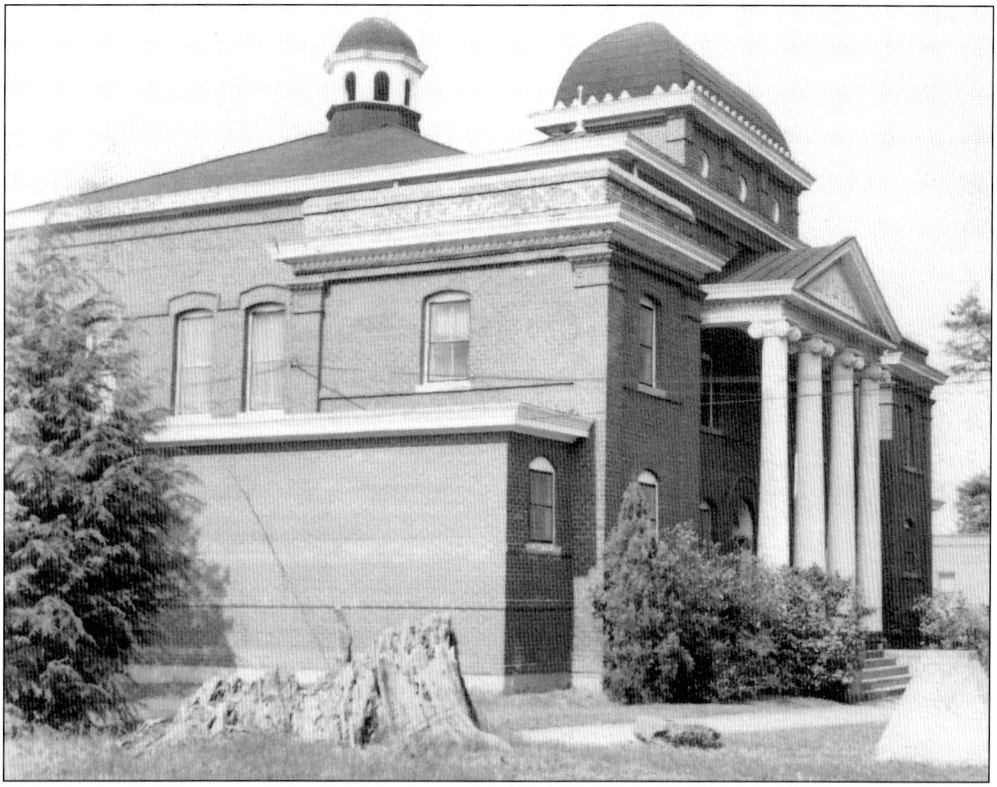

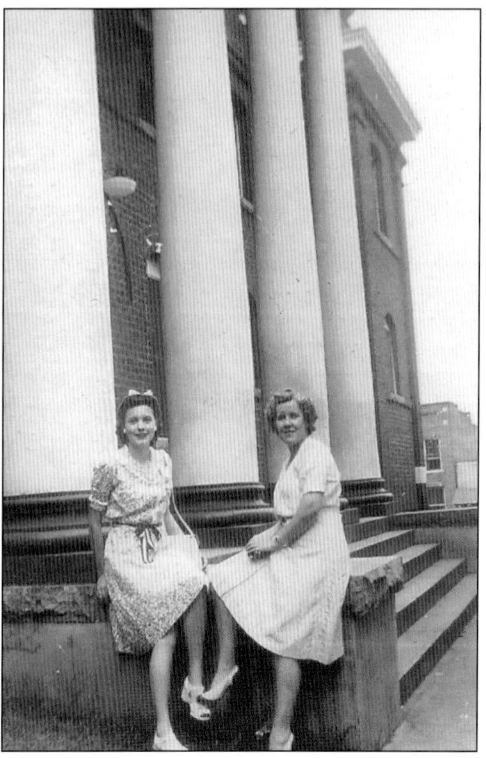

This photograph features the courthouse in the 1950s. Since its construction in 1904, very little changes have been made. A new wing was later added in order to increase space. (Courtesy of Jerry and Sarah Stephens.)

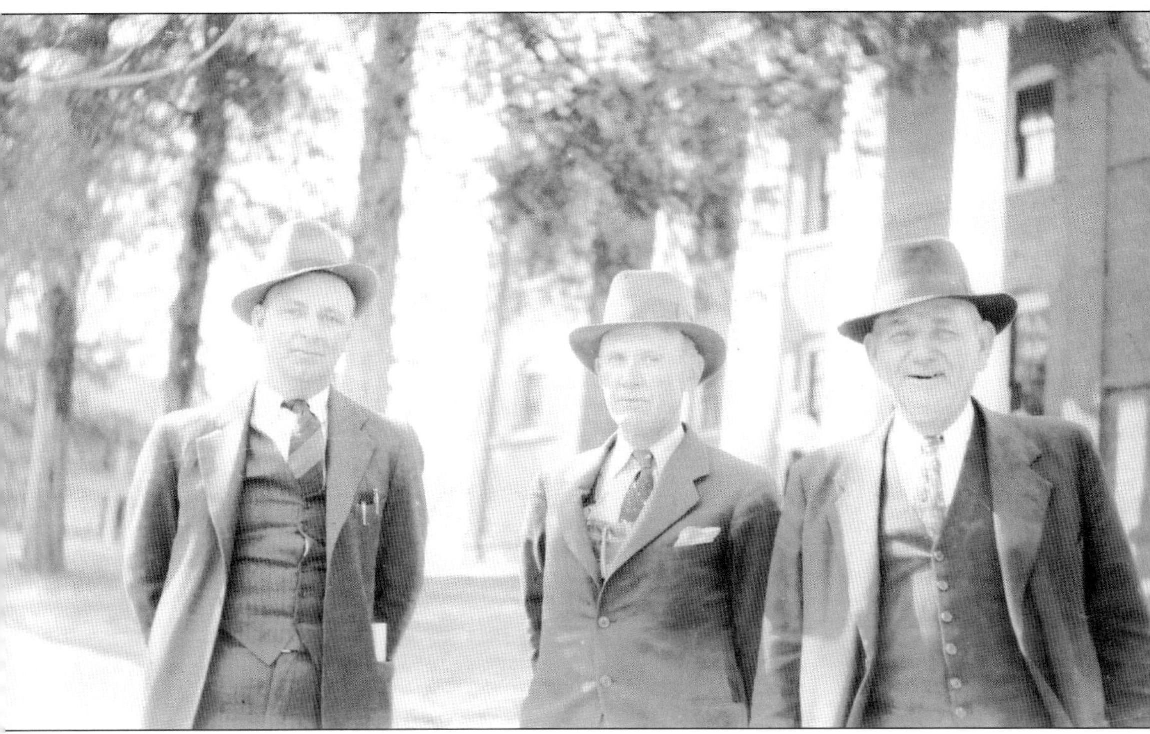

This early image captures (from left to right) Bill Fulton, Cary Carroll, and S.P. Christian in front of the courthouse in Danbury. Seen to the left is Moody's Tavern. (Courtesy of Barbara Fulton Tuttle.)

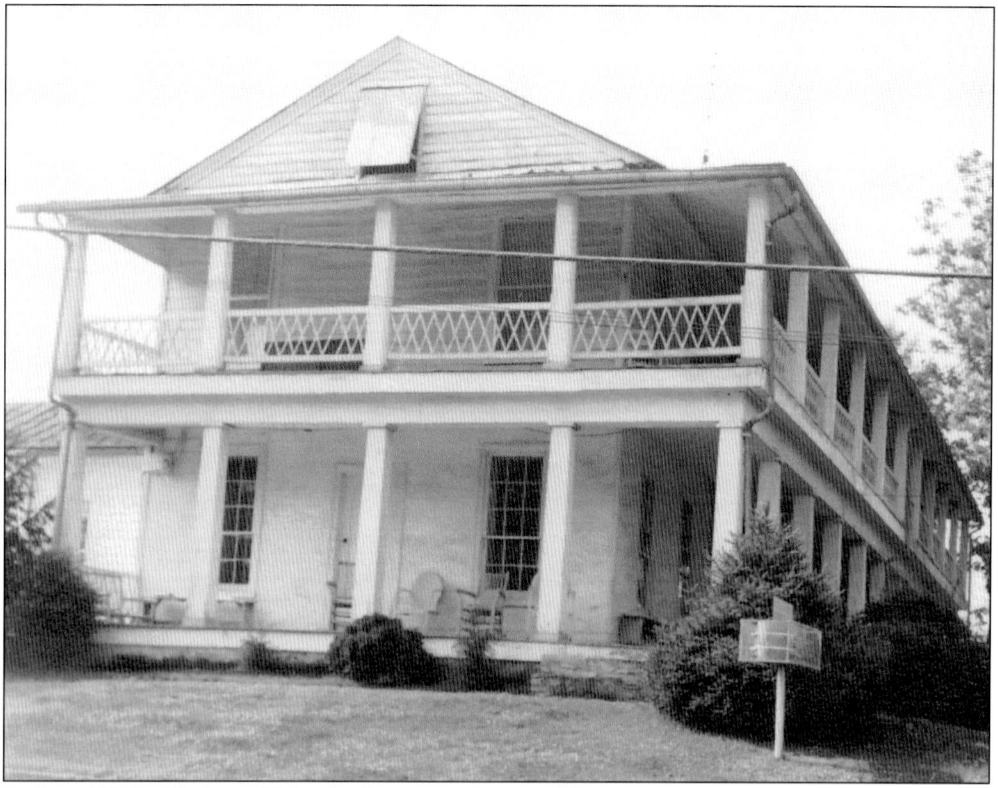

Built in 1854 by Nathaniel Moody, this tavern has much history. In 1864, Gen. George Stoneman raided the town of Danbury and occupied what was then the McCanless Inn for a while. This building has housed everything from apartments to the Stokes County Board of Education offices. It is now a private residence and is under renovation. (Courtesy of Jerry and Sarah Stephens.)

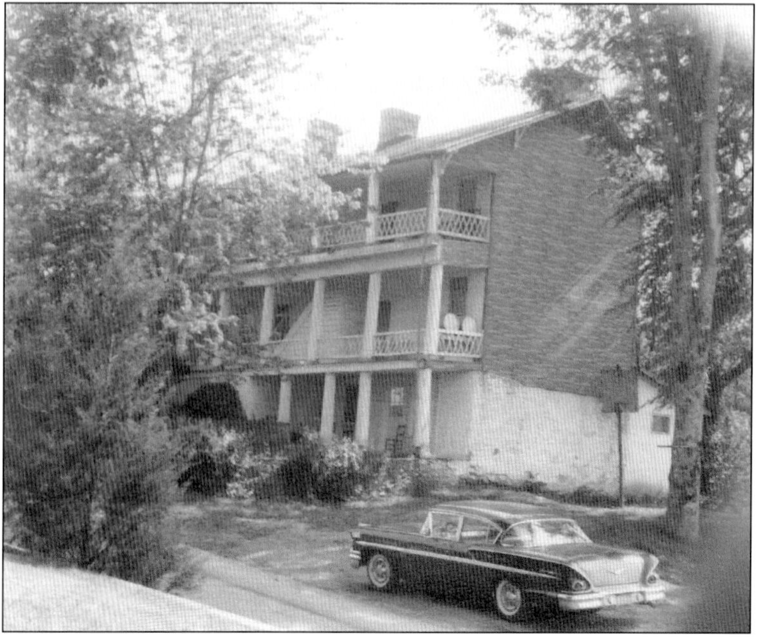

This photograph features the rear of Moody's Tavern during the 1950s. (Courtesy of Jerry and Sarah Stephens.)

Nathaniel Moody Pepper was an influential person of Danbury. Nathaniel was the son of Dr. John Pepper, who served as a medic assistant on the battlefield of the Civil War. In 1872, he purchased the equipment from the *Old Constitution* newspaper and named it the *Danbury Reporter.* Nathaniel ran the *Danbury Reporter* after his father's death in 1881 and passed the tradition down through the Pepper family for many years. This newspaper would evolve into what is known today as the *Stokes News.* (Courtesy of Stokes County Historical Society.)

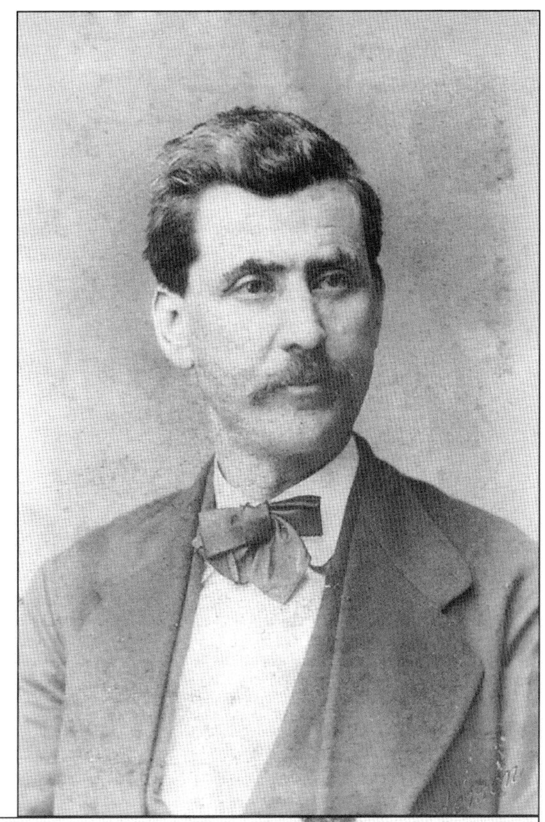

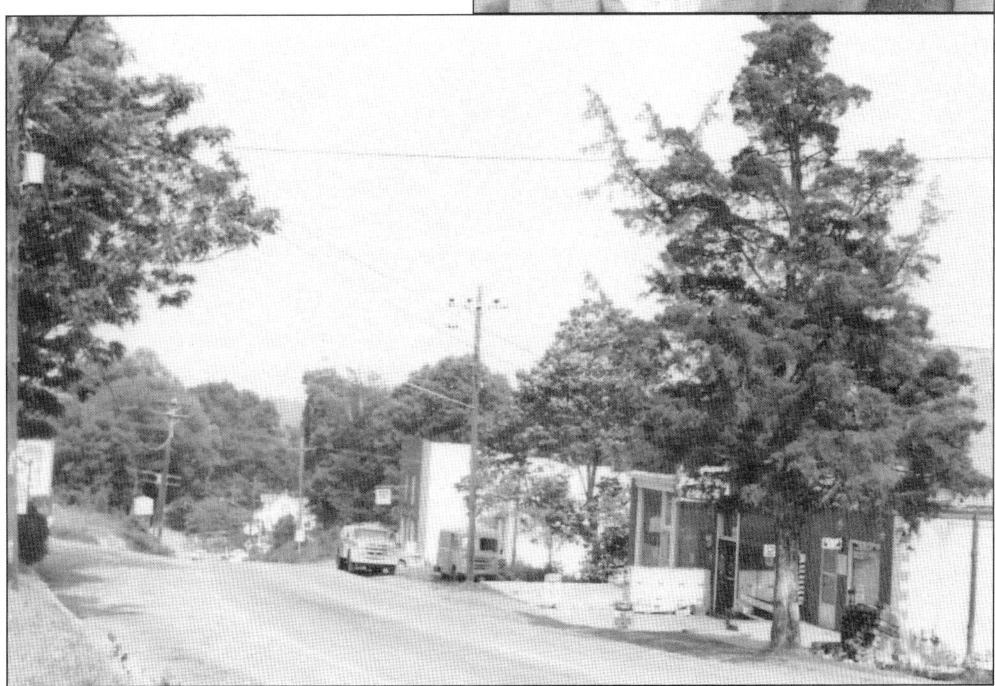

This view of Highway 8 in downtown Danbury, opposite of the old courthouse, highlights Zack's Barbershop and Petree Law Office. (Courtesy of Jerry and Sarah Stephens.)

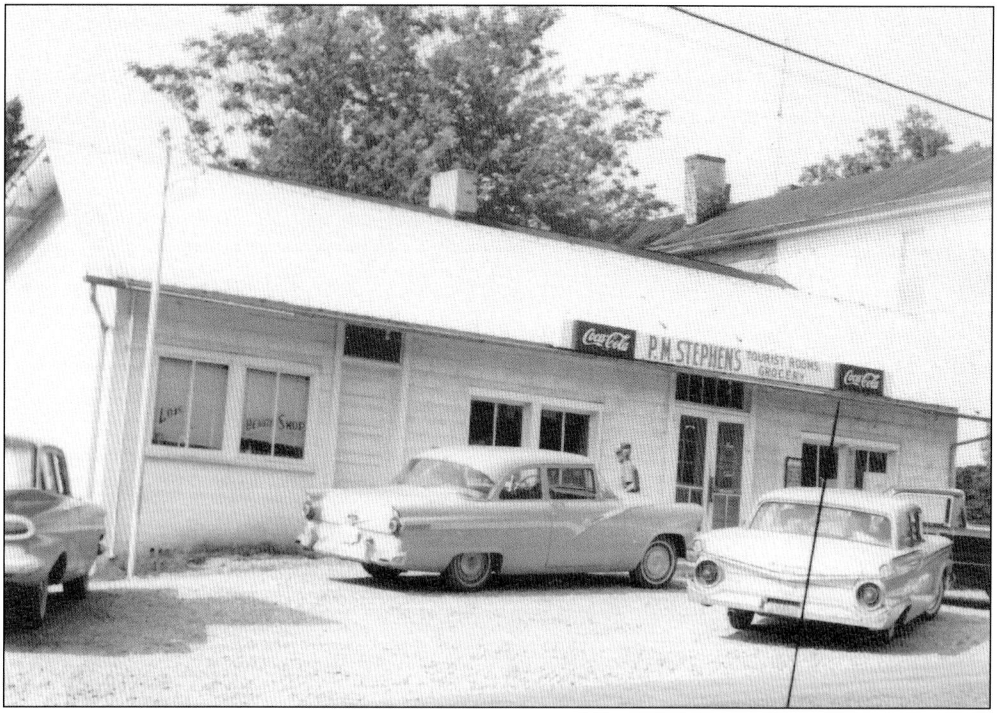

P.M. Stephens ran a store in Danbury and rented rooms to tourists in the old hotel. Also seen in this c. 1955 photograph is Lois' Beauty Shop. (Courtesy of Jerry and Sarah Stephens.)

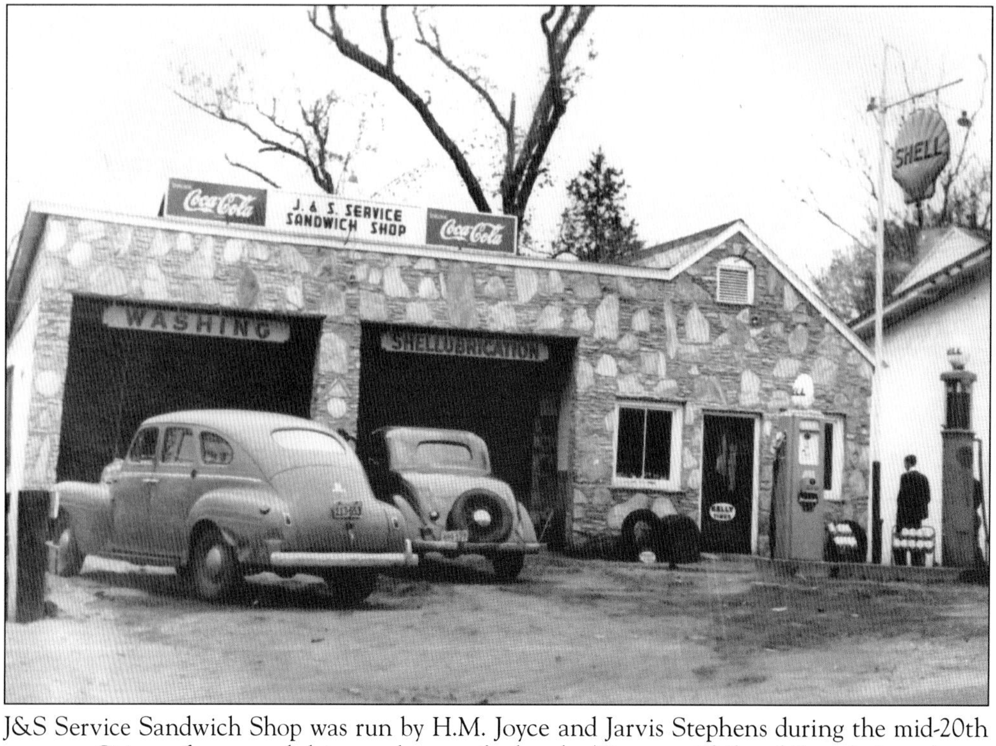

J&S Service Sandwich Shop was run by H.M. Joyce and Jarvis Stephens during the mid-20th century. Citizens frequented this popular spot for lunch. (Courtesy Phil and Pamela Joyce.)

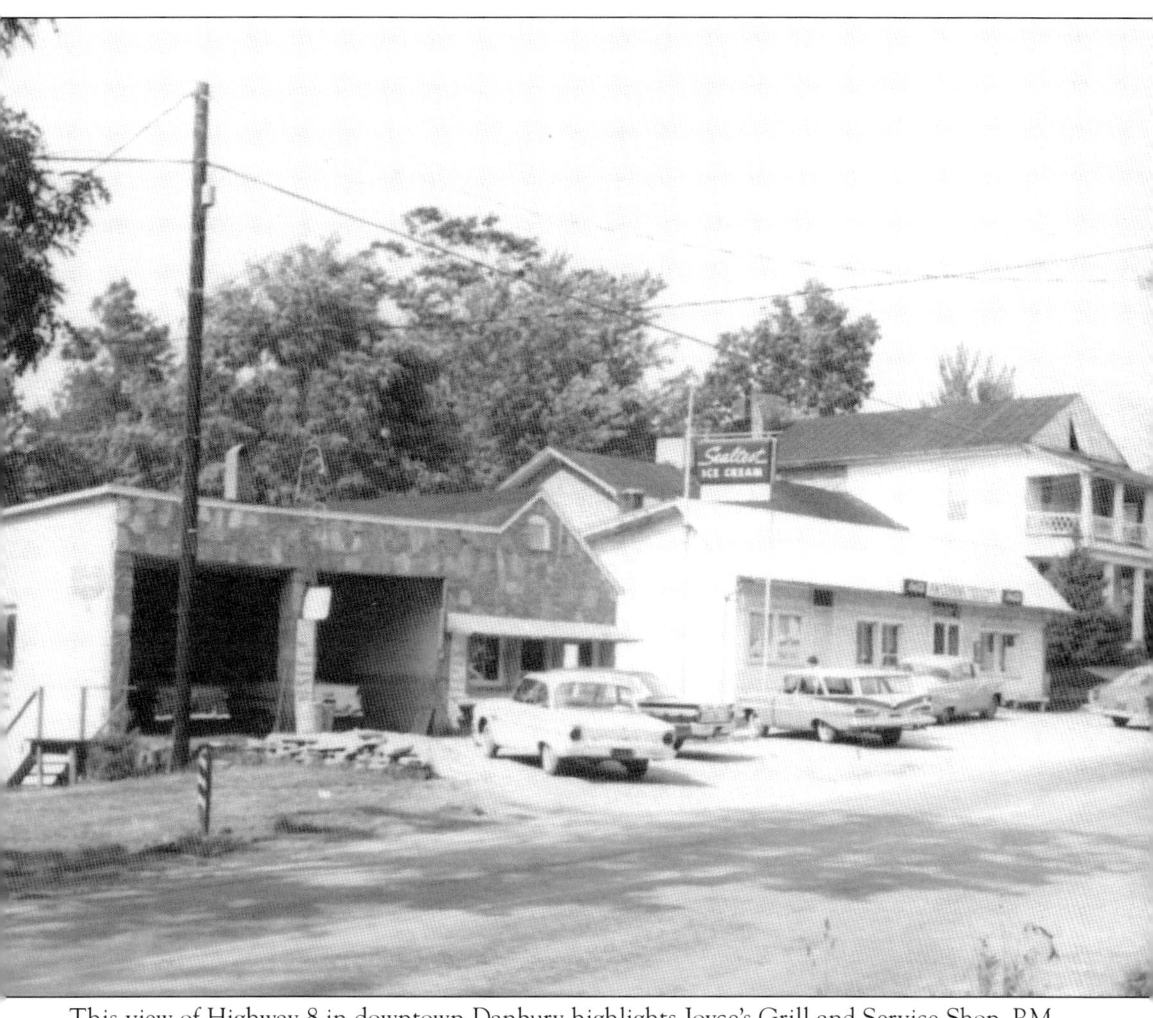

This view of Highway 8 in downtown Danbury highlights Joyce's Grill and Service Shop, P.M. Stephens Grocery and Tourist Rooms, Moody's Tavern, and the top of the courthouse around 1955. (Courtesy of Jerry and Sarah Stephens.)

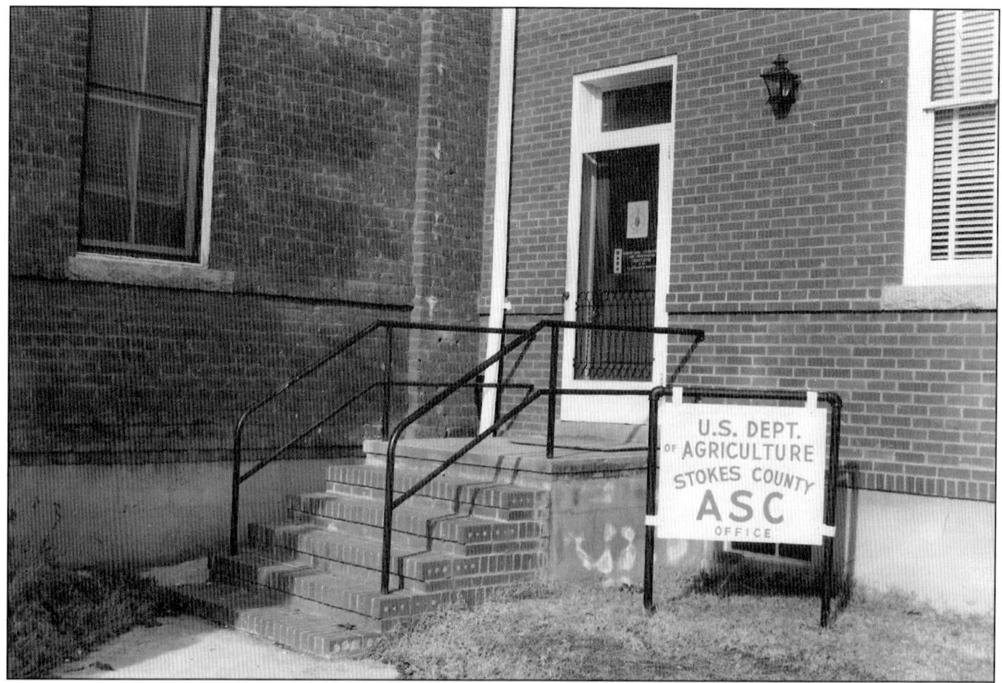

Pictured is the office of the Agriculture Conservation System program in Stokes County, which was part of the US Department of Agriculture. This picture was taken in Danbury in 1961. (Courtesy of Hazel F. Bowles.)

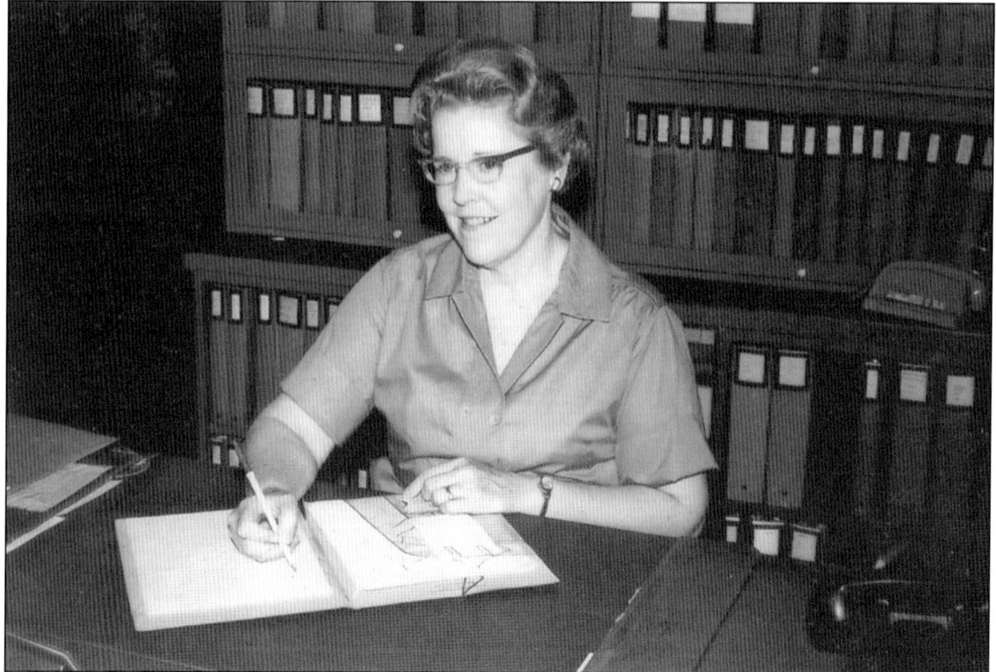
Hazel F. Bowles, director of the Agriculture Conservation System in Stokes County, is pictured here at her desk in the Agriculture Conservation System office in 1961. (Courtesy of Hazel F. Bowles.)

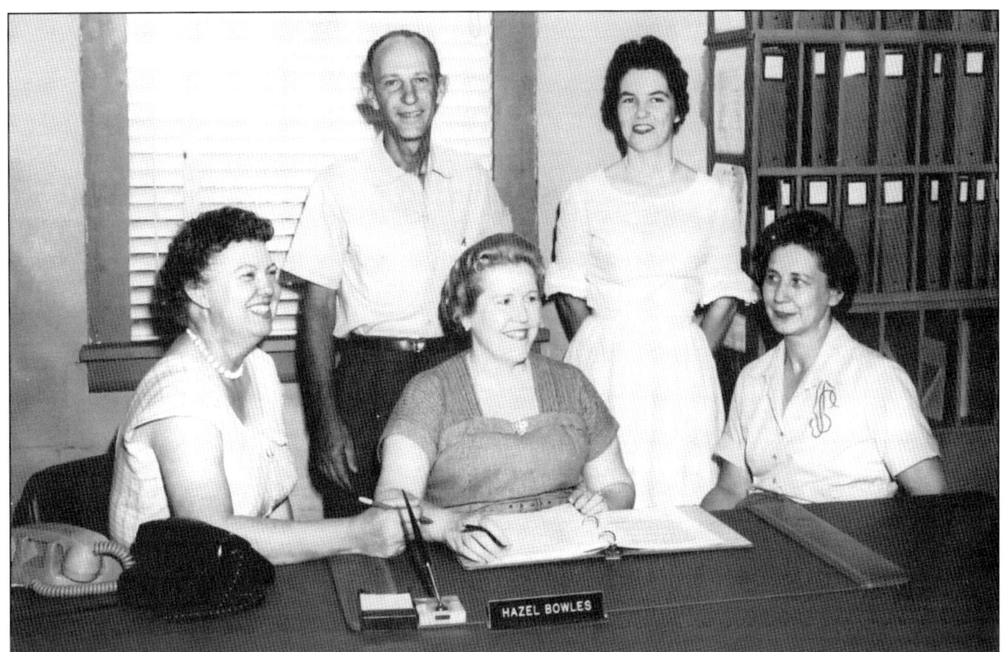

Pictured is Hazel Bowles with the Agriculture Conservation System office staff in 1961. From left to right are (first row) Hallie Martin, Hazel Bowles, and Bessie Flinchum; (second row) Francis Martin and Joice Gravitt. (Courtesy of Hazel F. Bowles.)

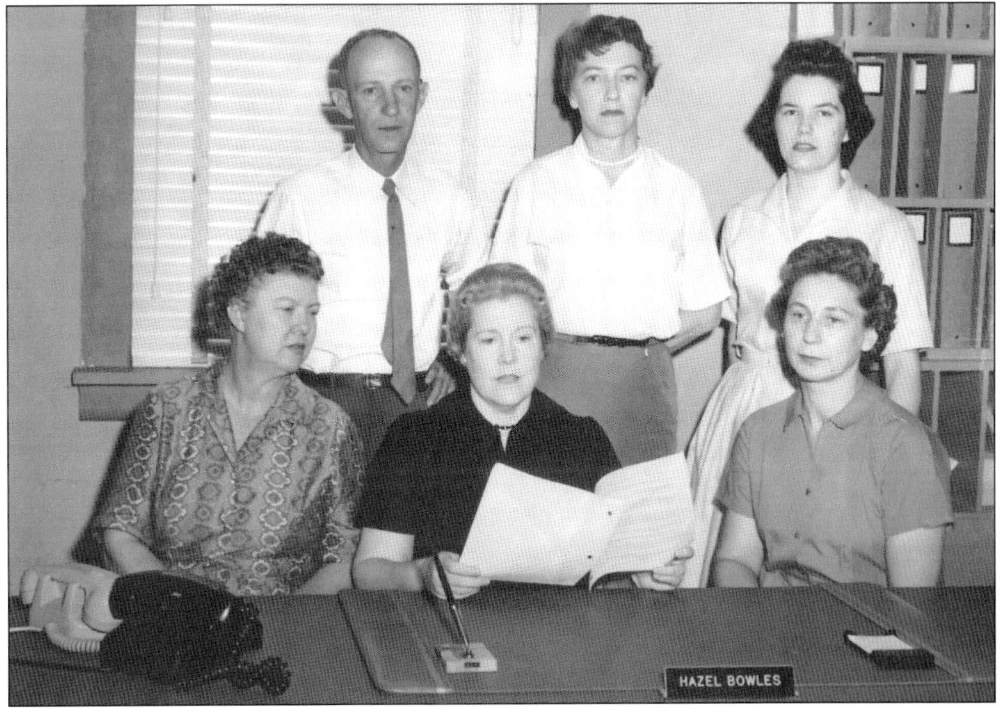

Pictured here again is the Agriculture Conservation System office staff. Standing in the center of the back row is Ellen Pepper Tilley, who is owed a great note of thanks for her efforts in the preservation of Stokes County history. (Courtesy of Hazel F. Bowles.)

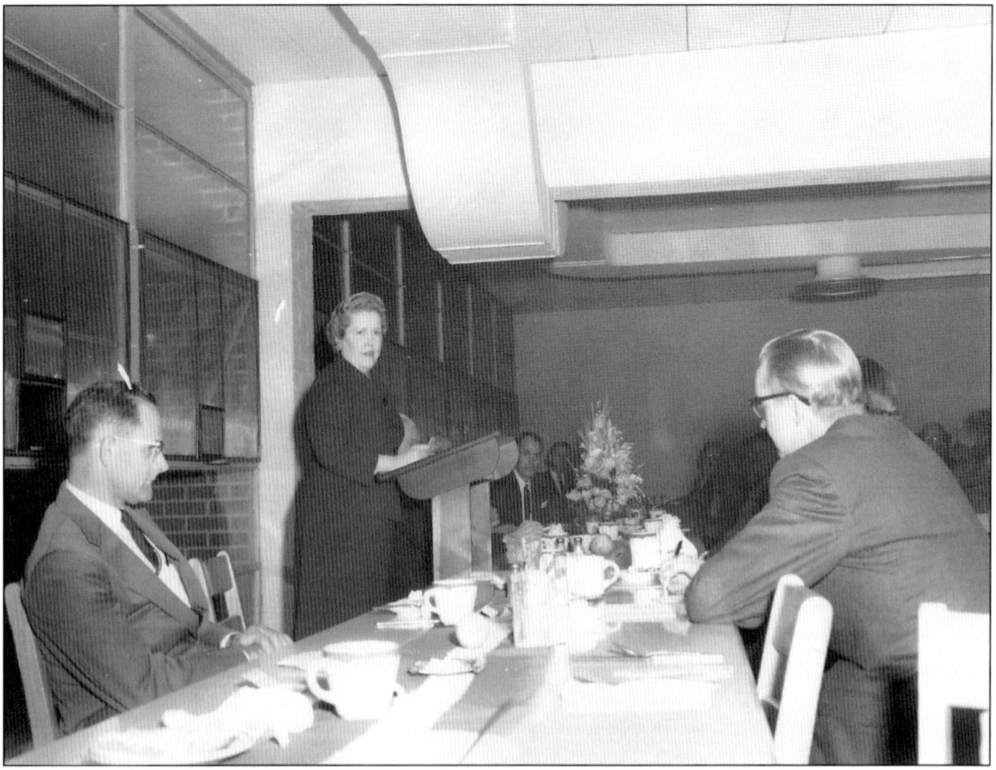

Pictured is a typical Agriculture Conservation System banquet. Hazel Bowles is delivering a speech at the podium. (Courtesy of Hazel F. Bowles.)

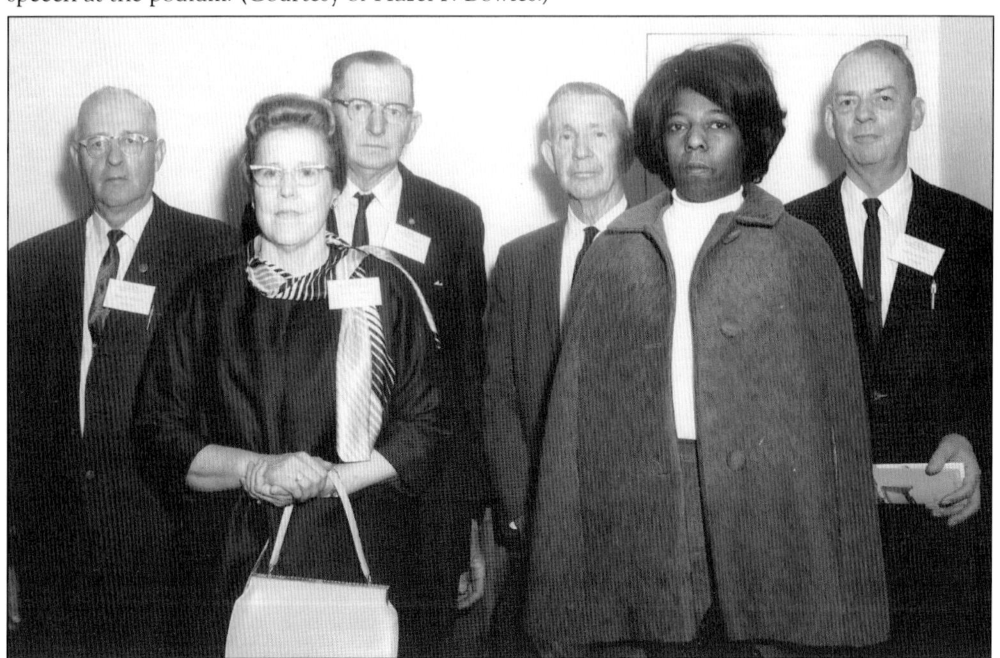

Seen in this photograph once again is the Agricultural Conservation System staff. (Courtesy of Hazel F. Bowles.)

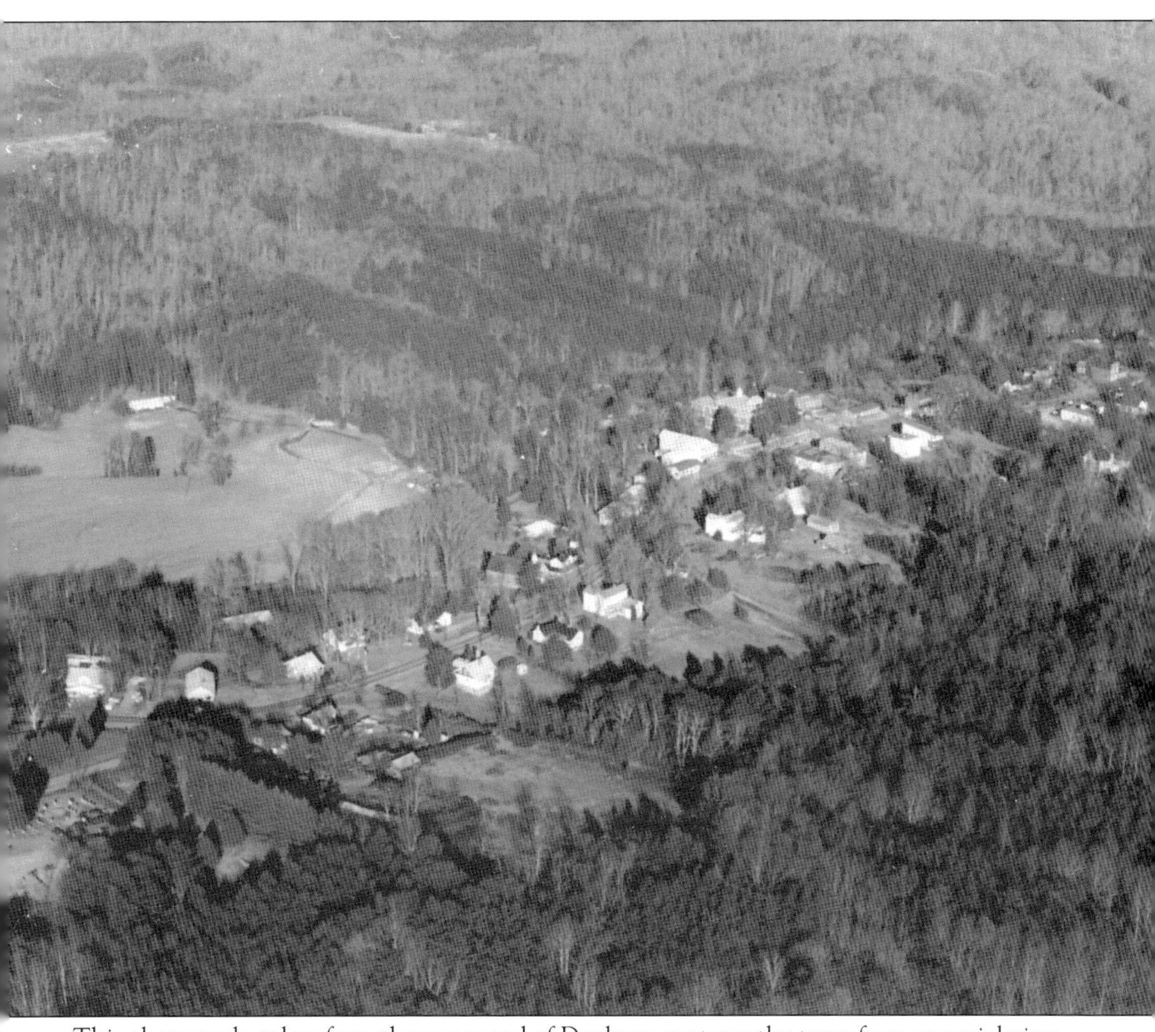

This photograph, taken from the upper end of Danbury, captures the town from an aerial view. Key buildings such as the old courthouse, Moody's Tavern, and the Wilson Fulton house can be seen. (Courtesy of Jerry and Yvonne Rutledge.)

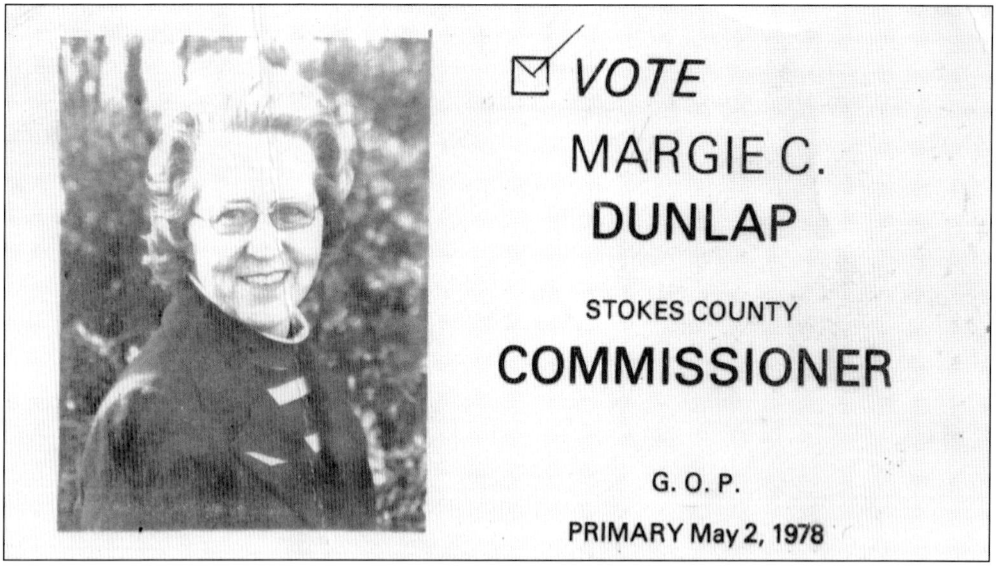

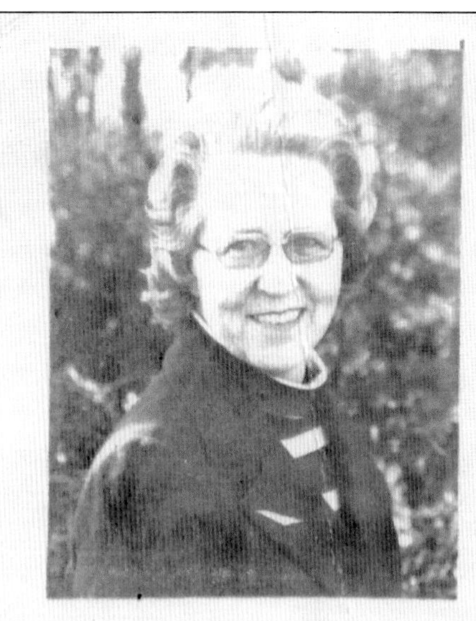

☑ VOTE

MARGIE C.
DUNLAP

STOKES COUNTY
COMMISSIONER

G. O. P.

PRIMARY May 2, 1978

This advertisement was mailed out as a campaign for Margie Dunlap, who would later be the first woman elected as a Stokes County commissioner. (Courtesy of Durwood and Patti Dunlap.)

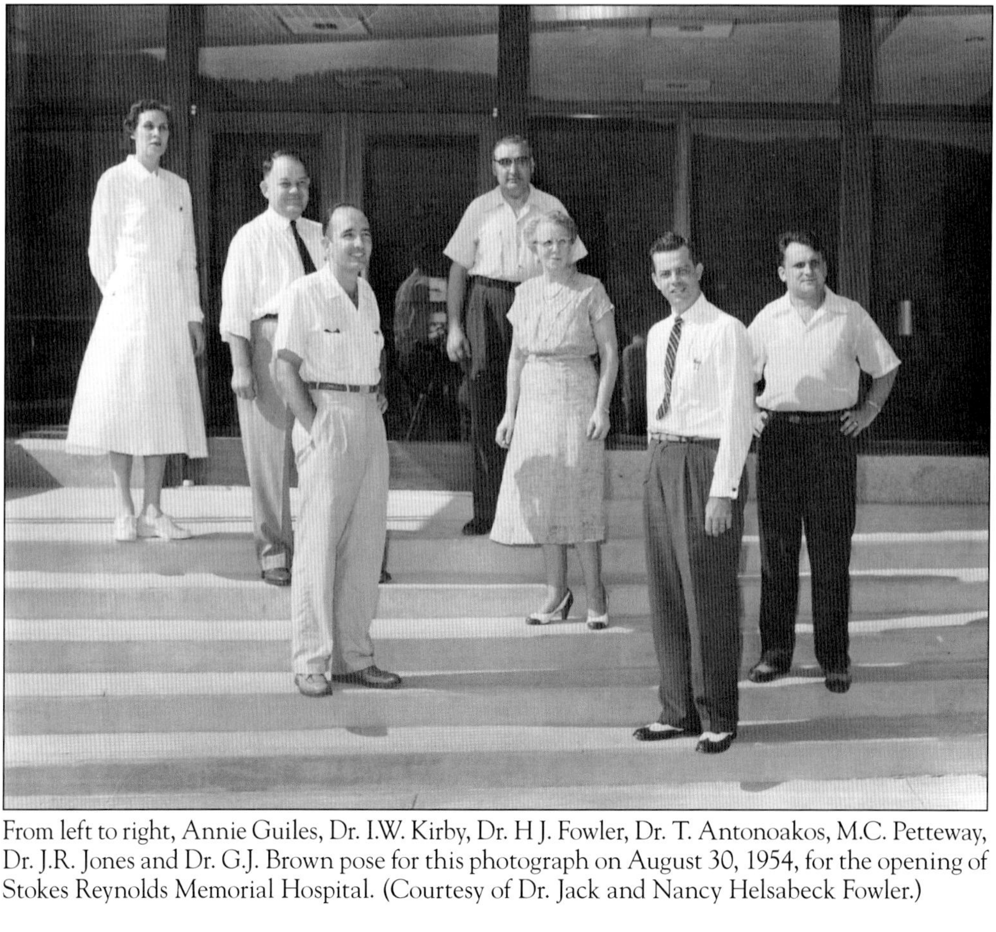

From left to right, Annie Guiles, Dr. I.W. Kirby, Dr. H J. Fowler, Dr. T. Antonoakos, M.C. Petteway, Dr. J.R. Jones and Dr. G.J. Brown pose for this photograph on August 30, 1954, for the opening of Stokes Reynolds Memorial Hospital. (Courtesy of Dr. Jack and Nancy Helsabeck Fowler.)

Five

The Springs of Stokes

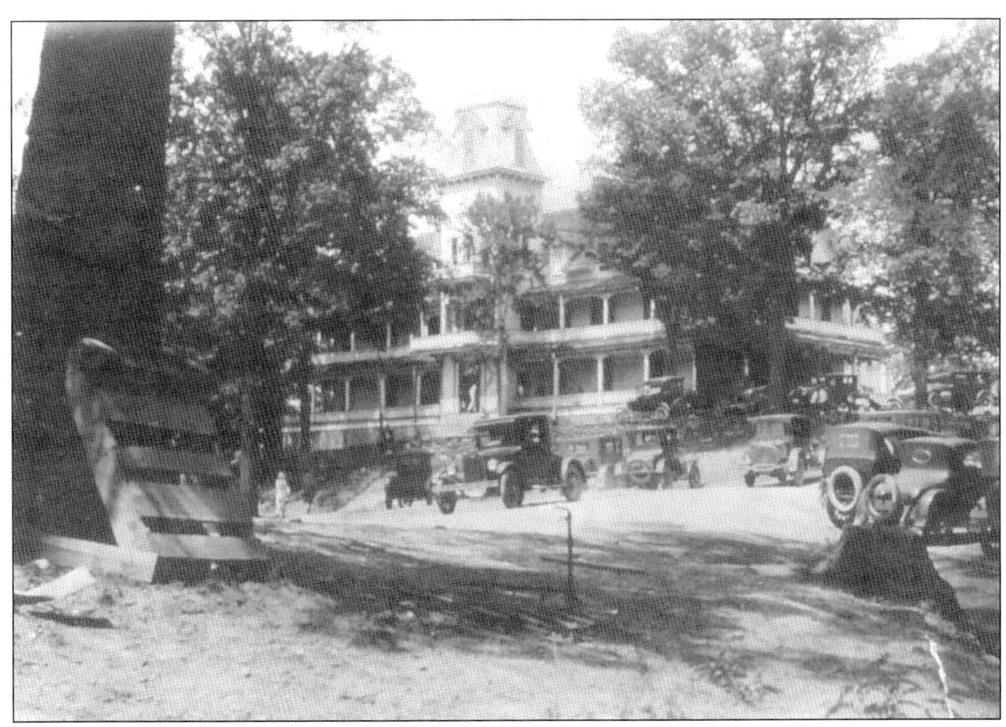

Piedmont Springs was the oldest resort to be built above Danbury. This photograph is a shot of the third hotel built at Piedmont Springs in 1889. (Courtesy of Charles Rodenbough.)

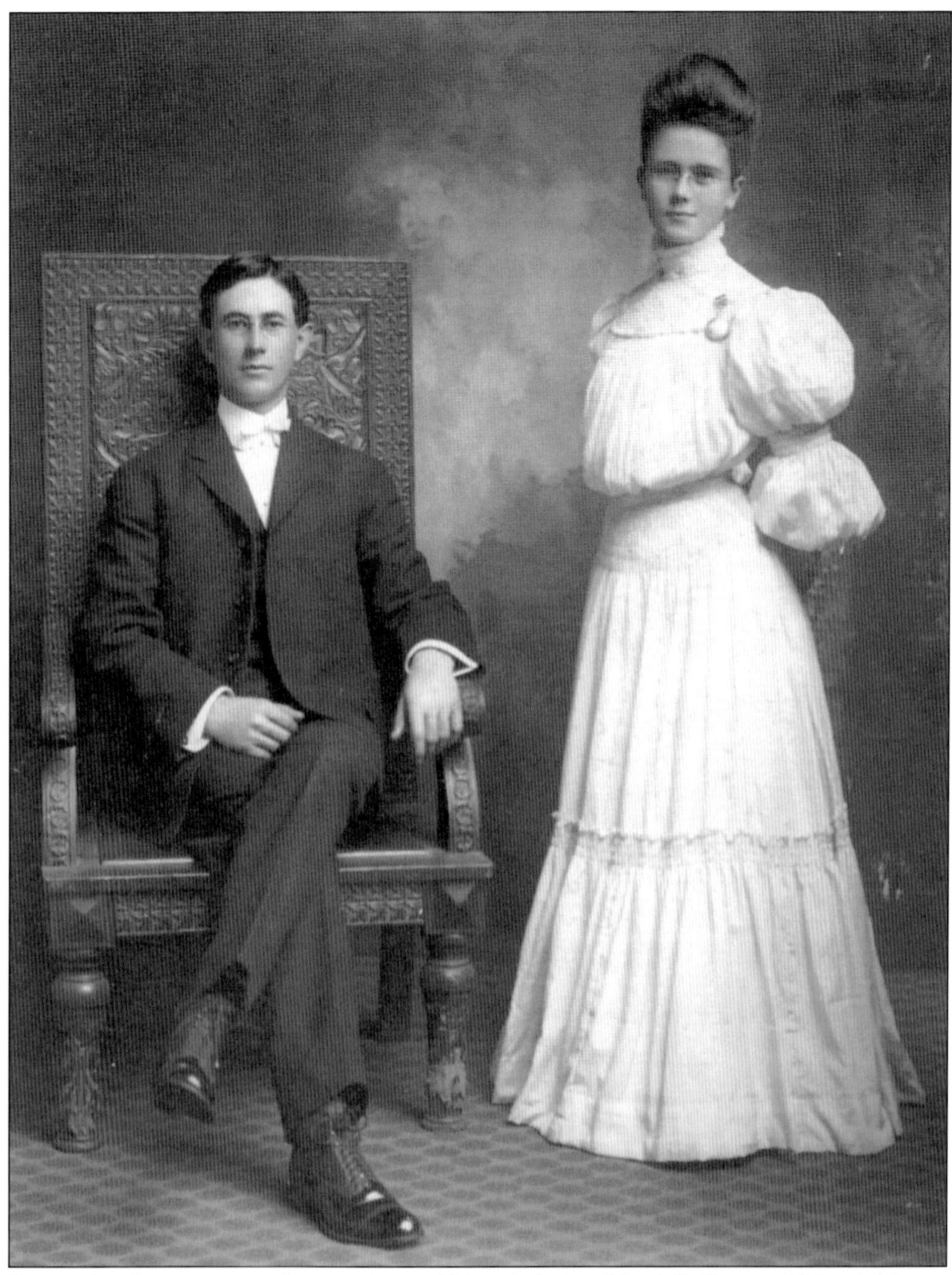

Depicted in this portrait are the proprietors of Moore's Springs Hotel, William and Minnie Moore. William was a cofounder of the resort with John Moore. William and Minnie owned the operation until about 1921, when it was sold. (Courtesy of Stokes County Historical Society.)

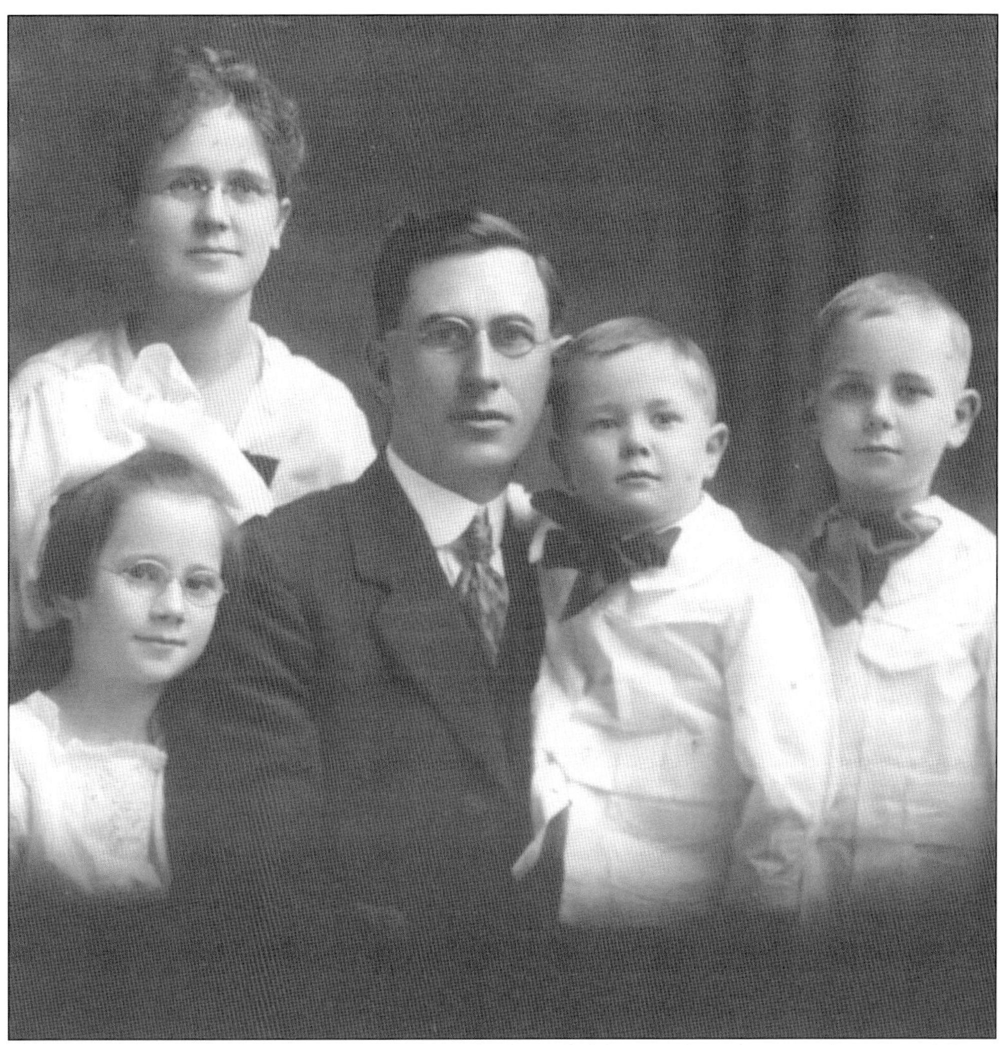

William Gabriel and Minnie Moore pose with their children in this photograph. Most of these children lived to be nearly a century old. Perhaps it had something to do with the "healing waters" at Moore's Springs. (Courtesy of Stokes County Historical Society.)

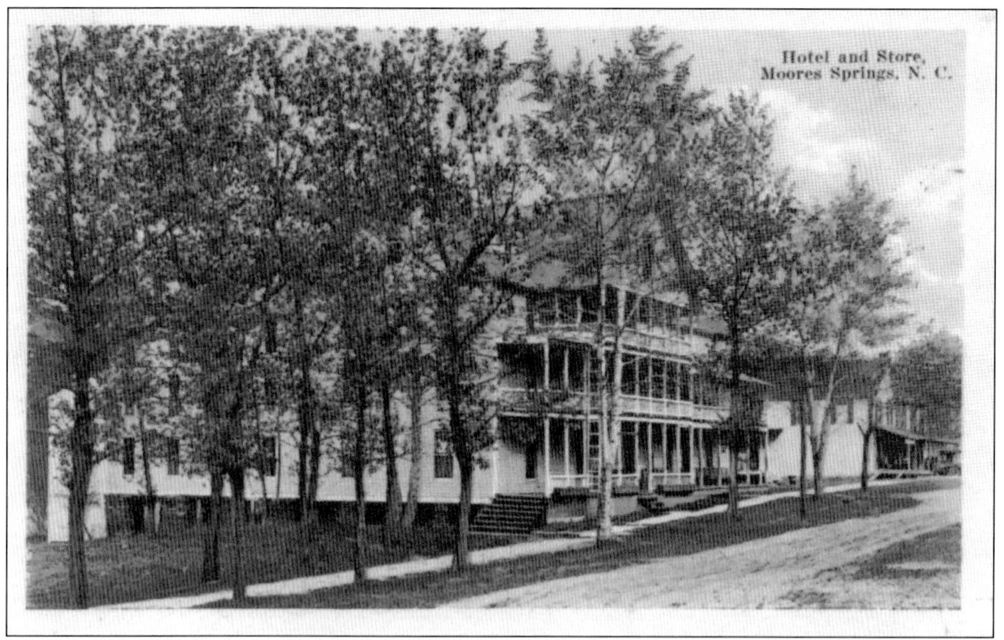

Moore's Springs Hotel and store are captured on this postcard. This hotel completely burned in 1925. (Author's collection.)

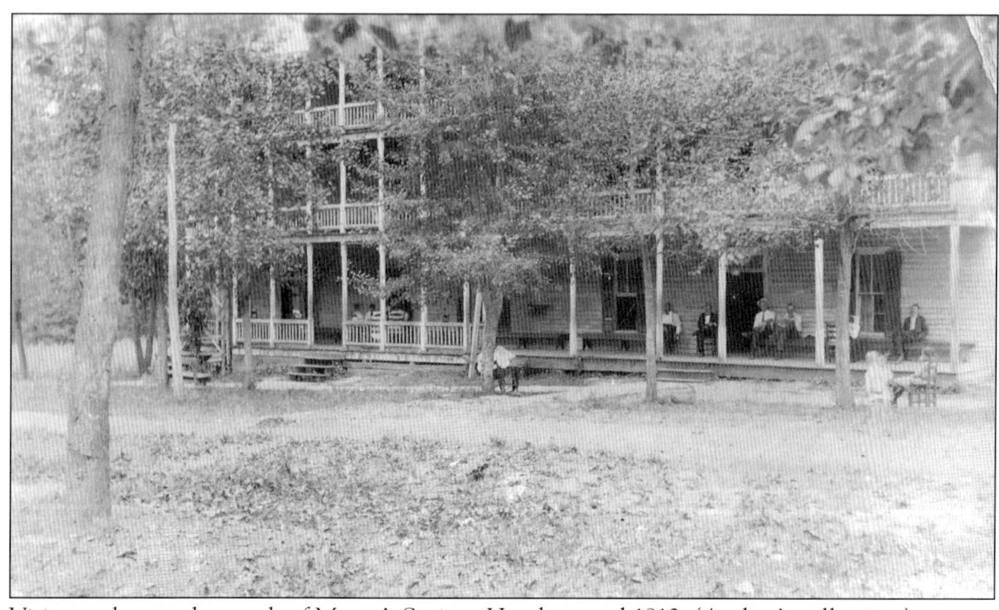

Visitors relax on the porch of Moore's Springs Hotel around 1910. (Author's collection.)

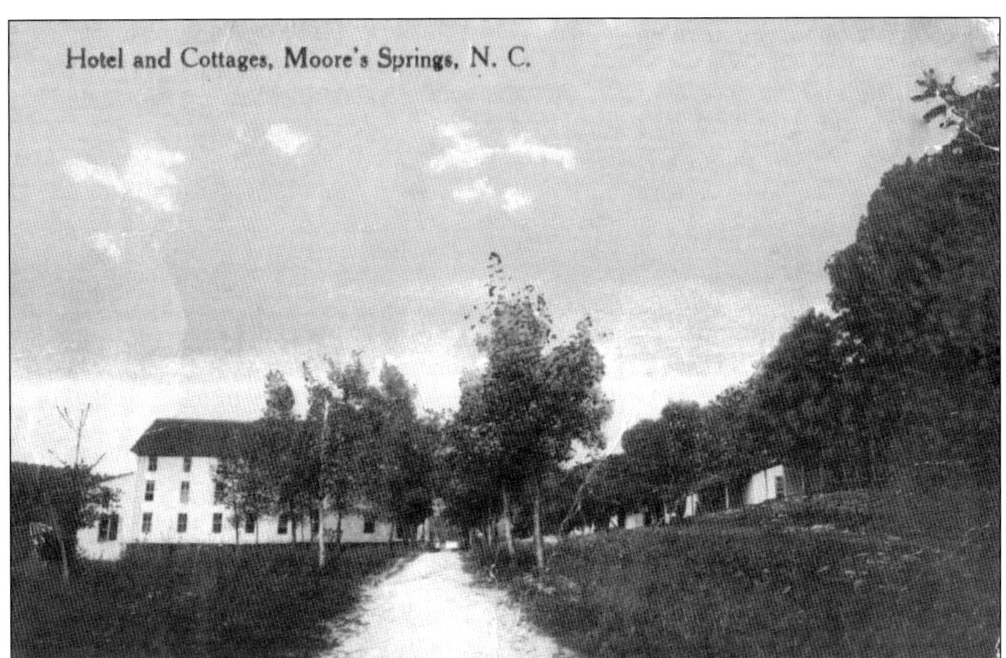

The side of the hotel at Moore's Springs can be seen on this 1915 postcard. Also, on the right-hand side of the road, guest cottages can be seen. (Author's collection.)

SPRING NO. 1	GRAINS PER GALLON OF 231 CUBIC INCHES
Sodium chloride	0.4430
Sodium sulphate	2.7488
Potassium sulphate	1.7809
Calcium sulphate	84.4705
Magnesium sulphate	5.4596
Magnesium carbonate	4.0715
Ferrous carbonate	0.3047
Cupric oxide	0.0817
Lithia, a very faint trace	
Silica	1.3075
Hydrogen sulphide, traces	
	100.6682
Water of crystallization, etc.	8.8965
Free carbonic acid, undetermined	
Total solids on evaporation at 212 degs. F.	109.5647

Moore's Springs Hotel

Rates: $2.50 per single day; $2.00 per day up to two weeks; $25.00 for two weeks; $45.00 to $50.00 for four weeks.

Moore's Mineral Springs Co.

Water shipped daily from Springs
12 ½ gallon bottles $2.00
Empty bottles to be returned Prepaid.

Moore's Mineral Water relieves constipation, indigestion, kidney and bladder trouble, skin disease, rheumatism, etc

SHIPPING POINT: RURAL HALL, N. C.

SPRING NO. 2	GRAINS PER GALLON OF 231 CUBIC INCHES
Sodium chloride	0.3808
Sodium sulphate	2.5553
Potassium sulphate	1.2010
Calcium sulphate	84.9241
Magnesium sulphate	4.8829
Magnesium carbonate	4.5933
Ferrous carbonate	0.3216
Cupric oxide	0.0584
Lithia, a very faint trace	
Silica	1.6461
Hydrogen sulphide	0.1080
	100.6711
Water of crystallization, etc.	8.3099
Free carbonic acid, undetermined	
Total solids on evaporization at 212 degs. F.	108.9810

Moore's Springs, N. C. August 24 191

Mr Thompson. atty.
Stuart Va

Dear Sir,-
I am Writing to know if you have Been inployed as Counsel for any of the Goins or Mr Weatherman. in any Suit Now pending in the Court of your State.
If not I want to Secure yours Services. Please advise me at once as I Will Need an atty at the comming Session of Court in your County. address me at Moores Springs N.C. -

yours Very Truly,
John Tuck.

This letterhead offers insight into the life of the Moore's Springs Hotel. It lists prices of both the water and hospitality. Also listed are the contents of the two springs at the resort. The water produced with these contents were legendary for healing purposes. (Author's collection.)

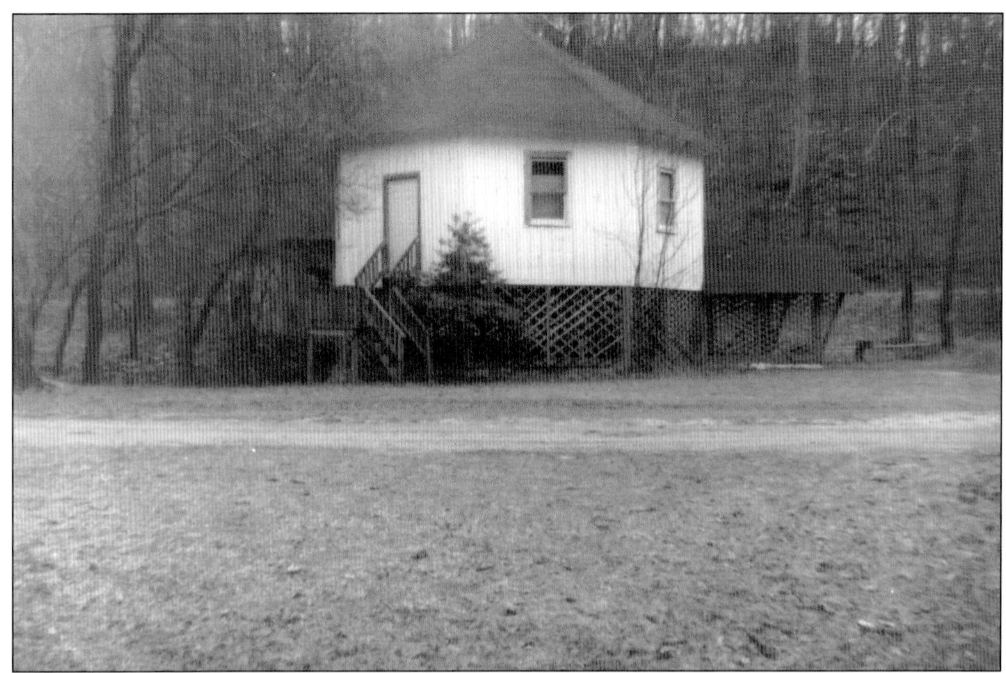

This is the springhouse at Moore's Springs, in which visitors to the resort would come to get water. (Author's collection.)

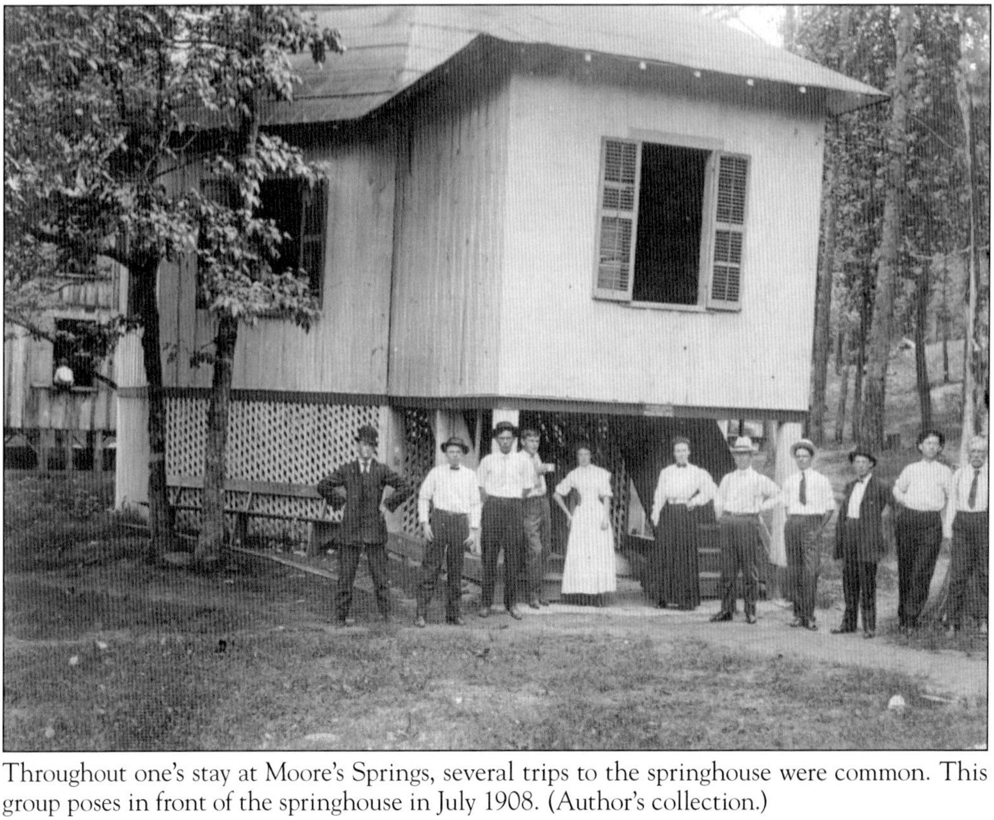

Throughout one's stay at Moore's Springs, several trips to the springhouse were common. This group poses in front of the springhouse in July 1908. (Author's collection.)

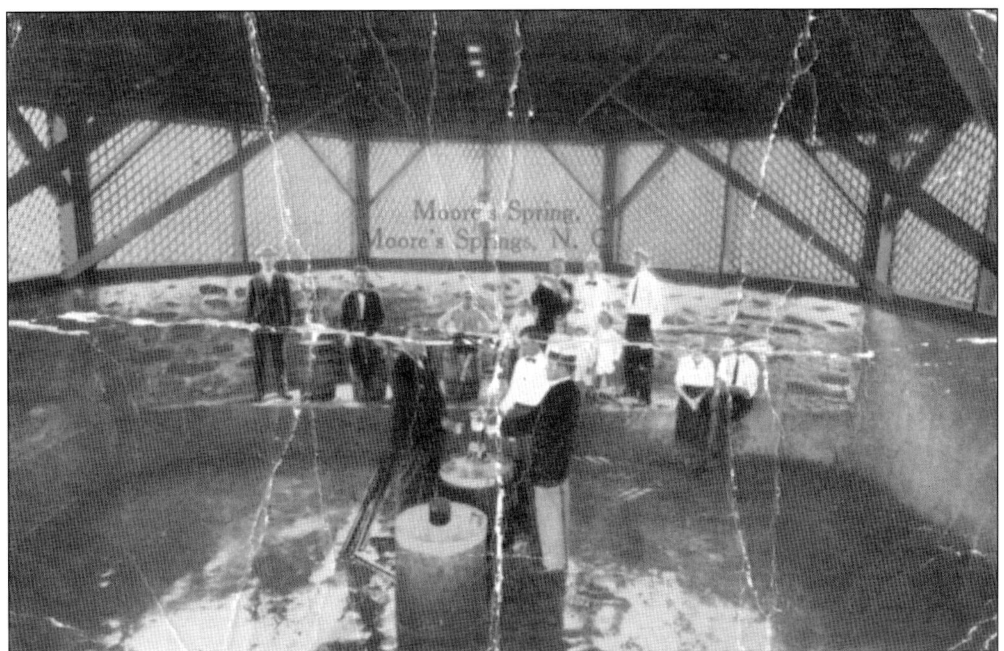

An interior view of the springhouse at Moore's Springs in 1915 shows men getting water. Notice the barrels of water in the background of the spring. (Author's collection.)

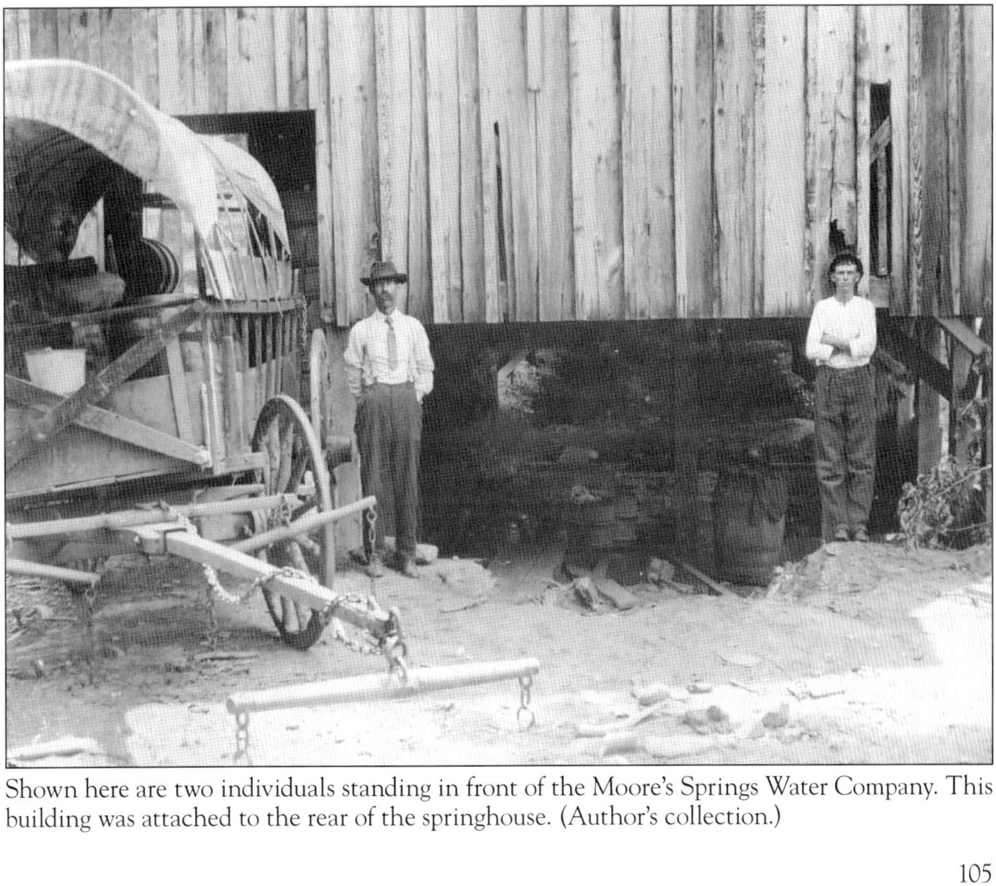

Shown here are two individuals standing in front of the Moore's Springs Water Company. This building was attached to the rear of the springhouse. (Author's collection.)

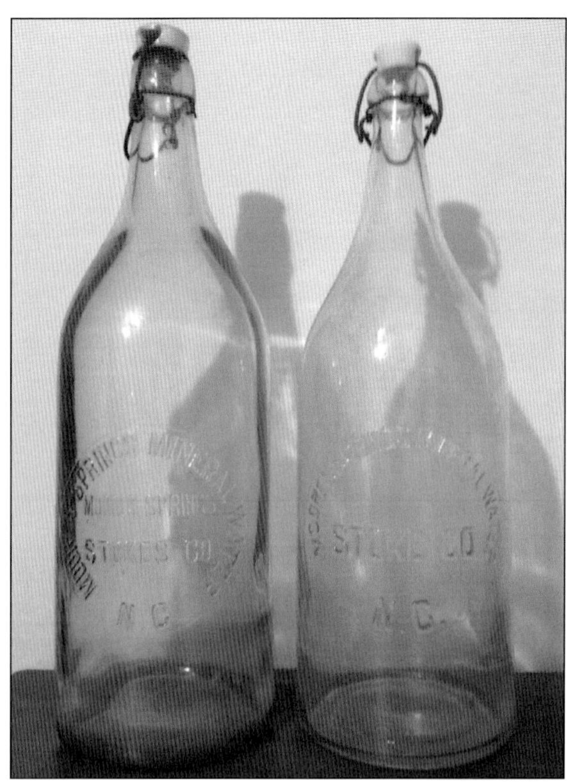

Shown here are the two variations of Moore's Springs water bottles. The one on the left is a typical Moore's Springs water bottle, while the one to the right bears the mistaken spelling of Stokes County as "Stoke County." (Author's collection.)

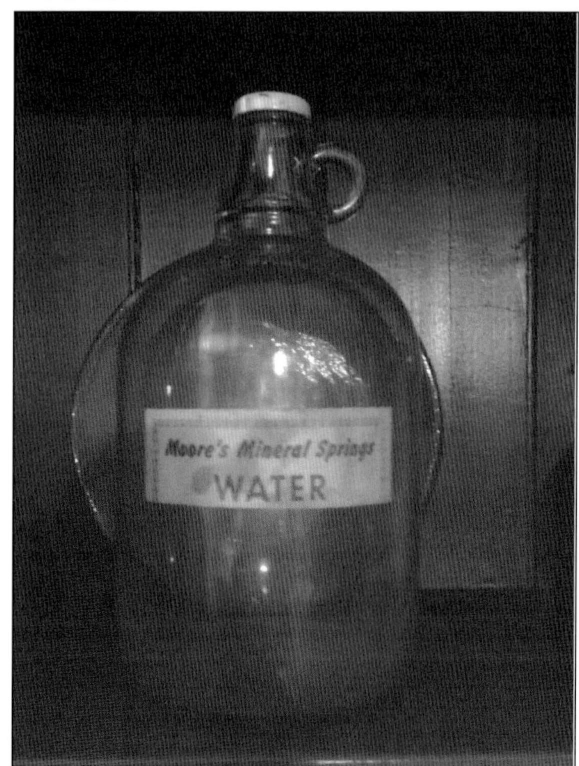

This jug was used to haul water from Moore's Springs in the 1950s by T.C. Petree. This was the last water hauled out of the springs for commercial use. (Author's collection.)

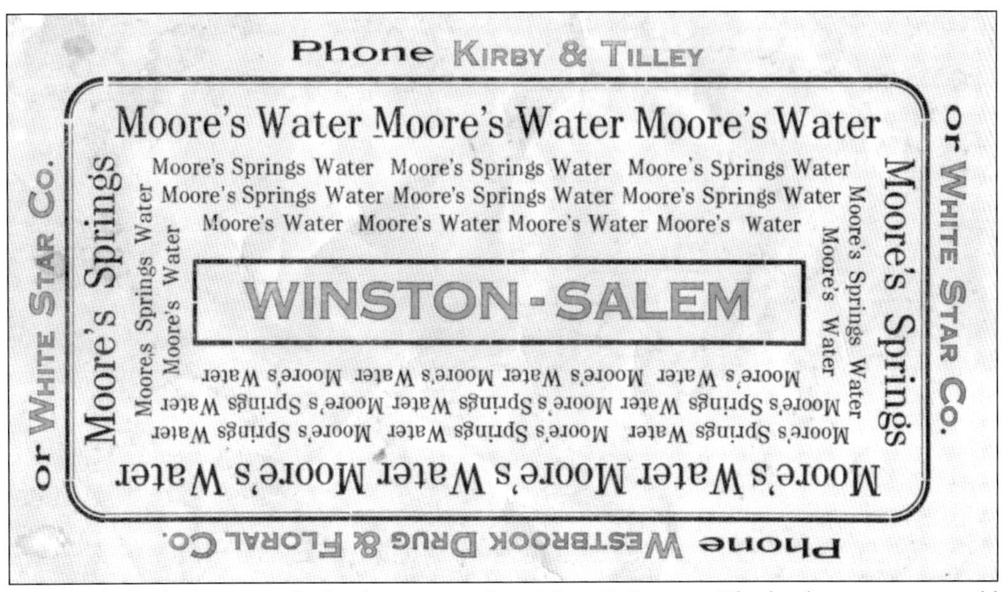

This trade card advertises the healing waters from Moore's Springs. The healing water was sold at these locations in Winston-Salem, North Carolina. (Author's collection.)

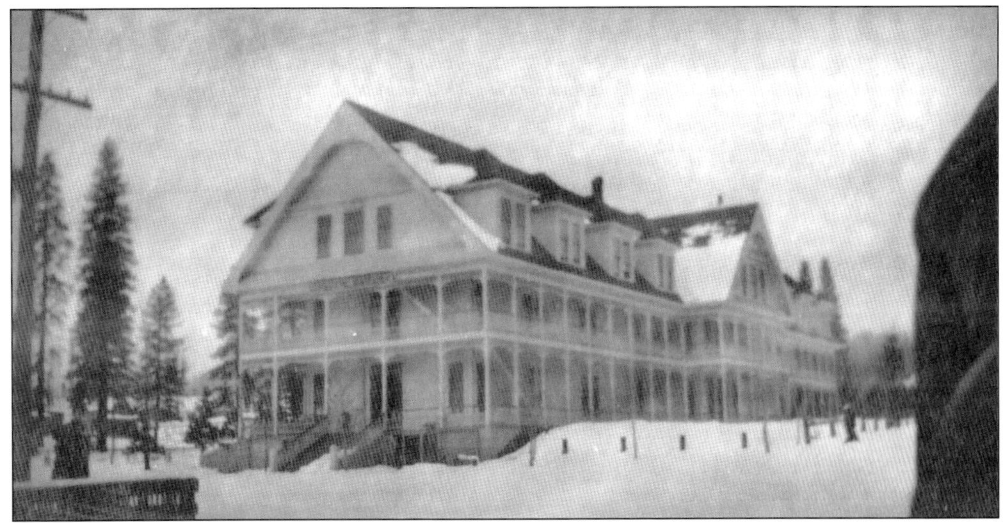

Established by the Vaden family in the latter part of the 19th century, Vade Mecum was the last resort to open. Photographed here is the early hotel at Vade Mecum Resorts, which was built in 1901. Fires were common occurrences at the resorts, and this hotel burned in 1908. (Author's collection.)

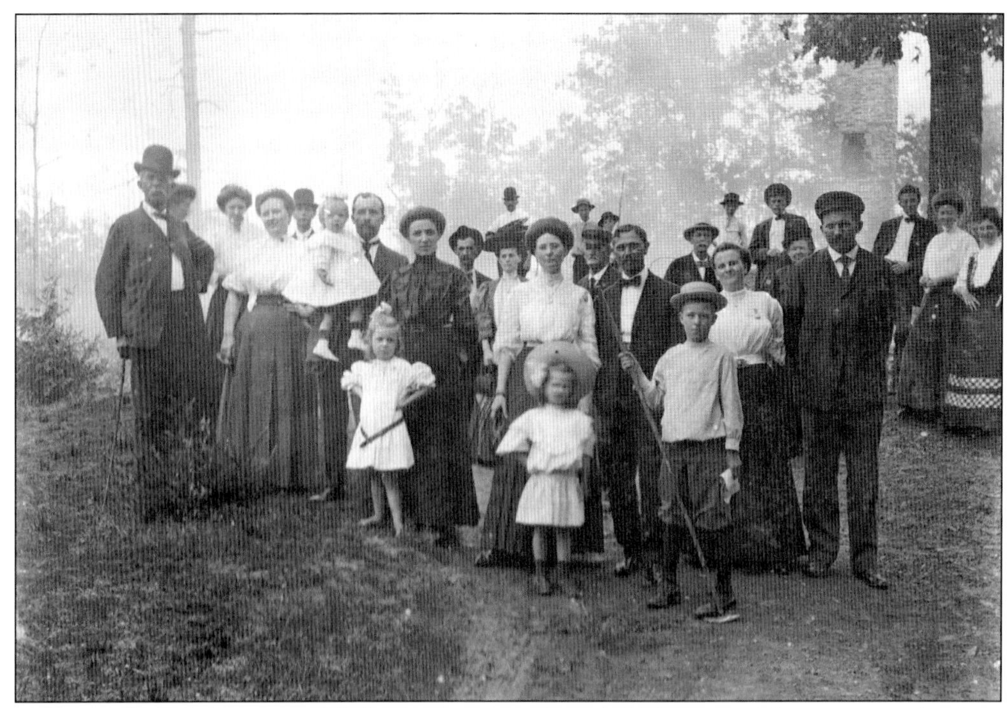

Fires swept through the resorts of the healing waters in the early 20th century. This group posed in front of the rubble of the burned hotel at Vade Mecum Springs in July 1908. (Author's collection.)

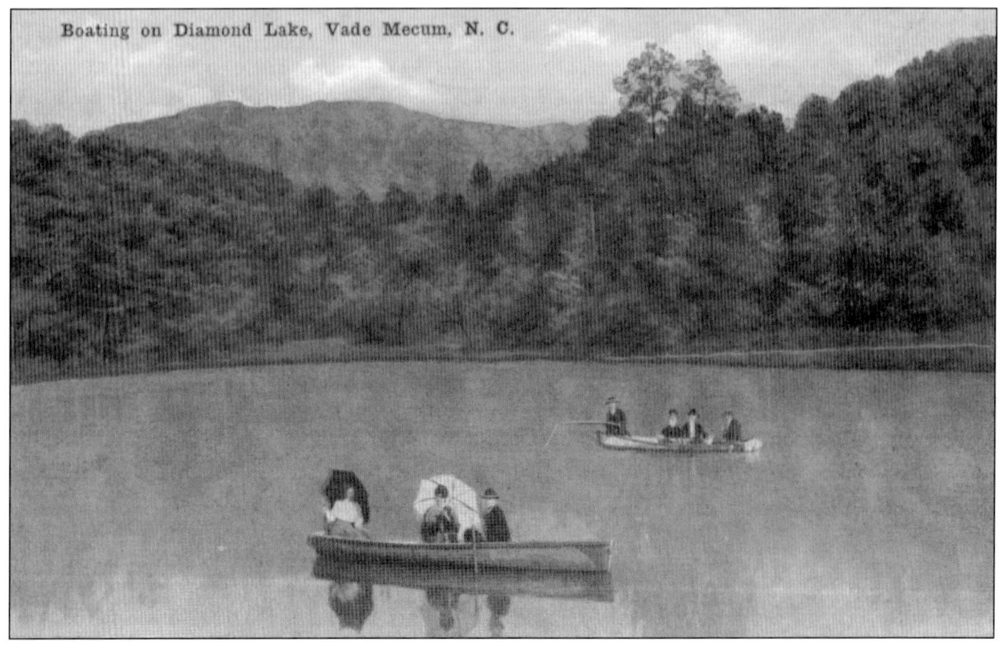

Seen in this postcard image are visitors to Vade Mecum boating on Diamond Lake. (Courtesy of Wayne and Louise Biby.)

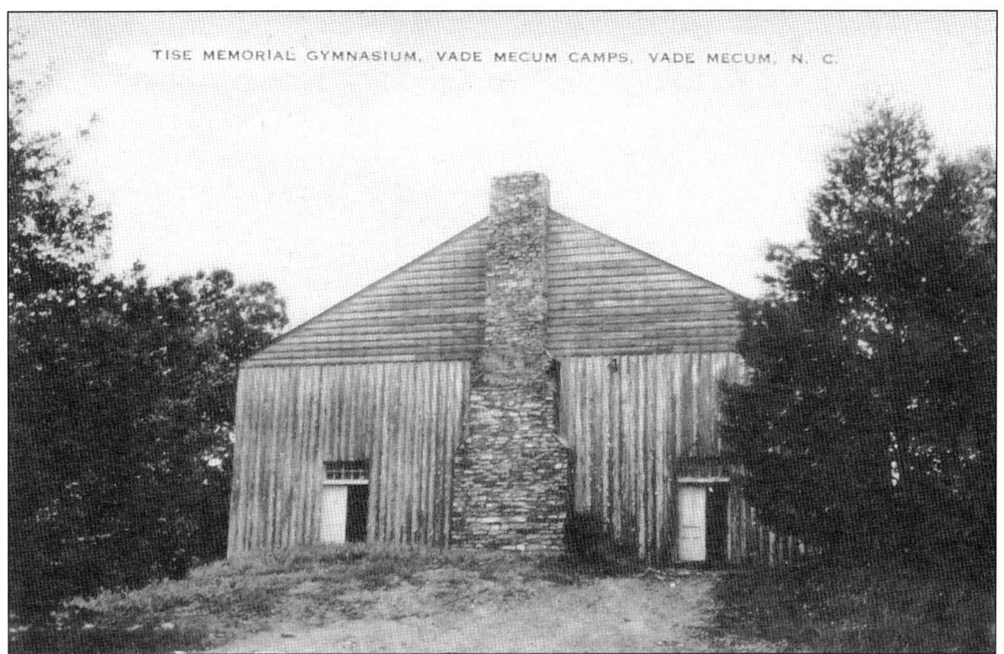

The gym located at Camp Vade Mecum was named for W.C. Tise, who was an early proprietor of the Vade Mecum Resort. The gym is still in operation at Camp Sertoma. (Author's collection.)

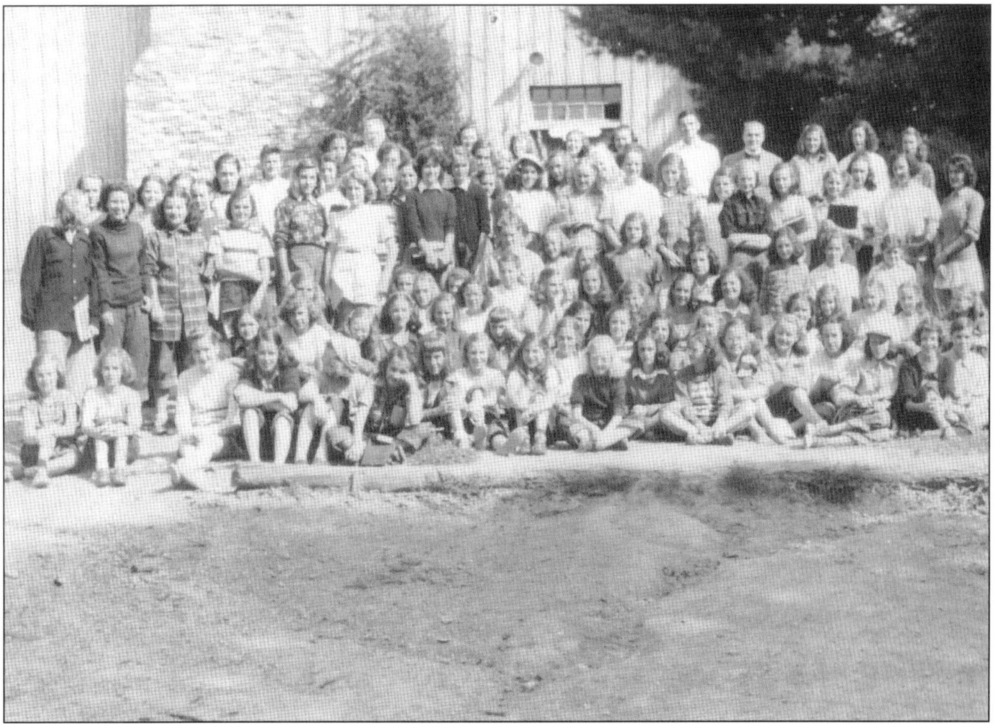

Camp Vade Mecum campers pose in front of the W.C. Tise memorial gym in the early 1940s. (Courtesy of Harold and Joice Lewis Gravitt.)

VADE MECUM FARMS
C. A. LEWIS, MANAGER
VADE MECUM, N. C.

This letterhead belonged to Claxton Abram Lewis, who was caretaker of Camp Vade Mecum from 1937 to 1953. This is an unusual reference to "Vade Mecum Farms." (Author's collection.)

STATEMENT
VADE MECUM, N. C., ______ 193__

M______

IN ACCOUNT WITH
C. A. LEWIS

This ledger paper was from Camp Vade Mecum when Claxton Abram Lewis was caretaker around 1938. (Author's collection.)

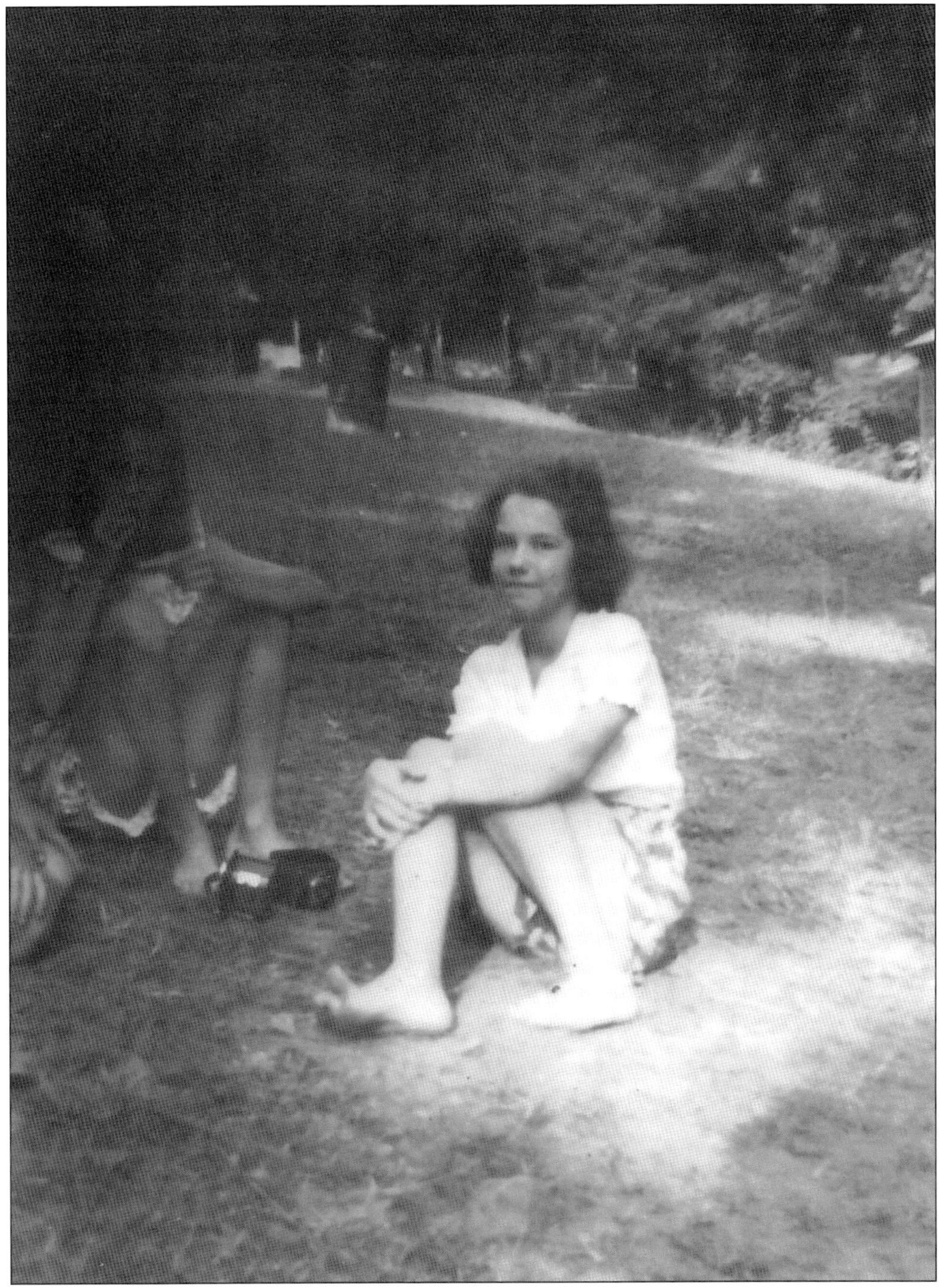

Joice (Lewis) Granitt was the daughter of Claxton A. Lewis, a caretaker at Camp Vade Mecum. She poses while enjoying a day at the camp. Cheshire Hall can be seen in the background. (Courtesy of Harold and Joice Lewis Granitt.)

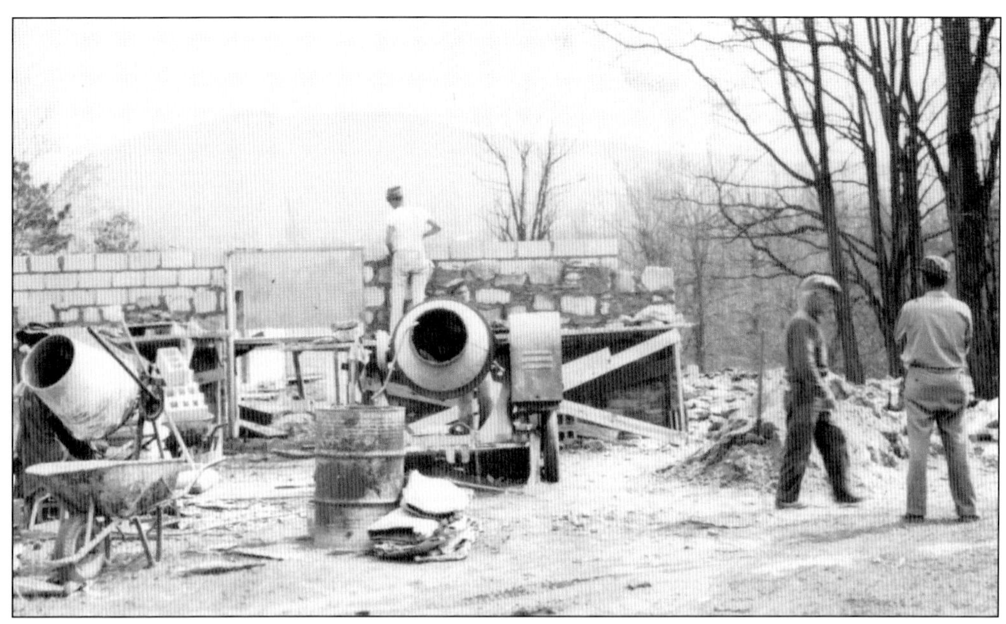

This is shot of the building of the Chapel of Thanks at Vade Mecum Episcopal Camp. In the background, one can see the hotel that was built when Vade Mecum was known for its healing waters. (Author's collection.)

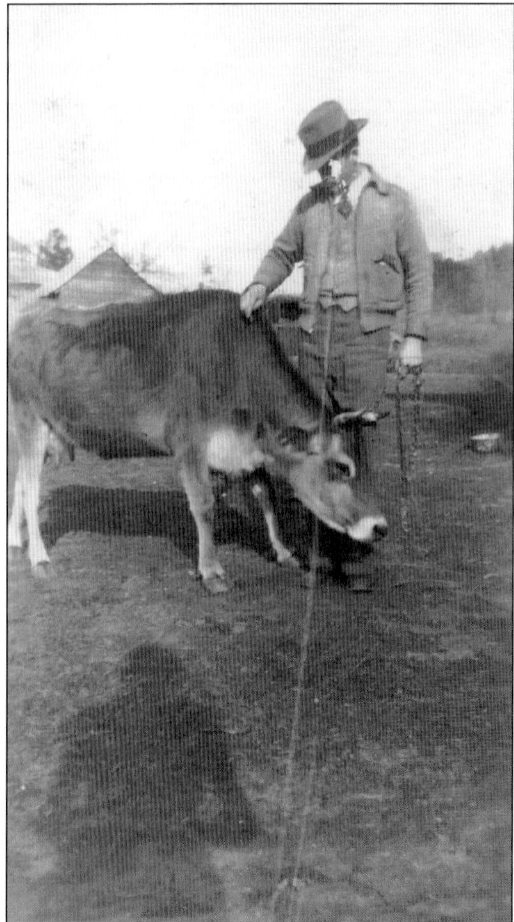

Claxton A. Lewis tends to his family's first cow, which he purchased for $25 while working for the Stokes County WPA in the early 1930s. (Author's collection.)

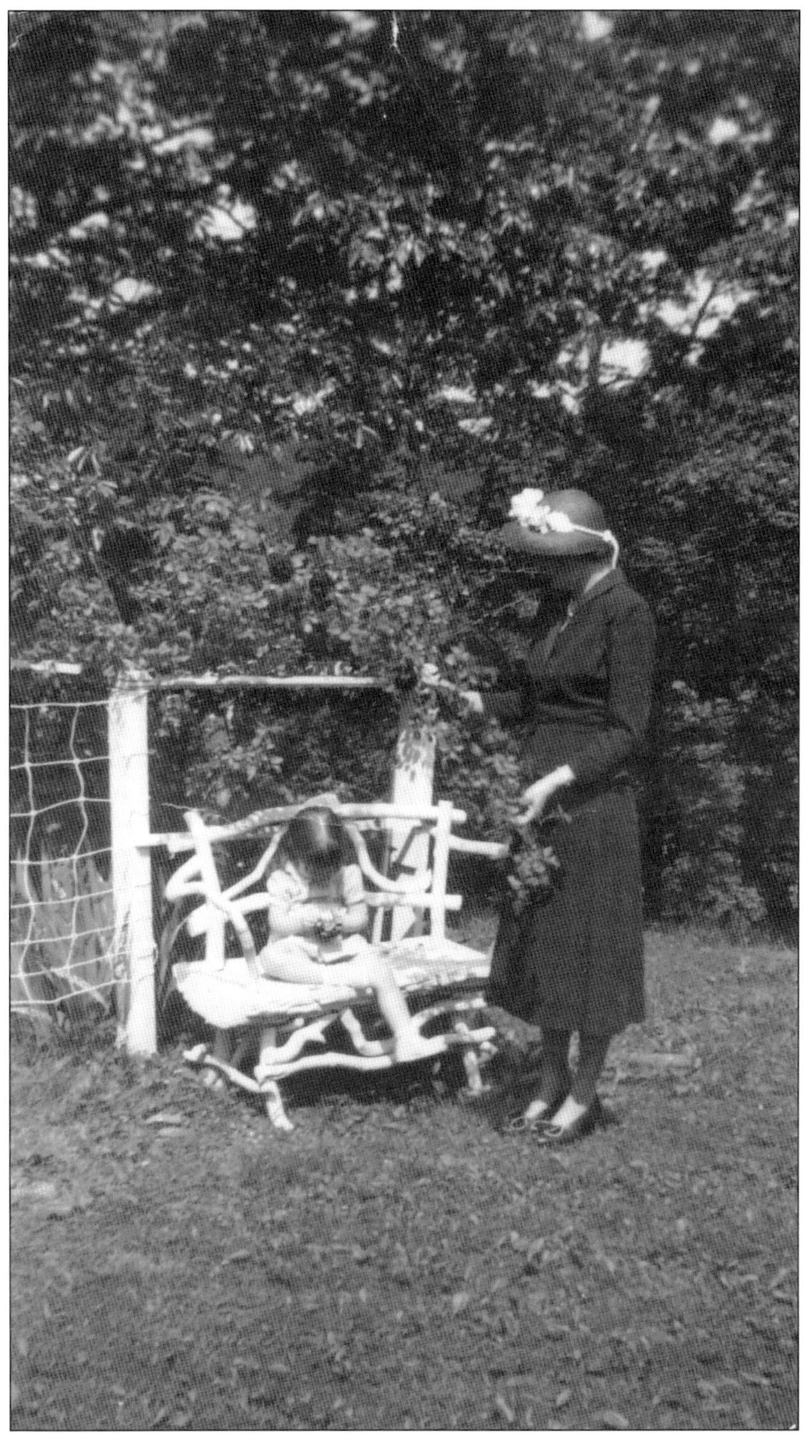

Pictured here are Ruby Rutledge Lewis, postmistress at Vade Mecum from 1949 to 1953, and her daughter Jane Lewis Berrier. Ruby's husband, Claxton Abram Lewis, a caretaker of Camp Vade Mecum, was the postmaster from 1937 to 1949. The Vade Mecum Post Office was located inside a home at the camp. (Author's collection.)

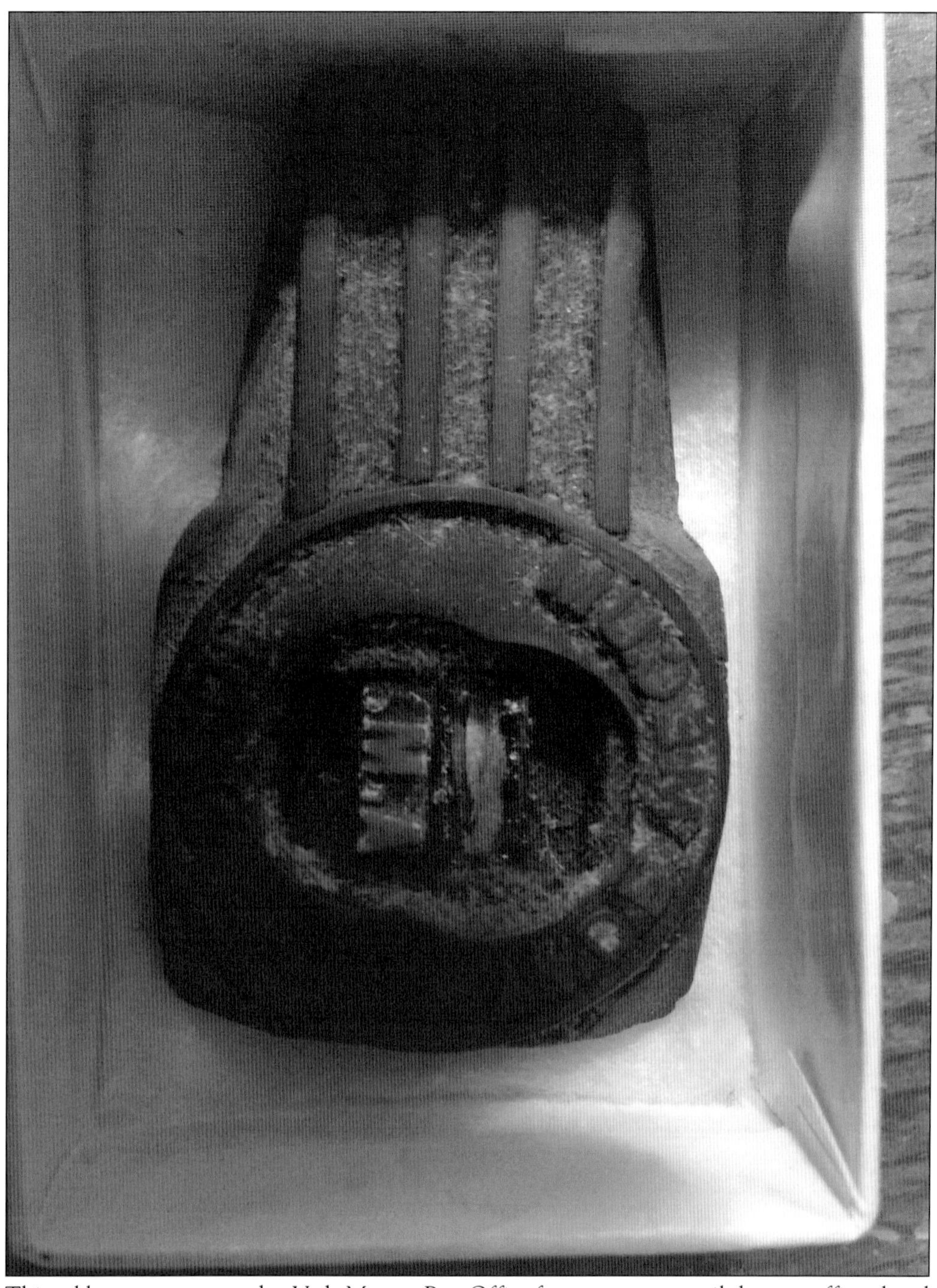

This rubber stamp was used at Vade Mecum Post Office for many years until the post office closed in 1953. (Author's collection.)

Six

Around Danbury

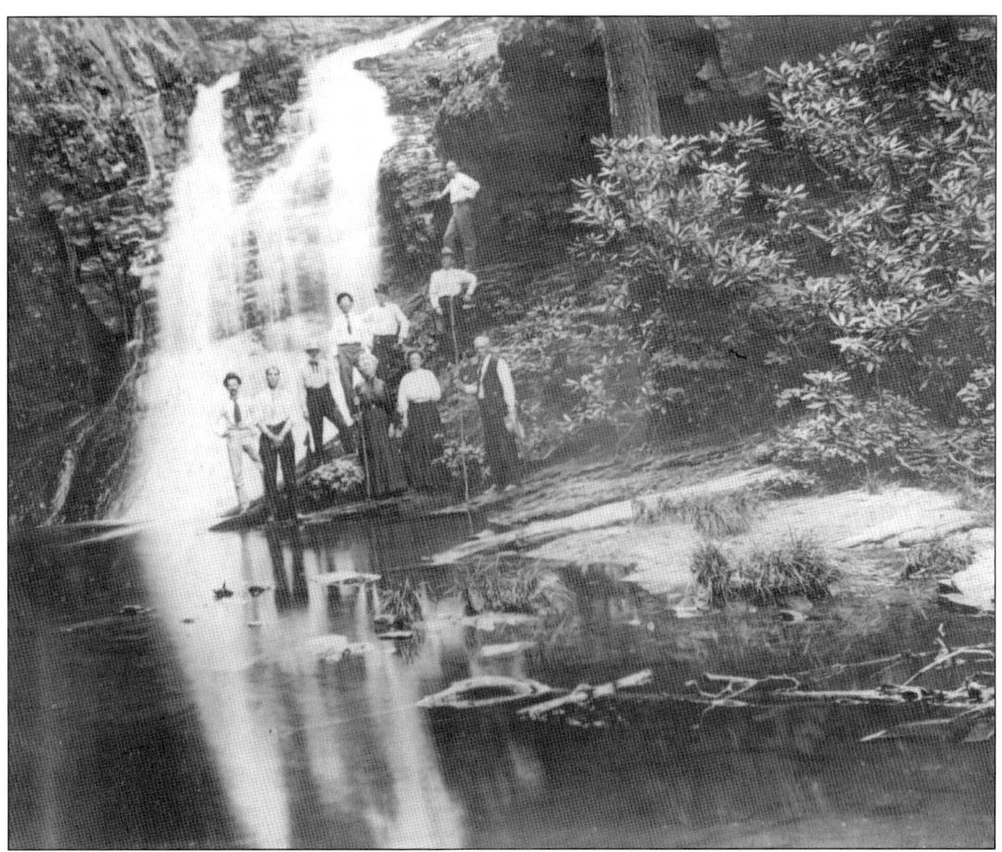

Cascade Falls has proven to be a popular place to take photographs since before the time this image was captured in 1908. Many visitors today still travel to the famous falls to recreate these pictures from long ago. (Author's collection.)

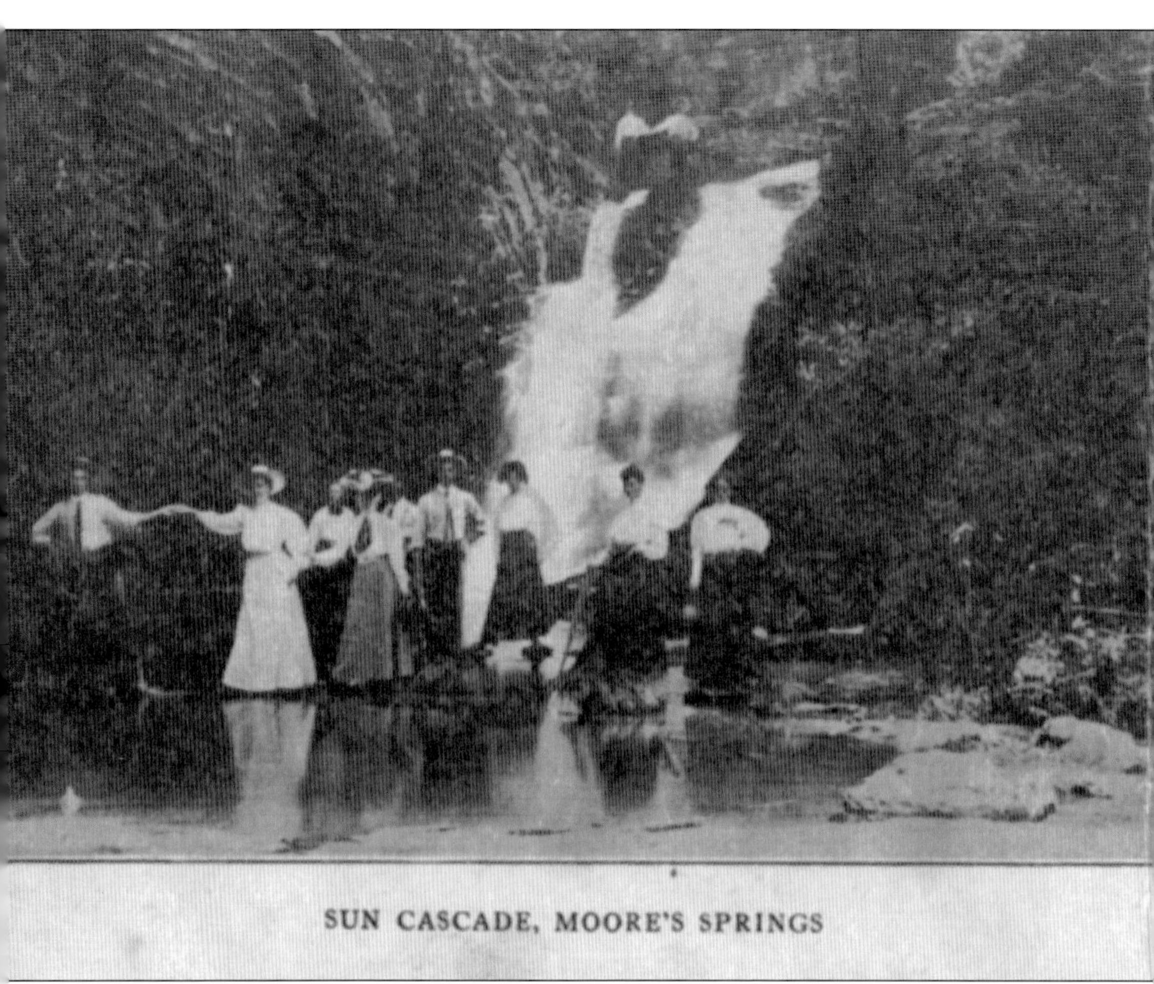

Another tour group is shown in front of Sun Cascade at Moore's Springs on this 1915 postcard. (Author's collection.)

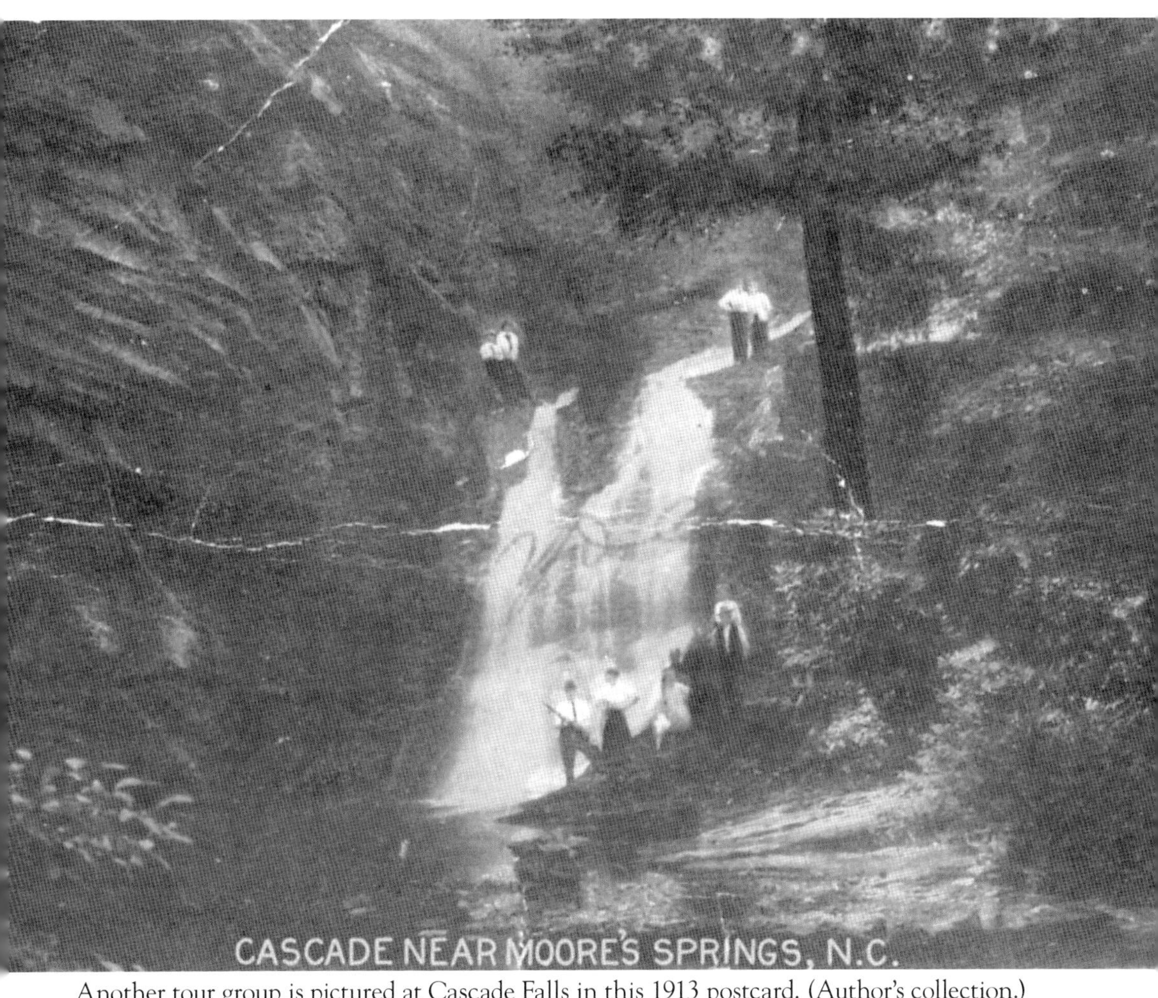

Another tour group is pictured at Cascade Falls in this 1913 postcard. (Author's collection.)

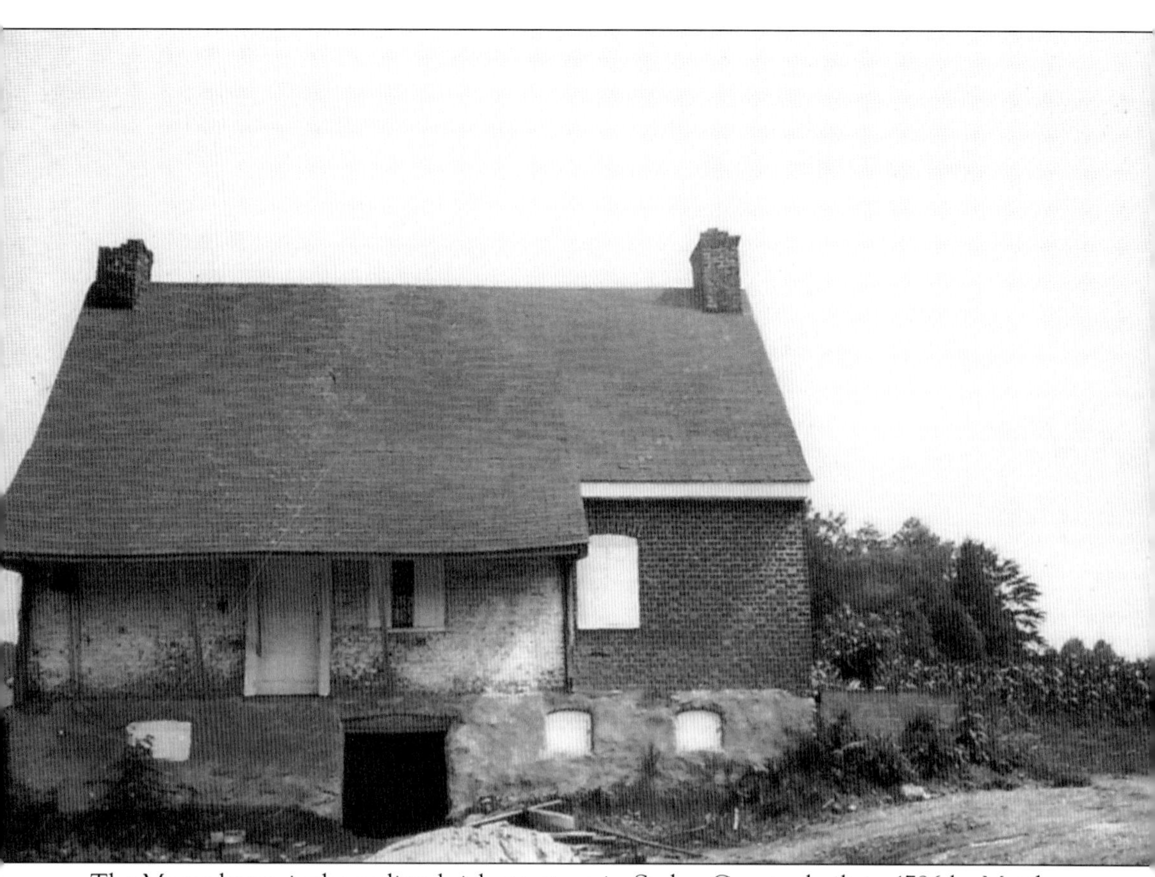

The Moore house is the earliest brick structure in Stokes County, built in 1786 by Matthew Moore. It is one of the few remaining structures with Moravian architecture in Stokes County. The Moore house is rumored to have been home to Hardin Reynolds, father of Richard Reynolds, for a period of time in the 1800s. (Author's collection.)

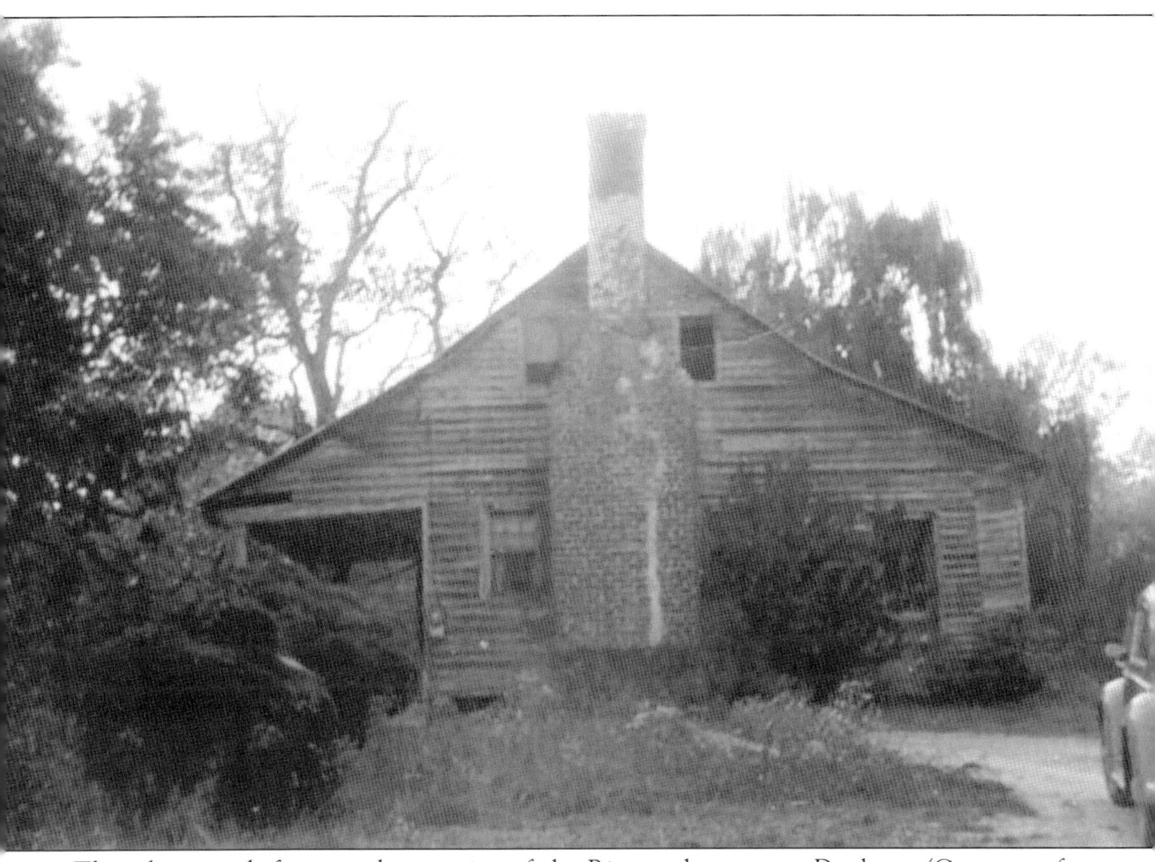

This photograph features the remains of the Rierson home near Danbury. (Courtesy of Charles Rodenbough.)

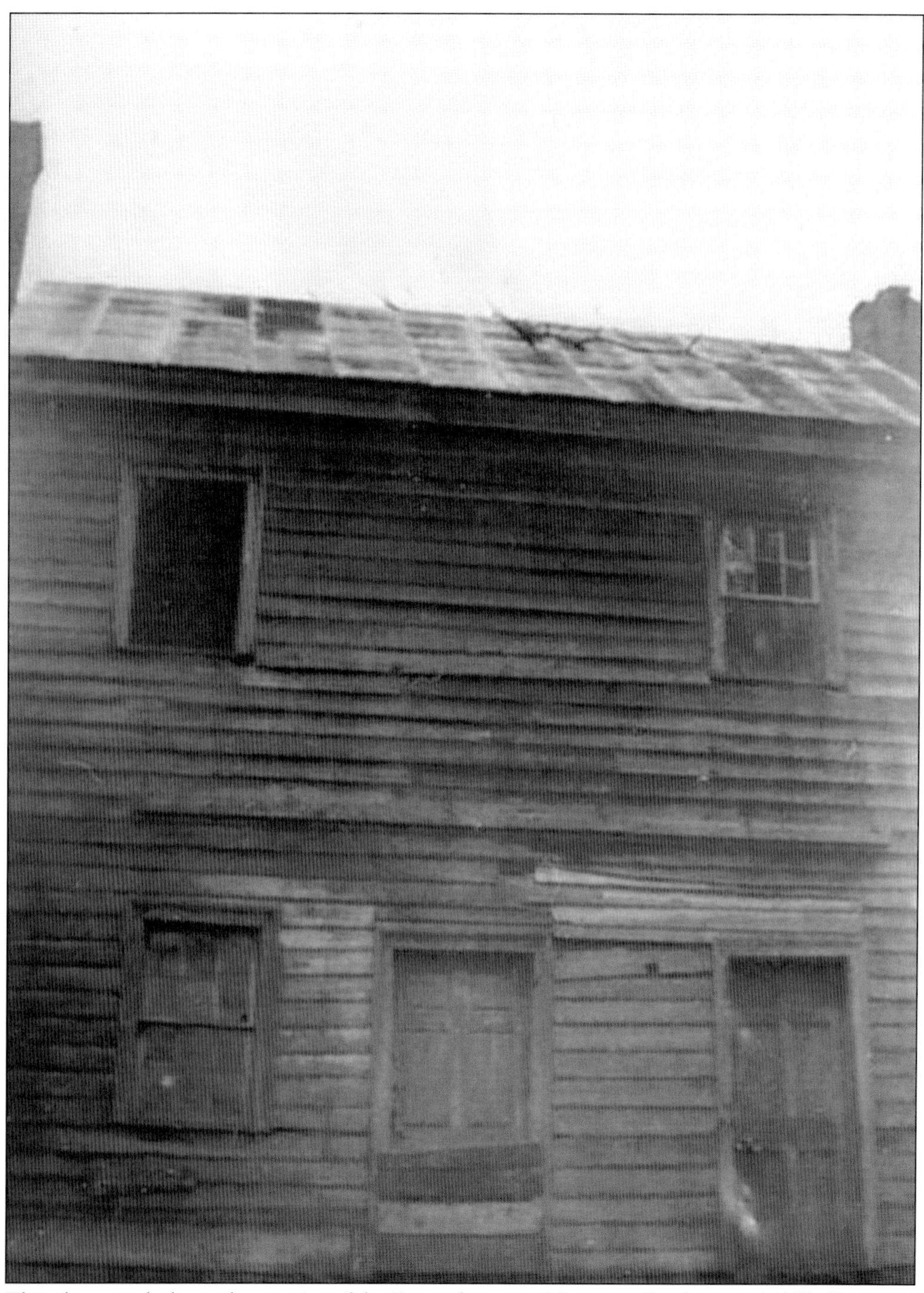

This photograph shows the remains of the Pepper house on Neatman Creek around 1955. (Courtesy of Charles Rodenbough.)

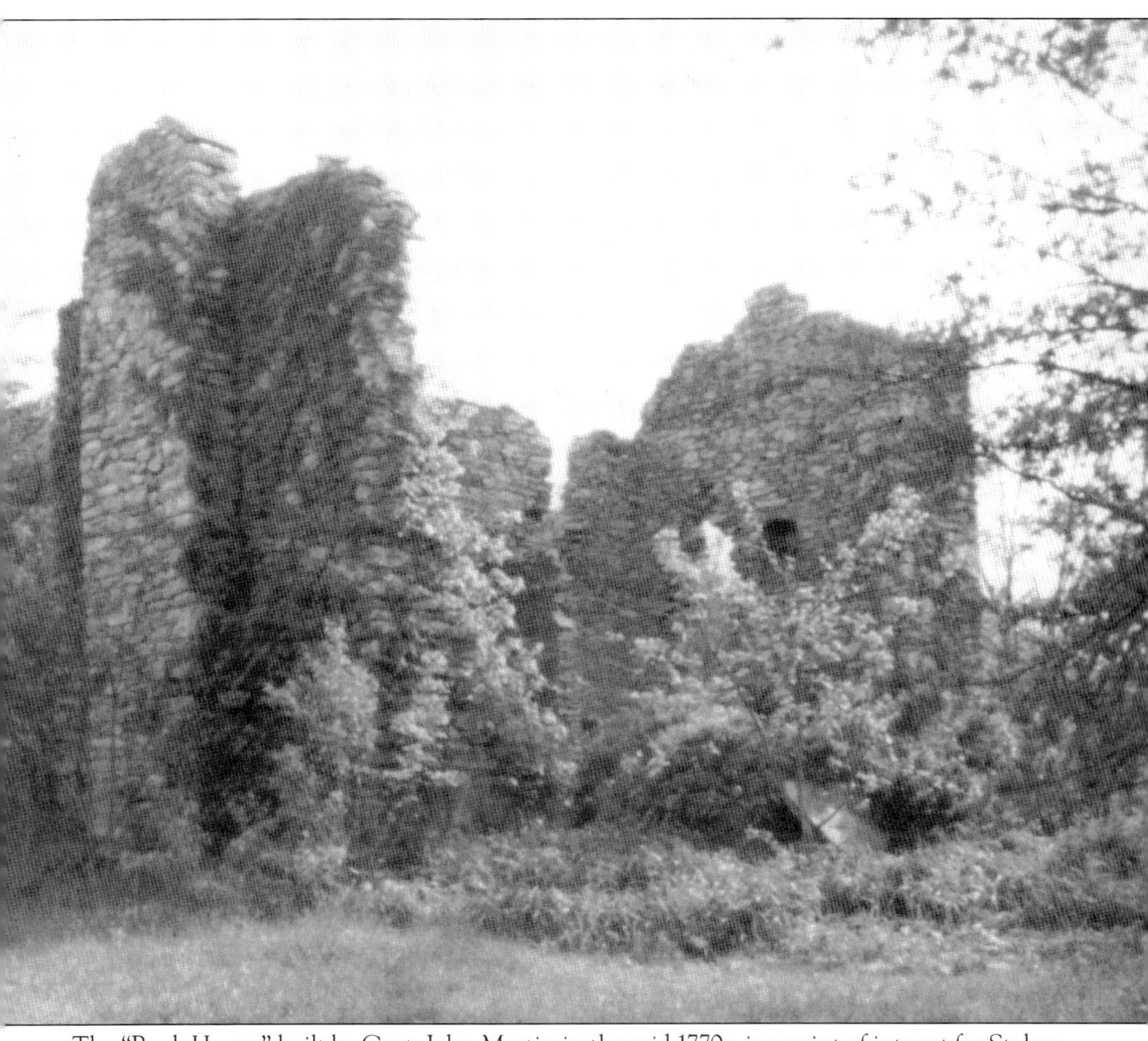

The "Rock House," built by Capt. John Martin in the mid-1770s, is a point of interest for Stokes County. Revolutionary War lore claims that this house served as protection from Tories and Indians. This photograph was taken before restoration. (Author's collection.)

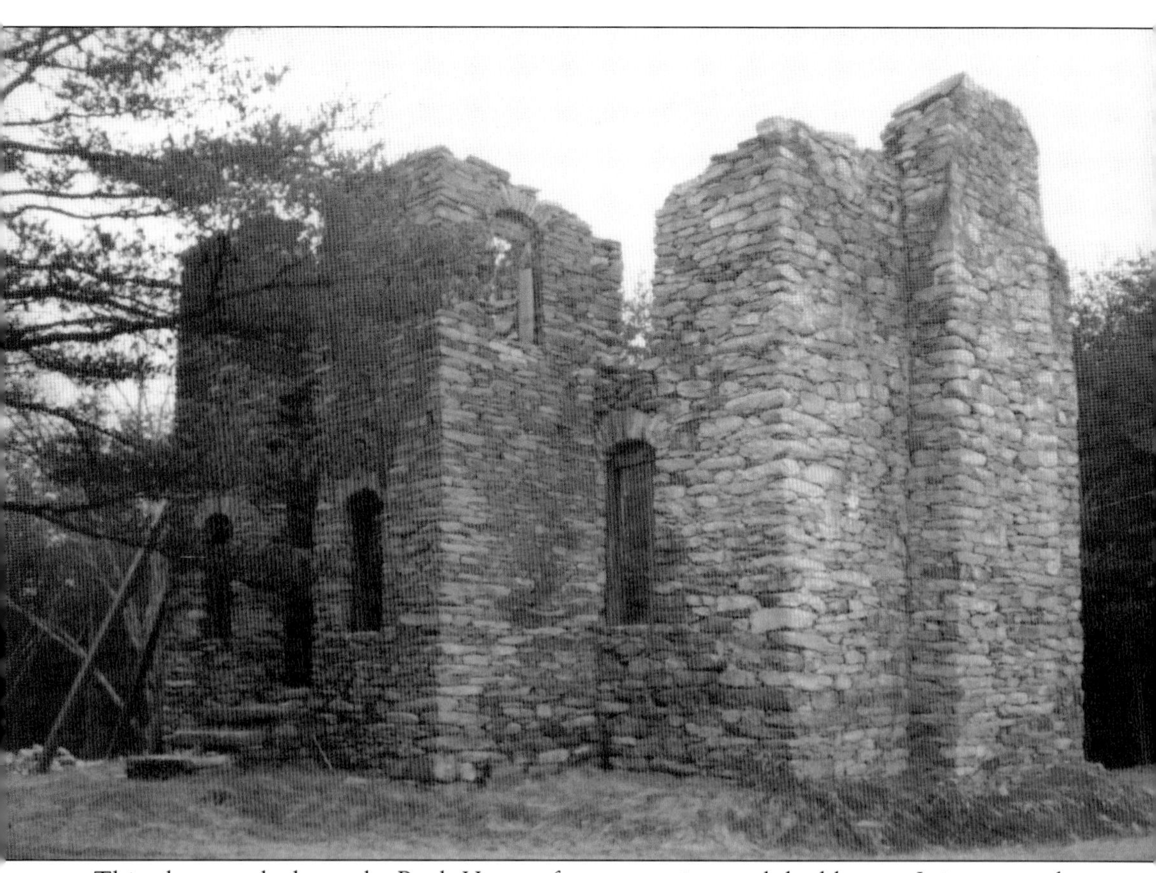

This photograph shows the Rock House after restoration work had begun. It is now under preservation by the Stokes County Historical Society. (Author's collection.)

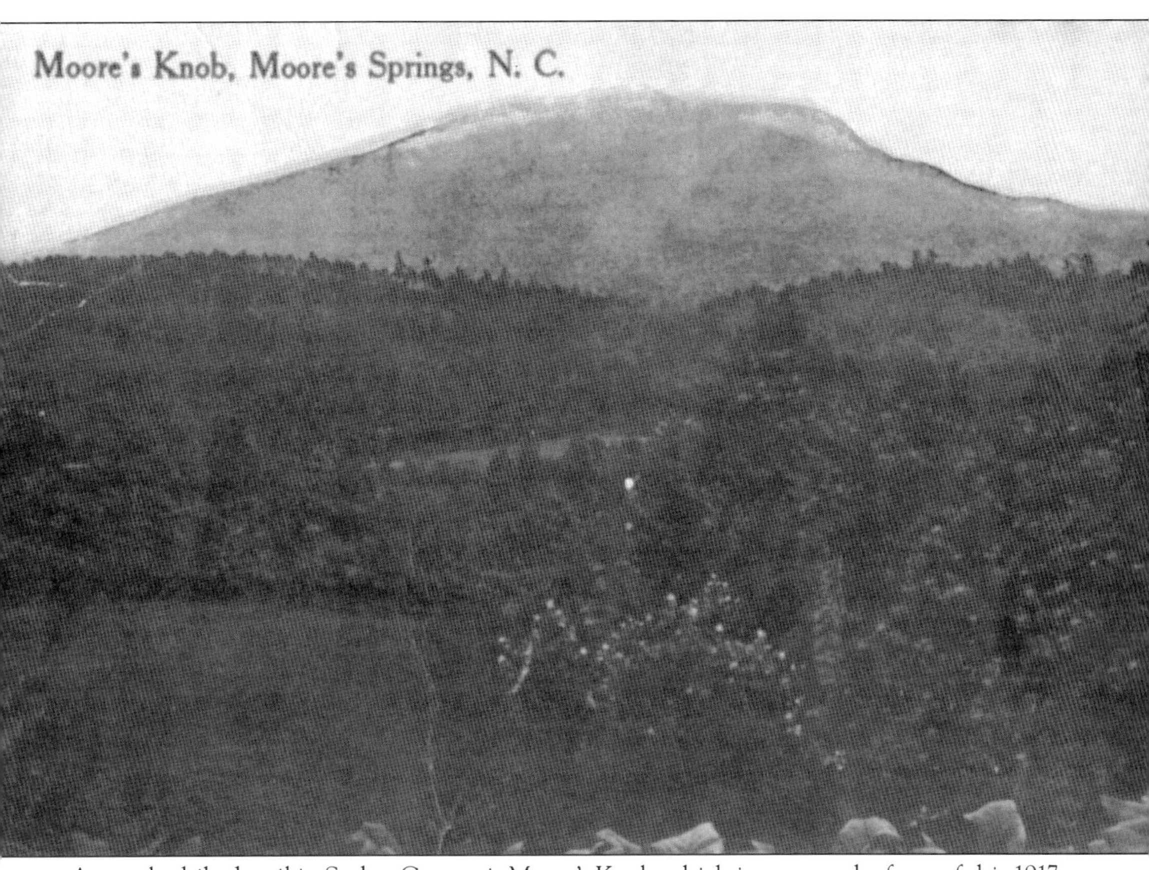

A popular hiked trail in Stokes County is Moore's Knob, which is seen on the front of this 1917 postcard. (Author's collection.)

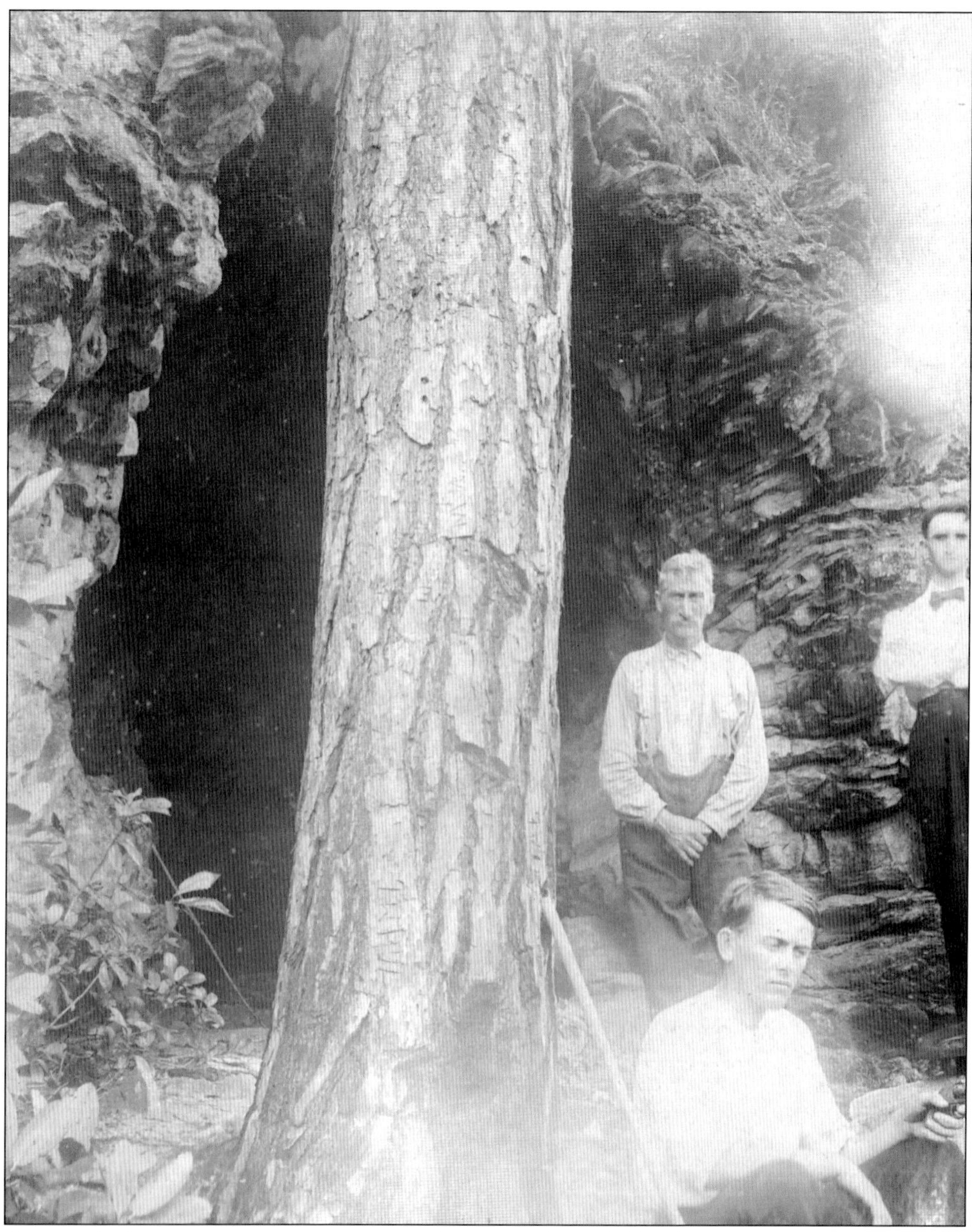

During the Revolutionary war, this spot, known as "Tory's Den," served as headquarters for the Loyalists in Stokes County. Legend has it that Col. Jack Martin's daughter was kidnapped by Tories and taken to Tory's Den. The locals discovered this cave and formed a militia to rescue Colonel Martin's daughter. This historical landmark is still visited by many each year. (Author's collection.)

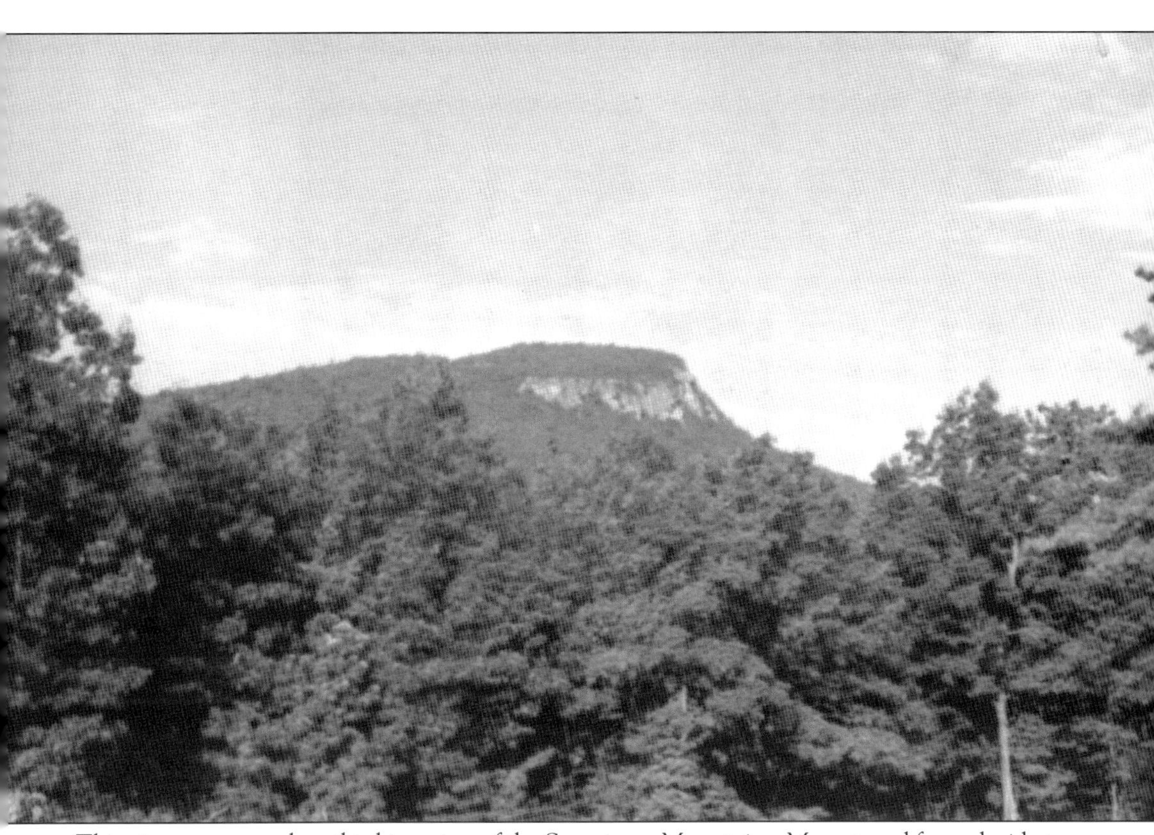

This view captures a breathtaking view of the Sauratown Mountains. Many travel far and wide to see this beautiful mountain range that almost begins and ends in Stokes. (Author's collection.)

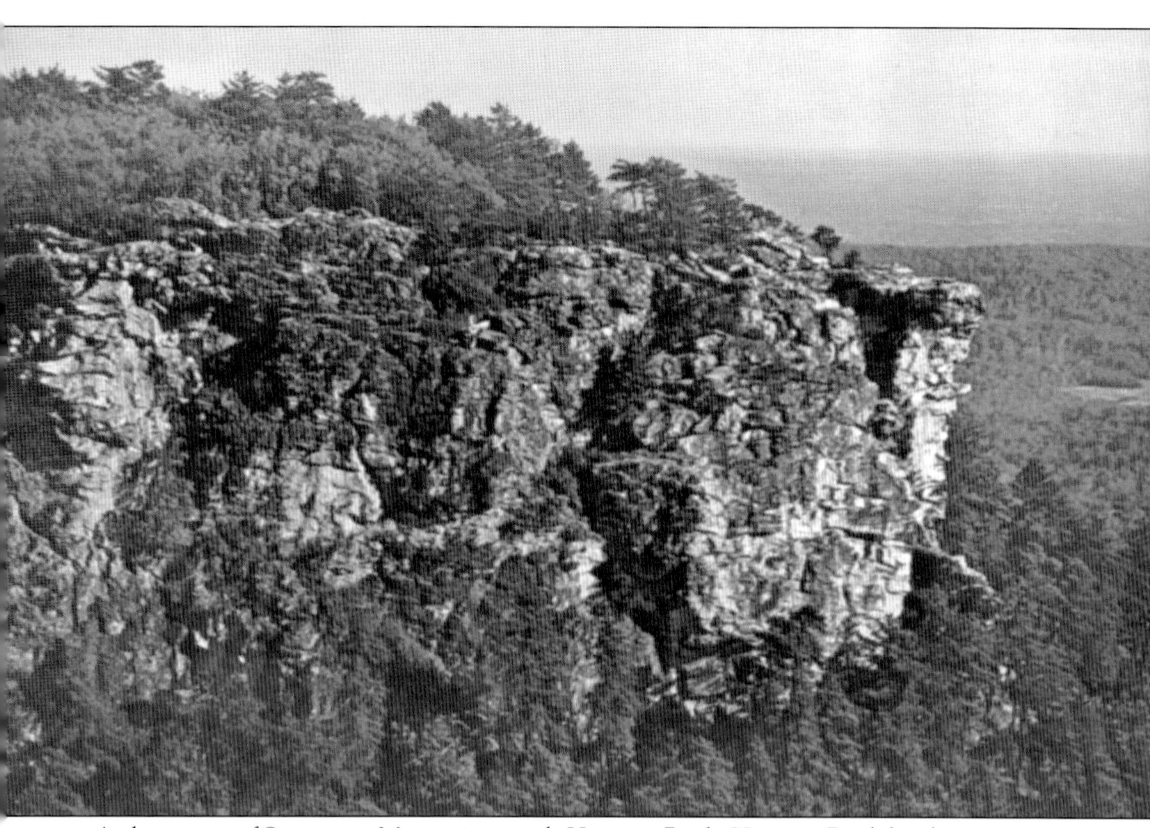

A closer view of Sauratown Mountain reveals Hanging Rock. Hanging Rock has become a state park and a nationally recognized destination. When hiking here, one can feel a sense of peace that only Stokes County can encompass. (Author's collection.)

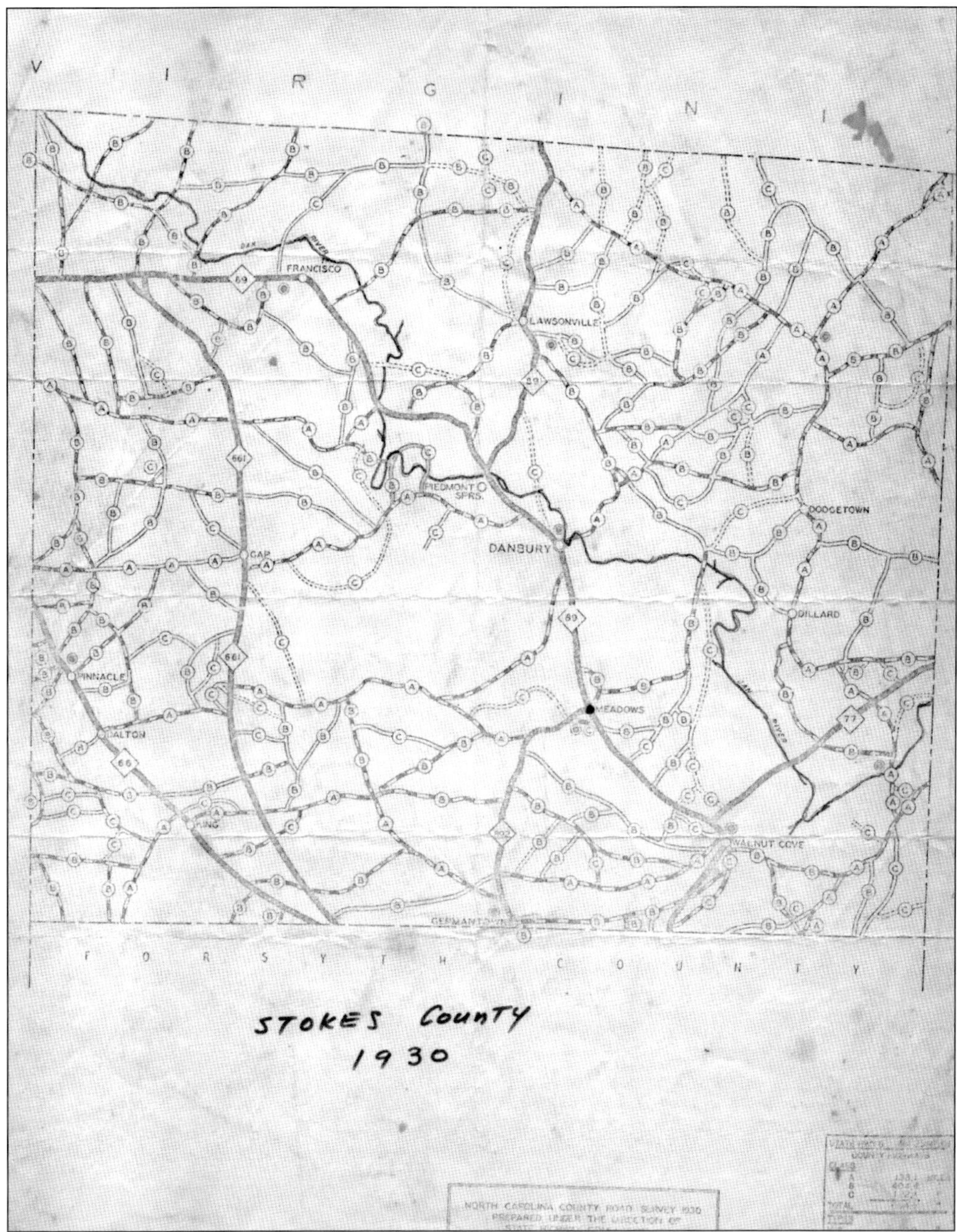

This 1930 map of Stokes County highlights the areas that *Around Walnut Cove and Danbury* has captured in cherished images. Many people pass through, but to its inhabitants, it is home. (Author's collection.)